TERRORISM

REDUCING VULNERABILITIES
AND IMPROVING RESPONSES

U.S.-Russian Workshop Proceedings

Committee on Counterterrorism Challenges for
Russia and the United States

Office for Central Europe and Eurasia
Development, Security, and Cooperation
Policy and Global Affairs

In cooperation with the Russian Academy of Sciences

NATIONAL RESEARCH COUNCIL
OF THE NATIONAL ACADEMIES

THE NATIONAL ACADEMIES PRESS
Washington, D.C.
www.nap.edu

THE NATIONAL ACADEMIES PRESS 500 Fifth Street, N.W. Washington, D.C. 20001

NOTICE: The project that is the subject of this report was approved by the Governing Board of the National Research Council, whose members are drawn from the councils of the National Academy of Sciences, the National Academy of Engineering, and the Institute of Medicine. The members of the committee responsible for the report were chosen for their special competences and with regard for appropriate balance.

This study was supported by Grant No. B7075.R01 between the National Academy of Sciences and the Carnegie Corporation of New York. Any opinions, findings, conclusions, or recommendations expressed in this publication are those of the author(s) and do not necessarily reflect the views of the organizations or agencies that provided support for the project.

International Standard Book Number 0-309-08971-9 (Book)
International Standard Book Number 0-309-52590-X (PDF)
Library of Congress Control Number 2004103935

A limited number of copies are available from the Office for Central Europe and Eurasia, National Research Council, 500 Fifth Street, NW, Washington, DC 20001; (202) 334-2644.

Additional copies of this report are available from the National Academies Press, 500 Fifth Street, N.W., Lockbox 285, Washington, D.C. 20055; (800) 624-6242 or (202) 334-3313 (in the Washington metropolitan area); Internet, http://www.nap.edu

THE NATIONAL ACADEMIES
Advisers to the Nation on Science, Engineering, and Medicine

The **National Academy of Sciences** is a private, nonprofit, self-perpetuating society of distinguished scholars engaged in scientific and engineering research, dedicated to the furtherance of science and technology and to their use for the general welfare. Upon the authority of the charter granted to it by the Congress in 1863, the Academy has a mandate that requires it to advise the federal government on scientific and technical matters. Dr. Bruce M. Alberts is president of the National Academy of Sciences.

The **National Academy of Engineering** was established in 1964, under the charter of the National Academy of Sciences, as a parallel organization of outstanding engineers. It is autonomous in its administration and in the selection of its members, sharing with the National Academy of Sciences the responsibility for advising the federal government. The National Academy of Engineering also sponsors engineering programs aimed at meeting national needs, encourages education and research, and recognizes the superior achievements of engineers. Dr. Wm. A. Wulf is president of the National Academy of Engineering.

The **Institute of Medicine** was established in 1970 by the National Academy of Sciences to secure the services of eminent members of appropriate professions in the examination of policy matters pertaining to the health of the public. The Institute acts under the responsibility given to the National Academy of Sciences by its congressional charter to be an adviser to the federal government and, upon its own initiative, to identify issues of medical care, research, and education. Dr. Harvey V. Fineberg is president of the Institute of Medicine.

The **National Research Council** was organized by the National Academy of Sciences in 1916 to associate the broad community of science and technology with the Academy's purposes of furthering knowledge and advising the federal government. Functioning in accordance with general policies determined by the Academy, the Council has become the principal operating agency of both the National Academy of Sciences and the National Academy of Engineering in providing services to the government, the public, and the scientific and engineering communities. The Council is administered jointly by both Academies and the Institute of Medicine. Dr. Bruce M. Alberts and Dr. Wm. A. Wulf are chair and vice chair, respectively, of the National Research Council.

www.national-academies.org

Preface

The first U.S.-Russian interacademy workshop on terrorism was held in Moscow in June 2001 with a focus on countering terrorist attacks that could cause catastrophic damage to civilian populations or to the economy or to both. In early 2002 the proceedings of that workshop were published in both English and Russian under the title *High-Impact Terrorism Proceedings of a Russian-American Workshop.*

The events of September 11, 2001, greatly heightened interest within both the National Academies and the Russian Academy of Sciences in expanded cooperation in addressing the challenges of the growing threats of terrorism. Therefore, in December 2001, at the invitation of the National Academies, the Russian Academy of Sciences selected seven Russian specialists to travel to the United States for further discussions with National Academies counterparts and with government officials and other specialists in the United States on many aspects of high-impact terrorism. Based on the recommendations emerging from the discussions among representatives of the academies at that time, in February 2002 the academies agreed to establish parallel committees consisting primarily of academy members with extensive experience in addressing topics of direct relevance to terrorism to develop an expanded program of cooperation in counterterrorism. The charter for these committees, acting jointly, is set forth in Appendix B.

The newly appointed committees decided to meet as soon as feasible to develop a broadened agenda for cooperation. The meeting was held in March 2003 after being postponed for three months because of delays associated with the seizure of hostages by dissidents during a stage production of *Nord-Ost* in Moscow in October 2002. In addition to the meeting of the joint committees, two one-day workshops on urban terrorism and cyberterrorism were held in Moscow just before the meeting. The cochairs of the workshops summarized the workshop conclusions at the meeting. In addition, some members of the committees and a few invited specialists with important insights on terrorism threats and vulnerabilities in their respective countries made technical presentations on topics of special interest. These proceedings include articles based on technical presentations at the two workshops and on selected presentations during the meeting of the committees.

Following the meeting, the Russian Academy of Sciences arranged consultations for the American participants with various Russian government ministries involved in counterterrorism activities (identified in Appendix A). Similar visits were made directly following the Moscow workshop in June 2001. Also, the National Academies arranged for the Russian specialists who visited in December 2001 to exchange views with representatives of U.S. government departments and agencies. These proceedings, together with the proceedings of the workshop in June 2001 and the related consultations with government ministries and agencies in both countries, provide a good basis for development of an agenda for sustained cooperation that should serve the interests of government officials and counterterrorism specialists. This agenda is currently in its formative stage. Six working groups were established by the joint committees to focus on urban terrorism, radiological terrorism, bioterrorism, cyberterrorism, the roots of terrorism, and the role of the nongovernmental sector, and they will help develop this agenda.

We have not attempted to summarize the papers or the discussions in these proceedings. The presentations are sufficiently important that we decided to publish them in their entirety.

ACKNOWLEDGMENTS

This publication was made possible by a grant from the Carnegie Corporation of New York. The statements made and views expressed are solely the responsibility of the authors and do not represent the positions of the Carnegie Corporation or the National Research Council, the Russian Academy of Sciences, or other organizations where the authors are employed.

In addition to a review by committee members, this volume has been reviewed in draft form by several individuals chosen for their technical expertise, in accordance with procedures approved by the NRC's Report Review Committee. The purpose of this independent review is to provide candid and critical comments that will assist the institution in ensuring that the report is as sound as possible and meets institutional standards for quality. The review comments and original draft manuscript remain confidential to protect the integrity of the process.

We wish to thank the following individuals for their review of selected papers: Seymour Goodman, Georgia Institute of Technology; Michael Moodie,

Chemical and Biological Arms Control Institute; and Raphael Perl, Congressional Research Service.

Although these reviewers have provided constructive comments and suggestions, they were not asked to endorse the content of the individual papers. Responsibility for the final content of the papers rests with the individual authors.

Special thanks are extended to Kelly Robbins for her tireless translation of the Russian language papers into English and her editorial services. We also wish to thank Jan Dee Summers, Christopher Holt, and A. Chelsea Sharber for their work in editing these proceedings.

Siegfried S. Hecker
Chair, NRC Committee on Counterterrorism Challenges for Russia and the United States

Glenn Schweitzer
Director, Office for Central Europe and Eurasia

Contents

CYBERTERRORISM

PAPERS PRESENTED TO THE NRC AND RAS COMMITTEES

URBAN TERRORISM

Analysis of the Threats and Consequences of Terrorist Acts in Urban Settings: Outline of a Protection System

*Vladimir Z. Dvorkin**
Russian Academy of Sciences Institute of the
World Economy and International Relations

This report presents selected results of the project "Terrorism in a Megapolis: An Assessment of Threats and Levels of Protection," which was completed in late 2002 by the Center for Political Research in Russia in cooperation with the Expert Innovation Center for Civil Defense and Emergency Situations and the National Anticrime and Antiterrorist Foundation.

The modern industrial infrastructure of highly developed states, in particular in megacities, includes many thousands of radioactive, chemical, and biological facilities and therefore presents a real opportunity for terrorists to inflict catastrophic damage even without using their own weapons of mass destruction, although their desire to obtain such weapons is clear. .

The tragic events in New York City and Washington, D.C., on September 11, 2001, represented the end point in the process of realizing the threats from mass-scale terrorist acts, many dozens of which were committed in the last decade of the last century throughout the world. However, it is impossible to disagree with Senator Richard Lugar, who emphasized that regardless of how monstrous the September 11 tragedy was, the death, destruction, and panic were minimal compared with what would have resulted if weapons of mass destruction had been used.

This tragedy and the obvious threats of variations on it have added powerful impetus to efforts to strengthen cooperation in the world community in all areas related to combating international terrorism, including the military operation in Afghanistan, exchanges of intelligence information, the blocking of illegal fi-

---

*Translated from the Russian by Kelly Robbins.

nancial channels, and the strengthening of control and protection measures for radioactive, chemical, and other materials.

Separate mention should be made of the sharply increased number of publications on problems regarding the analysis of sources, characteristics, and potential of international terrorism and ways of countering its threats. Several of these research areas are distinguished by their completely adequate scientific depth and logic; however, there is a clear lack of systemic research on the problems. At the same time, theoretical and applied systemic research on these problems would seem more than urgent for the development of practical antiterrorism approaches, inasmuch as systemic principles for the study of any types of threats primarily call for the most exhaustive possible structured knowledge of the enemy, including its goals and objectives; financial, material-technical, and professional potential; weapons; and many other characteristics. Potential terrorist targets must be categorized by their degree of accessibility and the level of damage their destruction would entail. These data represent the necessary foundation for organizing antiterrorism efforts. Bringing such research to an adequate level of completion requires the involvement of specialized organizations and a significant number of highly qualified professionals with experience working in these areas.

The results presented in this report are possibly the first (if not the zero) semblance of systemic research in this field. It does not claim to be a comprehensive presentation of all the issues listed above and is oriented primarily toward the problem of megacities.

An analysis of open informational materials and works on the problem of combating terrorist activities in megacities under the new conditions attests to the pressing need to develop a nearly exhaustive list of methods adequate to respond to the widest possible range of threats and types of terrorist activity. In addition to traditional methods, unique means without analogues in the military sphere may be used in the commission of terrorist acts. This is due to the fact that at its current stage of development, society is experiencing rapid and poorly controlled growth in the number of emerging ideas in the development and detailed study of fundamentally new strike effects. These ideas could serve as the basis for the accelerated creation of a wide and diverse array of technical means based on the application of physical, chemical, and biological principles and new technologies that were traditionally used by the terrorists of the past. A terrorist act could be planned over the course of years. The means to be used, the methods for using them, and the scope of the entire operation could be limited only by the availability of financial resources (often enormous) and personnel.

In addition, a certain backwardness of thinking has been observed toward the problem of counterterrorist activities in the political, operational-investigational, informational-analytical, and organizational spheres, and this backwardness gives rise to a shortage of fundamental support for timely decision making in the development of methods and means for conducting counterterrorist activities in megacities. One result of this could be difficulties in efficiently reorienting existing forces and resources and focusing them to meet newly emerging threats. We see the appearance of a specific sort of loss of control over the process of developing means and methods for counterterrorist activities in the interests of ensuring security. Therefore, an orderly structure of recommendations on the ways and means by which terrorist activities are conducted must be developed, as well as decisions on how to combat them within that structure.

An analysis of the consequences and measures involved in fighting nuclear, chemical, and biological terrorism has long been under way, and some impressive results have been achieved. Significant attention is also being focused on how to counter computer and electromagnetic terrorism.

The latter topic merits additional explanation. The possibility of using powerful electromagnetic impulses as a means of attack has become absolutely real because of the development of sources capable of creating peak output on the order of several gigawatts and the miniaturization of the elemental components of military and civilian radioelectronics, which makes these devices vulnerable to extremely low levels of electromagnetic wave energy. Danger lies in the use of electromagnetic signals against the components of computers, which are widely used in systems for managing vital public services in megacities, controlling technological processes in dangerous production facilities, and so forth.

Experiments have shown that components of distributed types of microprocessors and computers have crashed or stalled at field voltages in the ultrashort range on the order of 1 V/cm. At the same time, more complex systems (such as the PC-XT/AT and other more complex computers) were found to have problems with memory and display operations at the level of E < 0.02 V/cm. Unshielded general-use computers were most vulnerable to electromagnetic energy in the frequency range of 1–10 GHz.

A real device capable of producing a super-broadband electromagnetic impulse was developed in the late 1990s using military ammunition containing a common explosive substance. Such ammunition could in principle create an electromagnetic impulse of 0.1–1 MHz in length with an energy value of 0.1–1 kJ and a frequency band of several gigahertz. Progress in creating similar devices for stationary installation and multiple use was demonstrated for the first time in the United States in 1992 as part of the Mark N project.

Mobile generators mounted on heavy-duty trucks and having their own power sources have also been developed. The use of such generators would make it possible to bring down an unshielded system for public utility management in a megacity or a banking system, or it could disable control systems at dangerous production facilities. Therefore, these generators could be viewed as effective tools for carrying out terrorist activities.

The example of opportunities for electromagnetic terrorism attests to the expanding spectrum of violent means and methods of attack. This spectrum could also include space terrorism, which seems to be a far-off prospect. However, the growing number of orbiting satellites and the fact that third world countries will soon create their own space devices mean that the day is coming when space terrorism will be as realistic a possibility as the hijacking of an airplane. The commission of space terrorism would involve, first, the destruction of satellites and other space-based devices or the creation of obstacles that would hinder their normal operation. Second, it could involve the seizure and use of space-based devices to facilitate communications among terrorists or their use for terrorist military operations. Carrying out space terrorism is a task requiring significant financial, intellectual, and material resources; however, it would be inappropriate to fail to consider it as part of the arsenal of methods that terrorists might use in the future.

The listed means of terrorist acts are directly or indirectly related in varying degrees to their impacts on elements of megacities. These elements may be conditionally divided into the following three categories:

1. Elements of megacities that represent direct targets for attack. These include high-rise apartment buildings, places where large numbers of people gather, major transportation hubs, and so forth.

2. Elements through which terrorists plan to achieve their goals. This category includes water systems, through which contaminated drinking water could be widely distributed in one or more locations; various means of transportation; the postal system (mass or targeted delivery of potentially dangerous mail or freight); various computer networks; and so forth.

3. Elements of megacities that represent sources of heightened danger, the destruction or disruption of which would cause wide-scale accidents and catastrophes entailing consequences comparable to those resulting from the use of weapons of mass destruction. Objects in this third category primarily include facilities located in or near the megacity, such as various enterprises in the atomic and chemical industries, research centers that operate nuclear reactors or use dangerous radioactive materials, petroleum storage facilities, and so forth.

It should be noted that terrorist acts directed at sites in the third category and using methods aimed at artificially causing wide-scale accidents could have the most dangerous consequences and therefore require more detailed study consideration.

Despite the measures being taken to make industrial production facilities, the energy industry, and means of transportation more secure and environmentally safe, tendencies toward increasing the scope and level of danger of accidents have been observed. This is the result of the introduction and rapid implementation of new technologies; the inclusion of new substances with toxic, flammable, aggressive, and other harmful properties in production processes; increases in the energy requirements of production; increases in the power of individual pieces of equipment, the size of storage facilities, and the capacities of cargo vehicles; and increases in the speed of production and distribution processes.

The potentially destructive forces inherent in production facilities and technologies create the objective foundation for their focused use as means of attacks aimed at inflicting damage on the regions in which they are located. This could be accomplished by artificially creating conditions necessary for releasing and taking advantage of their destructive potential. Some examples include

- the creation of zones of catastrophic flooding by destroying dams
- the radioactive contamination of an area by destroying nuclear reactors
- the chemical contamination of the atmosphere and water by destroying chemical plants
- the setting of massive fires by burning forests or oil and gas wells
- the spreading of epidemics

It is clear that a megacity's industrial facilities and high population density make it very vulnerable to dangerous forces of an industrial nature that would be unleashed upon the destruction of such facilities by terrorist groups. In this case, nonnuclear means could be used to trigger other factors with uncontrolled and wide-scale destructive effects. As a result, industrial facilities and technologies could be viewed as weapons of mass destruction (WMD), with an attack on them representing a passive form of WMD warfare.

In compiling a list of potentially dangerous facilities in a megacity, we used the results of an analysis of the potential consequences of their destruction.[1] An example of such a list is presented in Table 1. This list, however, does not allow for the ranking of the facilities found in megacities by the level of threat they face from terrorists. This could be done using the following characteristics:

Accessibility of facilities to terrorist attacks:

1. no limitations on access—no services for maintaining overall order at facility
2. no limitations on access—facility has services for maintaining overall order
3. limited access to facility
4. facility under armed guard

Technical means required for carrying out terrorist attack:

1. common military weapons or up to 1 kg of explosives
2. more than 1 kg of explosives
3. vehicles, heavy weapons, or a substantial quantity of explosives
4. dangerous radioactive, chemical, or biological substances
5. special equipment or unique weapons not in the arsenals of troops of the ministries of internal affairs or defense

TABLE 1 Example of a List of Potentially Dangerous Facilities

Type of Industry	Facility or Type of Production (Technology)	Basic Types of Damage Factors	Possible Impact Exclusion Zones, km^2
Electric Power	Located inside city limits or proximal to megacity:		
	• nuclear reactors at atomic power plants	Explosions, fires, radioactive contamination	Up to several hundred km^2
	• storage facilities for spent nuclear fuel	Explosions, fires, radioactive contamination	From tens to several hundred km^2
	• dams at hydroelectric plant reservoirs	Flood surge	From tens to several hundred km^2
Atomic Power	Processing of spent nuclear fuel:		
	• radiochemical plants	Explosions,	Up to several
	• spent fuel storage facilities	radioactive contamination	thousand km^2
Fuel	Extraction and processing of oil and gas:		
	• oil and gas refineries, including units producing ammonia and other powerful poisons	Explosions, massive fires, chemical pollution of atmosphere	From tens to several hundred km^2
Pulp and Paper	Bisulfate production of pulp using powerful poisonous substances	Explosions, massive fires, chemical pollution of atmosphere	From tens to several hundred km^2
Food	Refrigerated processing and storage facilities	Explosions, massive fires, chemical pollution of atmosphere	Up to several km^2
Public Utilities	Water treatment plants and purification facilities	Explosions, massive fires, chemical pollution of atmosphere	Up to several km^2
Agriculture	Storage facilities for anhydrous ammonia and ammonia water for use as soil fertilizers and defoliators for cotton and other crops, central stockpiles of chemical pesticides and herbicides	Explosions, massive fires, chemical pollution of atmosphere	Up to several km^2

TABLE 1 (*Continued*)

Type of Industry	Facility or Type of Production (Technology)	Basic Types of Damage Factors	Possible Impact Exclusion Zones, km^2
Microbiological	Scientific research centers and test facilities:		
	• production of biological agents and mixtures	Pollution of atmosphere and local biospheres	Up to several km^2
	• production of biological livestock feed additives harmful to humans		
Transportation	Railroad tank and freight cars, tanker trucks, marine tankers, and cargo freighters	Explosions, fires, radioactive or chemical contamination of the environment	Up to several km^2
Chemical	General chemistry:	Explosions, fires, chemical contamination of the atmosphere and water	From tens to several hundred km^2
	• production of powerful poisonous substances (chlorine, ammonia, phosgene, hydrocyanic acid, organophosphorus compounds, anhydrous sulfur dioxide, hydrogen fluoride, inorganic acids, etc.		
	• nitrogen and phosphate fertilizers		
	• chemical herbicides and pesticides		
	• chemical fibers and threads		
	• synthetic dyes, resins, and plastics		

Level of expertise required for carrying out terrorist attack:

1. skills in handling firearms or minimal knowledge of explosives
2. experience in working with explosives, expertise in evaluating the direction and destructive potential of explosions
3. knowledge of specific details regarding the operation of the target facility, high level of skill and expertise in handling specialized equipment or dangerous special substances

Frequency of occurrence of conditions under which terrorist act would cause maximum damage:

1. constant
2. daily during peak hours
3. several times per month
4. several times per year
5. unique conditions that might be repeated only once every few years

Consequences of terrorist act at facility:

1. several dozen victims, localized damage, insignificant economic damage (on megacity scale)
2. about 100 victims, several square kilometers suffering destruction or contamination, normal life of the city paralyzed for several days, substantial economic damage
3. several hundred victims, tens of square kilometers suffering destruction or contamination, city infrastructure disrupted and requiring several weeks or federal government funds and resources to restore, economic damage comparable to the annual city budget
4. several thousand victims, several hundred square kilometers suffering destruction or contamination, consequences beyond the megacity, event of nationwide scope

A categorized list of a megacity's critical (most vulnerable) potential terrorist targets, including transportation networks, places where large numbers of people congregate (stadiums, shopping malls), chemical enterprises, research reactors, water supply sources, electric power plants, and so forth, ranked in terms of the above-listed criteria, would include more than 50 groups of facilities.[1] Rankings of points in megacities vulnerable to terrorist attack are captured in Table 2.

This list is one of the fundamental components in the development and implementation of the comprehensive targeted program "Megacity—Capital" (TsKP MS). The goals of the program are to create, introduce, and develop an integrated system for combating terrorism. Its objectives are to coordinate the efforts of the various ministries, departments, organizations, and institutions regardless of level of jurisdiction or form of property ownership with the aim of achieving the stated goals.

The Megacity—Capital Program must be an integrated set of subprograms linked through resources, implementers, and timetables. The subprograms include taking inventory, systematizing, classifying, identifying, and evaluating the characteristics and vulnerability levels of all of the megacity's high-risk industrial facilities and natural sites both as potential terrorist targets and as

TABLE 2   Example of a Categorized List of Critical (Most Vulnerable in Terms of Terrorist Threat) Points in a Megacity

Name of Megacity Facility	Typical number of facilities in megacity	Accessibility of facility	Technical means required for attack	Level of expertise required for attack	Frequency of conditions needed for maximum damage	Consequences of terrorist attack
Atomic power industry facilities in or close to megacity:						
• nuclear power plant	1	4	2–4	3	1	2–4
• spent nuclear fuel storage facilities	1–2	4	2–4	3	1	2–4
Industrial facilities:						
• chemical plants and enterprises using radioactive materials	about 40	4	2 or 3	3	1	2–4
• oil and gas refineries, including units producing ammonia and other powerful poisons	2–3	4	1–3	1 or 2	1	2–4
• petroleum depots	2–4	4	1 or 2	1 or 2	1	1–3
• water treatment stations with stockpiles of 330–350 tons of chlorine at each	4–6	3	1 or 2	1 or 2	1	1–3
• ammonia storage facilities at refrigeration plants (10–120 tons) or wholesale produce enterprises (2–170 tons)	about 10	3	1 or 2	1 or 2	1	1–3
• liquid rocket fuel plants (hydrazine, asymmetric dimethylhydrazine, dinitrogen tetrocide, etc.)	1–2	4	1 or 2	3	1	1–3
• explosives plants	3–6	3	1 or 2	1–3	1	1–3
• pulping plants using bisulfates and other powerful poisonous substances	2–4	3	1 or 2	1–3	1	2 or 3

continued

TABLE 2　*(Continued)*

Name of Megacity Facility	Typical number of facilities in megacity	Accessibility of facility	Technical means required for attack	Level of expertise required for attack	Frequency of conditions needed for maximum damage	Consequences of terrorist attack
• coking plants and facilities producing anhydrous sulfur dioxide, sulfuric acid, and other powerful poisonous substances	1–2	3	1 or 2	1–3	1	2 or 3
• storage facilities for anhydrous ammonia and ammonia water for use as soil and fertilizer and defoliator for cotton and other crops, central stockpiles of chemical pesticides and herbicides	3–5	3	1 or 2	1–3	1	2 or 3
• plants producing biological agents, mixtures, and livestock feed additives harmful to humans	2–4	3	1 or 2	1–3	1	1–3
• synthetic rubber factories	1–3	3	1–3	1–3	1	1–3
• chemical plants using synthetic organics (phenol, aniline, benzene)	about 10	3	1–3	1–3	1	1–3
Megacity water supply system:						
• water mains and wells supplying the city with drinking water	about 10,000 km	2	1 or 4	1 or 3	1	1 or 2
• water treatment facilities	20–30	3	1 or 4	1 or 3	1	1 or 2
• boiler plants	about 100	3	1 or 2	1	1	1
• sewer system	5000–6000 km	1	1 or 2	1	1	1
• storm drain network	about 6000 km	1	1 or 2	1	1	1
• water intake points	10–15	3	1 or 4	1 or 3	1	1 or 2

TABLE 2   (Continued)

Name of Megacity Facility	Typical number of facilities in megacity	Accessibility of facility	Technical means required for attack	Level of expertise required for attack	Frequency of conditions needed for maximum damage	Consequences of terrorist attack
City energy supply system:						
• gas pipelines and propane tank filling stations	about 100	2	1	1	1	1 or 2
• power plants supplying the city with electricity	20–25	4	2 or 4	1 or 2	1	1–3
• electric power lines	several thousand km	1	1	1	1	1
• substations	about 150	1	1	1	1	1
Places where large numbers of people gather:						
• stadiums	about 50	2	1–3	1–3	3	1 or 2
• movie theaters and concert halls	about 90					

possible sources of industrial accidents, catastrophes, and natural disasters. Other subprograms involve the development of a unified conceptual and terminological framework and a set of laws, regulations, and reference documents, as well as the implementation of a series of special research, design, industrial, socioeconomic, organizational, and other measures to ensure the effective handling of security problems related to combating high-tech terrorism. Integrating all existing security and public service systems will make it possible to create a systematic basis for protecting the population, facilities, and territories from various types of external and internal threats.

The difficulty in developing and implementing the comprehensive program for countering terrorism in megacities can, on the one hand, be overcome by organizing the system into threat classes, for example, radiation, chemical, radiological. However, in doing so, it would be even more difficult to categorize and identify the top priority targets for protection given the limits on available

resources. On the other hand, it would be expedient to develop and test procedures for implementing such a program in a typical district of a megacity, one
that includes examples of the types of facilities that would be potential terrorist
targets.

More detailed materials on the problems mentioned above may be found in
the previously cited publication of the Center for Political Research in Russia,
which its authors believe to be the first systematic attempt at a comprehensive
analysis of the problems of combating terrorism in megacities. The publication
also provides a basis for the initiation of a more in-depth systematic analysis of
these problems and the development of a set of practical recommendations and
organizational and technical measures for effectively meeting these new security
challenges.

NOTE

1. Terrorism in a megapolis: assessment of threats and levels of protection. 2002. Moscow:
Human Rights Publishers.

Urban Security and September 11, 2001, in New York City: Projection of Threats onto a City as a Target and Measures to Avert Them or Minimize Their Impact

George Bugliarello
Polytechnic University

Cities encompass a growing portion of the world's population—today, more than 40 percent and in the United States almost 80 percent. They are sites of concentrated economic and social activities and government operations and have extensive infrastructures. In the very nature of the activities they host, in their structures, and in their monuments, they also constitute powerful symbols that embody the pride of a nation. Cities, especially large ones, are particularly vulnerable because all their systems are interdependent, and the vulnerability of one system leads to that of other systems. For these reasons, historically, cities have been prime targets of terrorist attacks, exemplified by the bomb exploded in the World Trade Center in New York City in 1993; the attack and destruction eight years later on September 11, 2001, of the World Trade Center in New York City; the attack on the Pentagon in Washington, D.C., also on September 11, 2001; and the attacks in the Tokyo subway, in Tel Aviv, in New Delhi, and in a Moscow theater production of *Nord-Ost*.

Thus far, most attacks have been predominantly low-tech ones, executed with simple means. However, many other kinds of attack are possible, exemplified by the attacks with sarin in Tokyo and with anthrax in the United States and by the airplanes of September 11, 2001 (which were hijacked, however, with simple means). Cities have also been, historically, sites of major incidents of social violence—riots and street brawls, as well as civil internal wars and external warfare. A brief and by no means complete listing of what happened in the decade 1989–1999 is contained in Table 1.

An important characteristic of cities is that not only can they be targets of attacks, but they can be potential suppliers of what terrorists need to carry out their attacks (Box 1). They possess a large number of biological and chemical laboratories and stores, as well as, in many cases, biological and chemical indus-

TABLE 1 Cities with Major Incidents of Social Violence (1989–1999)[1]

Civil or Internal War or Urban Terrorism	Riots or Street Protests by the Civilian Population	External Warfare
Baku	Belgrade	Baghdad
Beijing	Bombay	Belgrade
Bogotá	Calcutta	Grozny
Buenos Aires	Dhaka	
Cairo	Jakarta	
Colombo	Los Angeles	
Kabul	Rangoon	
Karachi		
Kinshasa		
Lahore		
Lima		
London		
Madrid		
Manchester		
Mogadishu		
Monrovia		
Moscow		
New York		
Oklahoma City		
Paris		
Phnom Penh		
Port au Prince		
Tbilisi		
Tokyo		

tries; they can provide radiation sources in hospitals, laboratories, and instructional nuclear reactors; they have fuel depots, gas pipelines, liquefied natural gas storage, electronics stores, computer labs in universities that can give access to cyberterrorists, and vehicles that can be used in a terrorist attack—trucks, tankers, bulldozers, armored bank vehicles, as well as just cars. Cities are also large potential suppliers of human resources for terrorism and—in libraries, universities, and other institutions—of the information terrorists may need to plan and carry out their attacks. They can be significant sources of funding through banks and businesses and through associations and religious institutions that can organize fundraising drives.

The threats that can be aimed at a city are the well-known ones of chemical attacks (explosives and poisons); biological, radiological, and nuclear attacks; and cyber-, electromagnetic, and psychological attacks. These threats find the city a target-rich environment, housing a complex interacting system of people, buildings, infrastructures (utilities, roads, railroads, ports, airports), hospitals, schools, churches, businesses, government, military bases, and also of patterns of work, business, home life, leisure, and shopping activities that, all together, define a city's way of life. A potential target that has grown very rapidly is the

BOX 1
Cities as Potential Suppliers of Terrorists' Needs:
Examples of Terrorists' Needs

- Biological or chemical labs and stores
- Electronic supplies
- Hospital radiation sources
- Fuel deposits
- Gas pipelines
- University computer labs
- Vehicles, such as tankers, bulldozers, or armored bank vehicles
- Human resources, such as students
- Information, such as libraries and universities
- Sources of funding

so-called telecom hotels, facilities housing the devices that connect networks. Table 2 shows a recent accounting of their number in some American cities.

Each threat to a city can target one or more of these interacting systems or activities (Figure 1). Explosives can be targeted at people or structures; electromagnetic pulses can be directed at elements of the infrastructure, such as airports or utilities, which in turn can affect the functioning of hospitals, schools, and other institutions; and psychological threats can be aimed at people and organi-

TABLE 2 A Growing Potential Target: Cities with the Largest Number of Telecom Hotels[2]

City	Number of Telecom Hotels, 2001
New York	64
Los Angeles	46
Dallas	37
Atlanta	36
Seattle	30
Chicago	72
San Francisco	25
Miami	24
Phoenix	23
Austin	19
San Diego	17
Portland	17
Washington, D.C.	16
Denver	16
Las Vegas	14
San Jose	13
Pittsburgh	13
Philadelphia	13
Jacksonville	13
Minneapolis	12

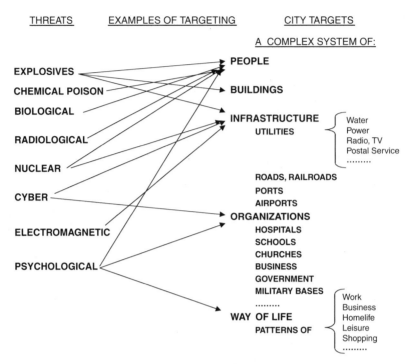

FIGURE 1 Cities' threats and targets.

zations to affect the way of life of the city's inhabitants. In protecting cities from terrorist threats, we frequently tend to focus more on the physical protection of people, structures, and organizations than on the powerful impacts of psychological threats.

In general, the threats can reach the targets with a variety of modalities of delivery. Countermeasures may address directly the threats, the modalities of their delivery, and the strengthening and resilience of the target (Figure 2). The countermeasures directly addressing the threats at their origin or in their transit toward the city, for example, in a ship, plane, or train, are basically the same whether an urban or nonurban attack is considered. However, many of the countermeasures against the modalities of delivery within the city and many of the countermeasures for protecting targets are peculiar to the urban environment. Modalities of delivery may range from cars in basement garages to the arrival of weapons of mass destruction in shipping containers, from the penetration of heating, ventilation, and air conditioning systems to attacks on subway stations. Means for counteracting them include sensors, reconfiguration of traffic patterns, as well as, of course, inspections and checkpoints. Countermeasures to increase the resilience of targets in an urban environment include hardening of

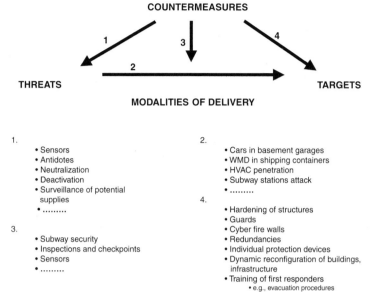

FIGURE 2 Countermeasures.

structures to explosives, fire, chemical, and biological attacks; cyber firewalls; redundancies; dynamic reconfiguration of buildings and infrastructure; and training of first responders in procedures to evacuate tall buildings.

Given the complexity of the system of targets in a city shown in Figure 1, an overarching need is a comprehensive system view of a city that explicitly addresses the interdependence of components and overall vulnerabilities. It is fair to say that, at this moment, such a view is by and large lacking. Integration of responses, starting with the issue of how persons in charge can coordinate the response to an attack in an integrated fashion, is also a critical need. There are increasingly, however, technological tools being developed, such as ad hoc computer platforms, that can help an incident commander in the integrated management of all the resources available.

PRINCIPLES AND OBSERVATIONS

From the aforementioned, 10 principles and observations emerge:

1. Given the nature of the city as a system of interacting systems, the importance of the weakest link is of overriding significance. Examples are cybersecurity vulnerabilities, dependence on the Internet, and the vulnerability of crowds

piling up against control points. Addressing these interacting systems and assessing and correcting the vulnerabilities of their weakest links are of vital importance and require advance modeling and simulations.

2. Sociotechnological interface factors often represent a weak link in the system of defense of cities. Failures of protective systems may be as much failures of social organization or human nature, as of a purely technical nature.

3. The intimidation and terrorizing of a population can be carried out by purely psychological means and deserves major attention.

4. Not everybody or everything can be protected in a city, making it essential to identify the critical components of infrastructures and organizations and give priority to their protection.

5. In designing the protection of a city, starting with that of its critical components, it is important to distinguish among what can be done now, what could be done in a relatively short time, and what will require a much longer time. Each of these time horizons needs to be addressed. Thus, immediate protection of a building may require guards and checkpoints, but in a longer time frame redesign of the building and development of sophisticated sensors may improve the efficacy of the protection and become more desirable.

6. The issue of centralization versus decentralization is complex. In some cases, decentralization is important for certain critical systems, as it is for major network nodes and telecom hotels, to reduce the vulnerability of the overall system. In other cases, however, the demands of the situation are not so simple. Thus, first responder systems need to be centralized to provide an organized response to an incident, but at the same time, they need to be decentralized in some fashion to reduce their vulnerability and make the response organization resilient even to direct attack and destruction of its command post.

7. Piggybacking on other systems, that is, the ability to use existing systems to which new functions may be added, becomes important given the magnitude of the task in providing a defense for a city. For instance, existing networks of air quality monitors can be enhanced with sensors for chemical and biological substances, and cellular phones can become elements of an incident information system.

8. Mobilization of private resources can contribute facilities and personnel and carry out important functions in response to terrorist threats or attacks. There are, in cities, very significant resources outside the government systems, such as medical departments of companies and private engineering firms or construction firms.

9. In water systems, the major vulnerability to chemical, biological, and radiological agents is usually more in the pipes than in the reservoirs. This fact may need to be taken into account in order to identify the critical vulnerability and deploy scarce resources in the defense of cities.

10. Preparation for and response to terrorist attacks places large demands on training. For instance, the operators of subway systems need to be trained to

understand the fundamental difference between the actions required in a fire and those required in a biological or poison attack. In a fire, the imperative is to attempt to vent the fire as much as possible to the exterior of the subway. In a biological or chemical attack, the imperative is to contain chemical and biological agents within the subway, so as not to vent them outside to the street level where they could cause a very high number of casualties, beyond the people trapped in the subway.

SOME SEPTEMBER 11, 2001, LESSONS IN NEW YORK CITY

The events of September 11, 2001, in New York City can provide a useful reminder of the technological challenges that a city faces when confronted by a terrorist attack. I offer a series of observations and assessments as a means to stimulate further discussion. Some of the weaknesses discussed here have been or are in the process of being remedied.

• The security checkpoints at the airports where the terrorists boarded the planes to attack the World Trade Center in New York and the Pentagon in Washington, D.C., were not effective. It is not totally clear why, but one of the contributing factors was that the box cutters used by some of the hijackers were not, at the time, prohibited as passenger carry-on items.

• In New York City, a lack of interoperability prevented the fire department and the police department from communicating effectively with each other. This was due to different frequencies and to incompatible devices, as well as, possibly, to sociological factors. Consequently, for instance, the police department had information on the conditions of the buildings attacked, as watched from helicopters, that could not be made available to the fire department.

• The incident commander of the fire department could not reach firefighters on high floors in the World Trade Center towers because of the inadequacy of the department's radio communications. This is a significant technological challenge.

• The city's emergency center was located in the World Trade Center—the most vulnerable target for the attack. The fire and police department command posts were located at opposite ends of the incident scene. Also, site and traffic control became difficult because of the large number of volunteers that tried to converge on the incident site and the lack of rapid assessment of the dimensions of the incident. All these incident management challenges are technologically relatively easy to address.

• More complex was the lack of immediate availability of building plans to the first responders. Timely availability of those plans would, in general, greatly facilitate the first responders' task of developing a response strategy and deploying their forces.

• Uncertainty about the possibility of further terrorist action might have led to an overreaction. This was prudent in light of what was known at the time, but lack of sufficient intelligence led to reactions that affected a large portion of the metropolitan area. The availability of intelligence and a broad citywide system model are major technological challenges that need to be addressed.

• The occupants of the World Trade Center buildings received conflicting guidance as to what action they should be taking. Escape routes inside the buildings were bottlenecked. Even more serious, blocked escapes to the roof above the floors that were hit by the aircrafts would have prevented evacuation from the roof, even if means had been available to do so. Evacuation from high floors when internal escape is impossible and the inability of helicopters, in general, to evacuate from the roofs of tall buildings in the presence of strong wind or fire are major technological challenges. Another challenge is providing inexpensive personal devices, such as simple masks and fireproof clothing, which would enhance the chance of a person to escape. (Some of these masks are commercially available.)

• There was a concentration of telecommunications network equipment at the target. Colocation of wire and wireless communications equipment at a target does not provide alternatives when their common site is destroyed.

• Structural steel elements in the two World Trade Center buildings had inadequate fireproofing, for reasons still to be fully understood. This would not have prevented the collapse of the structures but conceivably could have helped to slow it. The incident also showed the vulnerability of ultralight structures such as those of the World Trade Center towers. In the Pentagon, the resistance of structures that had recently been reinforced with strong cross-member connection showed the importance of structural design in limiting the damage.

• It was not possible to quickly assess the structural condition of the World Trade Center buildings—both those directly impacted and those surrounding them. This was a crucial factor in the indecision about evacuation of the towers and in determination of the actions that should have been taken for the other buildings not directly impacted. A technological challenge is to provide sensors that can determine the structural conditions of a building in order to alleviate the cumbersome and less effective means of optically observing possible structural movements with human operators around the clock, as had to be done at the World Trade Center.

• In the area of remediation, debris clearing in New York City was done in an exemplary fashion. It highlighted the technological and sociopolitical challenges presented by the magnitude of the debris, in coordinating the clearing actions, finding a site for the debris, and transporting the debris to outlying areas (outside Manhattan). A major technological challenge, of course, is remediation of the possible health effects of the incident. As yet, the long-term effects of the attack on the World Trade Center are not fully known.

• The issue of planning and public approval for the reconstruction phase after the attack has presented significant legal and social challenges.

In addition, other needs emerge from the experience of September 11, 2001. Some of them are mainly technical, while others are of a more sociotechnological nature. A partial list in no particular order might include

- secure communications networks for first responders
- ad hoc networks to enable all the emergency responders to communicate with each other and possibly with victims immediately after an incident
- self-healing grids for telecommunications and other utilities networks
- in-building repeaters optimally positioned for incident communication
- portable rapid sensors of biochemical and radiological threats
- supplemental technological means for guards where feasible or desirable
- robots for investigation and action (robots may be purely electromechanical or may also include human involvement)
- standard paradigms and programs for assessing overall vulnerabilities and risks of a city to various terrorist threats, singly or in combination
- virtual reality simulators to train emergency managers and first responders and to better visualize the interlocking vulnerabilities of the systems that make up the city
- data banks about previous incidents, pertinent science and technology information and resources, and so forth
- a better understanding of the behavioral patterns of decision makers, first responders, and the population at large when under stress
- a better understanding of the psychology and behavior of terrorists
- new design concepts for structures, networks, and supply systems
- improved interfaces between operations organizations and science and technology resources

THE ROLE OF POLYTECHNIC UNIVERSITY

Universities can be a significant component of the resources that a city can utilize in addressing threats to its security. Polytechnic University in New York is a case in point. The university has its Brooklyn campus located at Metrotech (an urban knowledge park)[3] two miles from the World Trade Center. In the wake of the September 11, 2001, attacks, it developed an Urban Security Initiative (USI) with the mission of addressing pressing urban security problems through the engineering, scientific, management, and educational capabilities of the university and collaborating institutions, industries, and public entities. The initiative is favored because Metrotech is also the site of the headquarters of the city's fire department; the Department of Information Technology, a major energy utility; and technological centers of major financial institutions.

The USI's current focus is on fire and emergency communications and operations, cybersecurity, biochemical sensors, and urban infrastructural systems, particularly water and energy utilities and transportation systems. These topics, and other emerging ones, are addressed through research and development, education and training, and conferences and symposia. USI is endeavoring to develop a repository of information on urban security issues and technologies. The scope of the initiative as a catalyzer of the expertise of Polytechnic University is shown in Figure 3, and the overall conception of its interaction with other organizations and institutions is shown in Figure 4.

FIGURE 3 The Urban Security Initiative at Polytechnic University as catalyst of the university's resources.

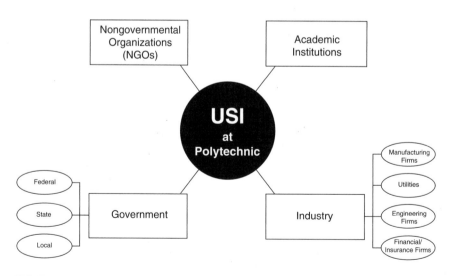

FIGURE 4 The Polytechnic University Urban Security Initiative: public-private partnerships.

CONCLUSION

The issue of urban security is immense and complex. This paper has attempted to provide an overview of some of its principal elements and characteristics, complemented by observations about the events of September 11, 2001, in New York City. The problems that cities face in confronting terrorism demand special attention and present major scientific and sociotechnological challenges.

NOTES

1. Mitchell, 1999, *http://www.ees.lanl.gov/EES5/Urban_Security/pdfs/cities_tatlissues.pdf.*

2. Evans-Crowley, J., E. J. Malechi, and A. McIntee. 2002. Planning Responses to Telecom Hotels: What Accounts for Increased Regulation of Colocation. Journal of Urban Technology 9:3 (December).

3. Bugliarello, G. 2002. Urban Knowledge Parks in Toward a New Agenda: Business, Social and Urban Development Impacts, Proceedings of the XIX IASP World Conference on Science and Technology Parks, International Association of Science Parks.

Lessons Learned from the *Nord-Ost* Terrorist Attack in Moscow from the Standpoint of Russian Security and Law Enforcement Agencies

Yevgeny A. Kolesnikov[*]
Russian Federal Security Service

It was not today or even yesterday when terrorism arose as a social phenomenon. Political terrorism became an international problem at the start of the twentieth century. While the activities of extremists were previously of a targeted nature, in our times they have victimized not only state leaders and prominent public and religious figures but also completely random citizens, and in most cases the terror strikes have been directed against these very individuals.

The tragic events that occurred in Moscow on October 23, 2002, represent one link in the chain of acts committed by international terrorists. At 9:05 p.m. that day, an armed band of terrorists headed by the Chechen field commander Movsar Baraev seized the Palace of Culture of the Moscow Ball-Bearing Factory, where a performance of the musical *Nord-Ost* was under way. There were more than 900 people in the building, including theater personnel.[1]

This act may be placed in the same category as crimes committed by members of al Qaeda, the Taliban, and other international terrorist organizations in the United States, Indonesia, and various countries of the Middle East. There is no doubt that this act represents the latest manifestation of international terrorism in its most extreme form and should be viewed as a blow against the entire international security system, affecting the interests of all civilized states. The true goal of the act was to harm the territorial integrity and security of the Russian Federation.

At 9:30 p.m. on October 23, 2002, dispatch services of the Federal Security Service (FSB) and internal affairs agencies received reports that a group of terrorists had seized a large number of hostages at the Moscow Cultural Center of

---

[*]Translated from the Russian by Kelly Robbins.

the State Ball-Bearing Factory, located at 7 Melnikov Street. At 9:35 p.m., after the reports were checked and verified, an alarm went out to special services personnel. Information on the seizure of the hostages was relayed to the president of the Russian Federation, the heads of federal ministries and agencies, and the Moscow city authorities.

In order to handle the situation and coordinate efforts to free the hostages, an operational headquarters was established, including representatives of the FSB, the Ministry of Internal Affairs (MVD), the Ministry of Emergency Situations, the Ministry of Defense, city administrative and management agencies, the Committee on Health Protection, and other specialists in rendering urgent aid in extreme situations.

On orders from the operational headquarters, heightened security was put in place around official government buildings and critically important elements of the city's infrastructure. Law enforcement units, special operational response detachments, personnel from the Ministry of Emergency Situations, and emergency medical and fire brigades were deployed in the area of the tragedy. The area was surrounded by police forces and MVD troops.

In accordance with plans that had been developed, forces from specialized detachments in the area deployed a mobile command center. A round-the-clock communications channel was established to exchange information with representatives of law enforcement agencies and special services of foreign states accredited in Moscow, which had provided detailed information on their countries' citizens who were among the hostages as well as offers of practical and technical assistance. Regularly scheduled briefings were organized for these partners.

Working under severe time constraints, the operational headquarters had to take many varied aspects of the situation into account. Thus, as new information was coming in about the circumstances surrounding the hostage taking and the situation inside the building, efforts were simultaneously under way to prepare action plans for various scenarios under which events could develop.

Already on October 23, the operational headquarters was informed of the existence of a facility identical to the Cultural Center of the Ball-Bearing Plant (the Meridian movie theater), and special assault units of the FSB Special Operations Center (SOC) began training exercises there. As a result of these exercises, on October 25, commanders of the operations units of the SOC outlined an overall concept for the military/law enforcement component of a possible special operation, developed various options for storming the building, and coordinated the details of cooperation with the various groups involved. They then informed the operational headquarters that they were standing ready to conduct the operation.

Meanwhile, the operational headquarters was also taking measures aimed at freeing the hostages by other means. International experience in conducting such operations has shown that although storming a building is, as a rule, extremely effective, it very often entails threats to the hostages' lives. Therefore, storming the building was not seen as the only option for resolving the situation. The preferred method, which could produce positive results under certain conditions, was to remove the terrorists from the building through negotiations. The plan was to gradually improve the situation for the hostages and then either force the terrorists to completely or partially give up their demands or neutralize them so that they presented the least possible risk to the captive citizens.

With that in mind, the negotiation process was initiated with the terrorists by means of the hostages' mobile telephones. The terrorists' demands were learned, and an understanding was reached regarding the parties with whom the terrorists were prepared to negotiate. Telephone contacts maintained with the hostages also made it possible to obtain information about what was happening in the concert hall on a real-time basis. To develop a scenario of what had occurred, individuals who had witnessed the seizure of the building were questioned on orders from the operational headquarters. Members of the Duma and representatives of public organizations and the media were included in the process of negotiations with the terrorists.[2] As a result of the negotiations, several groups of hostages were freed, including children less than 10 years of age.

From the first hours of the tragedy, the special services units involved took measures to assist the hostages. For instance, at 11:40 p.m. on October 23, during a reconnaissance of the perimeter of the theater complex, a metal door was discovered leading to a nightclub in the complex. Cries for help could be heard coming from inside. Following appropriate safety precautions, the door was opened, and about 40 people were freed from the building. During a search of basements, roofs, and the interior courtyard of the complex, three more escaped hostages were found. An SOC officer was wounded in a shoot-out with the terrorists while covering two women who had jumped from the second story of the Cultural Center. Overall, 113 people were freed by various means before the building was stormed.[3]

Officers from the screening group questioned the freed hostages and the individuals who had served as intermediaries in the negotiations. In particular, it was established that the terrorists were actively using methods of psychological pressure on the hostages and their relatives outside the building that had been seized. By telephone the terrorists were demanding that the relatives organize and conduct protest demonstrations in Moscow calling for the removal of federal troops from the Chechen Republic and the granting of independence to Chechnya. Out of fear for their loved ones, the relatives of the hostages were forced to attend those demonstrations.

Furthermore, to ensure their control over the situation in the concert hall, the terrorists used well-known psychological tactics by which some hostages characteristically begin to experience feelings of gratitude towards their captors under periods of stress despite the harsh treatment they are receiving. Thus, the hostages were for a long time deprived of food, water, and the ability to move around in the hall and were subjected to humiliations in performing essential natural functions. According to the estimations of health care specialists, hypodynamia, exhaustion, and dehydration had set in, with these conditions being capable of producing lethal consequences. The goal of these inhuman actions on the part of the terrorists was to subjugate the will of the hostages.

Based on information coming in from various sources, a map was drawn showing the placement of the terrorists and hostages and the locations where explosive devices had been set. From an analysis of the information received during the range of search, tactical, organizational, and technical operations that were carried out, the following scenario emerged. About 1,000 hostages were being held by a group of 35–40 terrorists in the auditorium of the Cultural Center. Two powerful explosive devices had been placed in the center of the hall and on the balcony, and mines had been placed on the stage and aimed into the auditorium. Some 15–18 female suicide bombers wearing belts with explosive devices were deployed around the perimeters and in the center of the seating area.

Terrorists armed with automatic weapons and grenades were located on the stage and in the balconies. Powerful explosive devices had possibly been placed under the weight-bearing structural supports of the building. The bandits had established observation posts and fire points in technical and maintenance areas on the second and third floors, making it impossible for tactical groups to make a covert entry into the Cultural Center building. In the opinion of explosives specialists, the simultaneous detonation of the explosive devices would have led to the complete destruction of the building and the certain deaths of all the hostages and tactical team members (more than 1,000 people).

It should also be noted that the number of victims could have been twice as high. There were 17 buildings in the restricted zone around the Palace of Culture alone. Of them, 10 were directly facing the building that had been prepared for detonation. The average distance from these buildings to the Palace of Culture was approximately 200 m. The structures included a military hospital, an educational institution, factory facilities, and apartment buildings, all of them hooked up to natural gas pipelines. If an intentionally or accidentally initiated explosion were to occur, the blast wave or debris could damage the gas lines. If sparks or pieces of burning debris were to fall into the factory grounds, they could ignite tanks of fuel or other chemical reagents or set off explosions of oxygen tanks—in other words, a major industrial catastrophe could result.

The operational headquarters took measures to resolve the situation peacefully, but it was not possible to achieve the desired results. The position taken by the terrorists ruled out any possibility of seeking a compromise solution. It was established that Baraev was not an independent figure and that decisions were being made by individuals located not only outside the building but also outside the borders of Russia. The terrorists' reconsideration of the agreement to release the foreigners, Baraev's October 25 statement that they would begin shooting the hostages at 6:00 a.m. on October 26, the deaths of four people (one woman and three men who were shot), and the previous behavior and personal characteristics of the terrorists reduced the chance of a peaceful outcome of the negotiations to zero and served as the basis for the decision to storm the building.[4]

From 5:00 to 5:30 a.m. on October 26, after all the necessary security measures were taken, assault teams were moved into their initial positions. It was obvious that in order to neutralize a large group of well-prepared terrorists with established positions in a building with a large number of rooms, individuals who had not only firearms but also an enormous array of explosives deployed in direct proximity to the hostages and at the most vulnerable points in the building's structure, the situation required an extraordinary plan of action that would preclude the possibility of any explosion. Therefore, the forward deployment of the assault teams was preceded by the use of special gas, which according to the plans of the operation's leadership would sharply reduce the capacity of the terrorists for resisting the assault. Taking into account the fact that the gas could affect the hostages as well, additional emergency medical service personnel supplied with the necessary antidotes were moved in close to the building.

As for the characteristics of the gas and the concentration used, these were selected by specialists with experience in this area. Fentanyl-based gas is widely used in surgery throughout the world, and it facilitates the temporary reduction of patients' movements without threatening their lives or health.

The assault teams included explosives specialists. The teams gained entry to the building through three access points—the nightclub, the central entrance, and the lobby windows. In a very short time, after overcoming the armed resistance of the terrorists, the assault teams burst into the auditorium and began defusing the explosive devices and evacuating the people.

During the special operation, which resulted in the elimination of 41 fighters led by Movsar Baraev, more than 750 hostages were freed, including 60 foreigners. Four members of the special forces units were wounded; two of the four were hospitalized. A number of individuals suspected of being accomplices to the terrorists were also detained during the course of the special operation around the theater complex.

Emergency medical assistance was provided to all the victims; however, 129 people died, including 8 foreign citizens. With regard to these victims, the loss of whom was unfortunately impossible to avoid, the main factors that increased the likelihood of their deaths were as predicted by health care specialists, namely stress, hypodynamia, hunger, dehydration, and the consequent exacerbation of preexisting illnesses, which are absolutely to be expected in people in a weakened state.[5]

During the operation, many automatic weapons, ammunition, and 76.6 kg of explosives were discovered and taken from the terrorists, including 17 automatic rifles, 20 handguns, 25 homemade explosive devices, so-called suicide belts, 2 homemade bombs in the form of metallic tanks filled with OF-540 artillery shells (with a total weight of 12 kg of explosives), 106 grenades (90 of which were homemade from VOG-17M and VOG-25 grenades for automatic grenade launchers), and more than 5,000 rounds of ammunition.

These are the basic figures characterizing the results of the operation. However, an analysis of the events of those days provides a basis for a broader range of conclusions and evaluations that have been drawn not only by law enforcement agencies and the special services but also by Russian society in general. Even the most reliable arguments pointing out that casualties were unavoidable under the circumstances and that there would have been far more victims if the start of the special operation had been postponed will not bring back those whose lives were taken by the plague of our times, international terrorism.

The Moscow city prosecutor's office has initiated criminal case No. 229133 based on Article 30 Part 3 (preparation for crime), Article 205 Part 3 (terrorism), and Article 206 Part 3 (hostage taking) of the Criminal Code of the Russian Federation.

Evidence gathered during the investigation includes documentation of repeated attempts to force Russia's senior leadership to hold talks with Aslan Maskhadov, as well as the prerecorded message from the terrorists that was broadcast by the al-Jazeera network, the psychological pressure that was placed on the hostages to force them to sign an appeal to the Russian president, the placing of telephone calls to the hostages' relatives and to the media asking them to organize and conduct rallies in support of the terrorists' demands, and the well-developed campaign conducted in the media. All of this evidence illustrates once again that the action was planned in advance and was supported in circles opposed to Russian government policy in the North Caucasus.

By means of coordinated investigations and operational efforts, the Moscow city prosecutor's office, the FSB, the Main Administration for Combating Organized Crime of the MVD Criminal Militia Service, and the Moscow Main Administration for Internal Affairs have done a great deal of work to clarify the circumstances of the hostage taking, determine who actually participated in the terrorist act, uncover the connections between the terrorists and their accomplices, and obtain information about terrorist acts that might be in preparation.

An analysis of the evidence gathered during the investigation illustrates the unbreakable link between this crime and the designs of the ideologists of international terrorism, who plan and finance broad-scale terrorist acts throughout the world. The methods used in developing and implementing the preparatory phase and the act of hostage taking itself were characteristic of those used by extremist organizations associated with al Qaeda, the Taliban, and other criminal groups espousing terrorism and violence as a means of achieving their goals.

The unshakable links between international terrorist organizations and fighters operating in the North Caucasus are also confirmed by the fact that Baraev's bandit group included foreign citizens from the Middle East. International terrorist leaders were involved in preparing and committing the terrorist act. They provided moral and material support to Baraev's group, including support sent from abroad, and took part in the leadership of this act. This is illustrated by the repeated attempts made immediately before the terrorist act, including some attempts from abroad, to force Russia's senior leadership to negotiate with Aslan Maskhadov.

Among the materials gathered for the criminal case are a video cassette of an interview given by Maskhadov on October 18, 2002 (five days before the events), in which he threatens to carry out terrorist acts, and a video of an August 2002 meeting of Maskhadov, Shamil Basaev, Movsar Baraev, and Abu Omar, the Arab mercenary and spiritual mentor of the fighters, at a conference of bandit group leaders in the Chechen Republic, where Baraev received his final orders and blessing to carry out the planned act.

In addition, evidence has been gathered indicating that not only Maskhadov and Basaev but also such major international terrorist figures as Movladi Udugov and Zelimkhan Yandarbiev were involved in planning and carrying out this crime. It should be noted that the latter two criminals are living abroad fully legally and are continuing their vigorous anti-Russian activities.

Up to now, the bodies of 34 of the fighters who were killed have been identified, and efforts are under way to identify the other 7.[6] Investigations are being conducted to determine the routes by which the terrorists traveled and the channels through which they obtained weapons and explosives. The routes and means of transportation (rail, air, or bus) used by some of the fighters have already been established. Official inquiries have ascertained that some of the terrorists were using passports with false information. One channel has been discovered through which false documents were created and delivered to the fighters. Operations and investigations are still under way in connection with three individuals in custody. Individuals involved in recruiting the female suicide bombers have been identified and are being sought.

Information has been received indicating a connection between the car bombing at the McDonald's restaurant on October 10, 2002 (2 Pokryshkin Street, Moscow) and the seizure of the hostages at the Palace of Culture of the Moscow State Ball-Bearing Factory. Expert assessments have established that the types of homemade explosive devices used in both incidents were identical. Certain individuals have been discovered to be involved in both cases.

During their operations, investigators have uncovered apartments used by the terrorists who participated in the hostage-taking incident. These apartments were also used as transfer points for the storage of weapons and explosives. When these locations were searched, officers found and seized firearms, ammunition, communications devices, and other equipment for carrying out terrorist acts, including 21 belts used in making *shahid* belts for the female suicide bombers.

Of course, more information will become available after the investigation is completed. However, I would like to emphasize that the operation to free the hostages on October 26, 2002, was and remains one of the most important landmarks in the struggle being waged by the law enforcement agencies and special services of the Russian Federation against the forces of terrorism. The events associated with the seizure of hostages at the Dubrovka theater complex revealed shortcomings in the organization of antiterrorism activities at the federal level, particularly with the process of providing information about the counterterrorist operation through the media. It is essential to understand clearly that the primary goal of terrorist acts is to attract broad public attention to certain processes, to instigate social confrontation within society, and to attempt to put pressure on the authorities and state administrative structures.

While noting the generally well-coordinated and selfless work done to free the hostages, we must also state that there are a number of problems objectively hindering the conduct of such operations. Many of them are of a narrowly specialized nature, and solutions for them are being worked out by the relevant agencies.

Cooperation between law enforcement and the media plays a special role in the process of resolving difficult conflict situations. During this operation, the operational headquarters could not achieve the necessary level of mutual understanding and coordination of actions with representatives of the media. Some correspondents covered the events associated with the freeing of the hostages in a tendentious manner and used the situation for their own particular aims. We must continue to work with journalists in improving our relationship in such situations.

The main conclusion to be made is that the overwhelming majority of citizens supported the action that was carried out, which attests to the consolidation of all segments of society in opposing attempts to destroy the Russian Federation and supporting the struggle against extremism and its ultimate form, terrorism.

We are deeply grateful to the international community for the support provided to Russia in those tragic days. Special thanks go to law enforcement agencies and special services of the partner states that declared their readiness to participate directly in efforts to free the hostages and in the investigation of the circumstances surrounding this crime.

Russia is ready to do everything in its power to promote measures to disseminate the experience it has gained in conducting such special hostage rescue operations, to exchange information on the weapons and equipment used, and to organize joint training exercises for both command and special operations units.

NOTES

1. At least 920 people were taken hostage, including 111 minors (39 of whom were small children), a number of pregnant women, and 68 foreign citizens.

2. Those involved in the negotiations included Iosif Kobzon (October 24, 1:37 p.m. and 3:35 p.m.), Irina Khakamada (October 24, 3:35 p.m.), Leonid Roshal (October 24, 5:50 p.m.; October 25, 1:37 a.m. and 2:50 p.m.), Grigory Yavlinsky (October 24, 11:37 p.m.–12:58 a.m. October 25), Anna

Politkovskaya (October 25, 2:50 p.m. and 7:40 p.m.), Sergei Govorukhin (October 25, 5:00 p.m.), Dmitry Beletsky (October 25, 5:00 p.m.), Yevgeny Primakov (October 25, 7:40 p.m.), Aslanbek Aslakhanov (October 25, 7:40–8:24 p.m.), Ruslan Aushev (October 25, 7:40 p.m.), *Sunday Times* journalist Mark Franchetti (October 25, 3:15 p.m.), four journalists from the Russian television network NTV (October 25, 1:40 a.m.), two Jordanian doctors (October 24, 5:50 p.m.), and five representatives of the Red Cross (October 25, 12:00 noon).

3. Of the 113 people freed before the building was stormed, 69 escaped (including 5 children) and 44 were rescued (including 25 children under age 14 and 3 older teenagers).

4. The following people were shot by the terrorists: (1) Olga Nikolaevna Romanova, born 1976, salesperson at the L'Etoile store in Moscow; (2) Konstantin Ivanovich Vasiliev, born 1967, chief specialist in the personnel department of the Main Administration for Military Court Operations of the Supreme Court of the Russian Federation; (3) Denis Petrovich Gribkov, born 1972, glassblower from the Laser-Neon company in Moscow; and (4) Pavel Georgievich Zakharov, born 1979, engineer from the Federal Registry of National Building Codes and Standards in Moscow.

5. According to data from the Moscow City Healthcare Committee, 650 people (including 9 children and 32 foreign citizens) were released from inpatient treatment facilities after rehabilitation.

6. Of the 41 terrorists killed, there were 19 women and 22 men. Thirty-four have been identified, and seven bodies (one woman and six men) remain to be identified.

Preventing Catastrophic Consequences of Bioterrorism in an Urban Setting

*Vladimir G. Ivkov** and Yevgeny A. Permyakov*
Russian Academy of Sciences Pushchino Science Center
Russian Academy of Sciences Institute of Biological Instrument Development

Potentially catastrophic consequences of acts of bioterrorism in urban settings are associated both with the particular ways in which modern megacities function and with the unique characteristics of the potential bioagents themselves. The special features of the city include many locations where people congregate, sizable transport flows, an integrated infractructure, numerous food distribution channels, and the complexity of managing the behavior of the population. The special features of bioagents include ease of dissemination, potential for covert use, presence of a latency period before their use is discovered, potential for person-to-person transmission, potential for the use of other organisms as vectors (insects, rats, and so forth), difficulty of detection and identification because of their extremely low effective concentrations, and the powerful psychological effect of bioterrorism itself.

Preventing acts of bioterrorism is extremely difficult and sometimes simply impossible; therefore, crucially significant factors include early detection, anticipation of potential scenarios of use, education of the public, advance planning to shape their behavior, and a clear-cut system for managing the situation with the help of educated, trained, and well-protected personnel.

Defining potential scenarios and training to respond to them is essential for the adequate functioning of the management system. This includes staff training (gaming), analysis of existing organizational response capabilities, identification of the most vulnerable elements in the protection system, and planning of prevention and suppression measures.

---

*Translated from the Russian by Kelly Robbins.

The most vulnerable points in a large city include the subway system, shopping centers, stadiums, mass gatherings at holidays and festivals, and grocery stores. Terrorist acts could lead to massive casualties because the use of a bioagent could go unnoticed during its entire latency period (usually 7–14 days).

Example 1: Just 1 g of anthrax spores represents 10 million lethal doses. Unless antibiotics are administered before the first symptoms appear, the mortality rate from anthrax could reach 85–90 percent. The simultaneous release of anthrax in several subway stations (perhaps by throwing a packet of spores in the path of a train arriving in the station), further dispersed with the aid of air currents produced by the movement of the trains, could under conditions existing in Moscow lead to the infection of several million people. Furthermore, taking into account the flow of passengers through Moscow to other regions, infected individuals would simultaneously appear at the end of the latency period in almost all regions of Russia. The result would be a general catastrophe, panic, and great difficulty in determining the source of the infection. Given current capabilities for detecting pathogens in air samples, such a scenario is completely possible.

Example 2: Anthrax spores could be dispersed using flares or fireworks set off during crowded holiday events (at stadiums, on New Year's Eve, at public festivals, and so forth). Such fireworks could also be set off on the roofs of tall buildings with the help of remote-control devices. To prevent such occurrences, the use of low-temperature explosive devices (fireworks and flares) by private individuals could be banned, and much tighter controls on the organization of large public events could be instituted.

Example 3: Let us reconsider the situation involving the use of anthrax spores, as this bioagent is the most accessible to potential terrorists and does not require complex technologies for acquisition and use. In this case, the scenario would involve the use of pilotless aircraft. The simplest would be helium-filled balloons, which are common at all public festivals. A floating balloon with a toy dangling from it would not attract anyone's suspicions; meanwhile, this "toy" could be a container dispersing spores. Taking into account wind direction, such a delivery device could infect tens of thousands of people (at stadiums, squares, festivals, amusement parks, and so forth), and the individual committing this terrorist act would face no risk in doing so.

Even these very simple examples demonstrate how vulnerable the modern city is. It is clear that even if the source and transmission path of the infection are discovered, decontamination measures (cleaning of the subway or parts of the city) could paralyze the operation of the city's infrastructure for a long time.

In addition to the creation of possible attack scenarios, systems for the early detection of the most likely dangerous bioagents will become a very important element in the system for countering bioterrorism. Critical characteristics of such systems include sensitivity, processing time, and reliability (absence of false positive signals), as well as the number of agents that can be identified. The need for widespread utilization of such devices requires that they must be capable of automatic operation. However, such warning devices will never be absolutely reliable; therefore, it is important to develop methods for confirming the identification of bioagents. One example of such methods is the molecular colony method (solid-state PCR [polymerase chain reaction] identification method) developed by the Russian Academy of Sciences (RAS) Institute of Protein at the RAS Pushchino Science Center. During a visit by our American colleagues to Pushchino, the inventor of the method, RAS corresponding member Aleksandr B. Chetverin, clearly demonstrated its capabilities and advantages.

The development and production of detection and identification devices for Russia could be organized at the RAS Institute of Biological Instrument Development (IBI) at the Pushchino Science Center. IBI was established in May 1994 on the basis of the Biopribor Research and Production Association (the former Special Design Bureau for Biological Instrument Development, which was founded in 1965). Along with other RAS institutes, IBI is part of the RAS Pushchino Science Center (Moscow Oblast, Russia).

In the years since its founding, the organization has amassed substantial scientific, technical, and production potential. Since 1965 the organization has developed more than 200 new scientific devices and pieces of equipment for both unique and routine research purposes, and about 4,000 devices have been shipped to institutes in Russia and abroad.

The main areas of scientific research and experimental design work at IBI include

- devices for studying the thermodynamic properties of biological systems (differential adiabatic scanning and titrating microcalorimeters, viscosimeters, densimeters)
- spectral and optical devices and equipment for the visible and ultraviolet spectral ranges, including broad-range spectrofluorimeters and spectrophotometers, photometers for immunological research, optical detectors for chromatography, interference filters, and quartz and glass cuvettes
- equipment for culturing microorganisms
- devices and equipment for biochemical research (trace DNA amplifiers, peptide synthesizers, chromatography and electrophoresis equipment, lyophilizer freeze-dryers and vats, membrane and peristaltic pumps, micropipettes, shakers, thermostats, sterilizers, chemical and biological test systems, and so forth)
- equipment for cell research, including micromanipulators, equipment for cell microsurgery, and equipment for electrophysiological research
- equipment for the automation of biological experiments (electronic systems for the collection, processing, and visualization of experimental data, as well as systems for the electronic control of biological experiments)
- devices and equipment for energy conservation (frequency regulators, automatic control switches for luminescent bulbs) and resource conservation (carbon extraction furnaces, equipment for the extraction of flavonoids)

The scientific and production potential of IBI can also be brought to bear in the development and production of devices and equipment for combating bioterrorism.

It is clear that if terrorist acts involving the use of biological weapons are carried out successfully, it will remove the psychological barrier that currently keeps them from being used throughout the world, and especially against such countries as the United States and Russia, by various extremist and separatist organizations. For this reason, it is extremely appropriate and mutually beneficial that we should take joint steps aimed at creating a protection system that would, if not prevent the use of biological weapons, make the efforts of bioterrorists ineffective.

Taking into account U.S. successes in developing systems for detecting and identifying potential bioagents as well as the enduring potential of Russian scientists, such a joint project at the RAS Pushchino Science Center (including the capabilities available at the State Research Center for Applied Microbiology in Obolensk) could play a substantial role in the creation of an international system to provide protection against biological terrorism.

Toxic Chemicals and Explosive Materials: Terrorism-Related Issues for the Research Community, Chemical Industry, and Government

Alexander MacLachlan
E. I. du Pont de Nemours & Co. (retired)

After almost 36 years in the chemical industry, I have found myself called on recently to participate in several studies and forums that deal with various aspects of terrorists' use of chemicals. While by no means an expert in terrorist matters, I will draw on my experiences as a longtime participant in the chemical industry and a participant in recent studies to suggest ways to make life more difficult for would-be terrorists. To prepare for this meeting I have also spoken with colleagues still active in the chemical industry to gain an understanding of what they are doing today. I am certainly not a spokesperson for that industry, however.

Two recent National Research Council studies with which I have been involved deal directly with chemical-related terrorism. They are *Containing the Threat from Illegal Bombings: An Integrated National Strategy for Marking, Tagging, Rendering Inert, and Licensing Explosives and Their Precursors* and *Making the Nation Safer: The Role of Science and Technology in Countering Terrorism*, published in 1998 and 2002, respectively. A study related to the first report, *Black and Smokeless Powders: Technologies for Finding Bombs and the Bomb Makers,* published in 1998, was also a source for this talk. The black powder and the illegal bombing reports were the direct result of two horrendous incidents, the bombing at the Alfred P. Murrah Federal Building in Oklahoma City and the first World Trade Center attack. The report on making the nation safer was initiated following the events of September 11, 2001.

Chemical-related terrorist opportunities fall into several categories:

- use of acquired or stolen chemicals to make bombs or poisonous substances to kill, maim, and frighten citizens

• theft of toxic chemicals for placement in water supplies, foods, and pharmaceuticals
• sabotage of chemical plants to cause releases of toxic materials into the
air or water supply
• sabotage of chemical transportation vehicles such as trucks, trains, and
ships

Terrorist targets may include individuals, places where large numbers of
people aggregate, prestigious monuments, critical infrastructure, and transportation systems. Unfortunately there is no end to targets.

The aforementioned studies all concluded that the strategies to thwart terrorists could for the most part be thought of as increasing difficulty for terrorists to obtain dangerous or precursor chemicals and to make it more likely that
those who do obtain possession of such materials will be caught. Absolute
prevention of terrorist acts is impossible. However, this "raising-of-the-bar"
philosophy was supported by all government and law enforcement officials
interviewed in the United Kingdom, Switzerland, and the United States. Interviews with chemical industry representatives suggest the same philosophy pre-
vails in the industry.

The recommendations of the reports and the recent interviews with chemical
industry representatives lead to the following broad categories of needed technology developments:

• more sensitivity in detecting and tracking dangerous products or their
precursors whenever they are being moved among locations
• limiting access to these materials through increased security or more stringent laws and regulations or both
• rendering materials unsuitable for terrorist use
• developing new technologies for more efficient cleanup of deliberate con-
taminations

All these approaches involve combinations of technology use or development, government actions, and the cooperation of industry.

EXPLOSIVES AND THEIR PRECURSOR CHEMICALS

The reports that dealt with illegal use of explosives and black powder examined a number of protection concepts:

• the addition of detectants to explosives and designated chemicals to make
them susceptible to sensitive mass screening devices or animals (dogs)
• the incorporation of information-containing markers into commercial explosives and certain precursor chemicals so that before or after a terrorist attack,

information can be gleaned that will give valuable insight as to the origin of the materials

• the rendering of precursor chemicals inert or not useful for explosive fabrication

• the limitation of criminal access to explosives and precursor chemicals

Both reports agreed that detectants added to commercial explosives had merit, but serious concerns about effecting the usefulness or safety of these materials prompted the study teams to recommend against this approach. More research was recommended to overcome the perceived shortcoming of current concepts. The exception to this general conclusion is the manufacture of plastic and sheet explosives. Since 1998 under the International Civil Aviation Organization (ICAO) one of four dectectants will be added to these explosives. These detectants have enough volatility that they can be readily picked up by screening equipment and dogs. Obviously, this approach will take a long time to permeate the market, and its effectiveness will only be seen if a terrorist uses smuggled military explosives covered by the treaty.

The addition of taggants, which can be used to provide critical source and date information before or after an explosion, to commercial explosives was examined and found not to be practical in the United States at this time. Taggants are used in explosives manufactured in and imported into Switzerland and have been credited with solving several crimes. While supportive of the concept, the relevant report recommends more research to overcome the perceived difficulties of cost and environmental contamination. The latter problem was particularly serious for bulk explosive materials, such as ammonium nitrate, used in mining and earth moving. Many taggant concepts were analyzed, but most were merely at the idea stage. However, some, such as the use of isotopic labeling, were intriguing and did seem to hold promise for use in certain precursor chemicals whether used in explosives or for toxic chemical synthesis.

Rendering explosive materials inert through additives has received quite a bit of study in various countries. Most of the focus is on ammonium nitrate fertilizer and urea. Early claims of having "inerted" ammonium nitrate were later shown to be incorrect or approaches that could be easily bypassed. Development of effective means to make ammonium nitrate inert is still considered worthy of support, however. Key considerations concern effectiveness, cost, and food safety.

In the United States, limiting access to explosives emerged as a major concern. U.S. laws to control commercial explosives range from extremely stringent in some states to remarkably lax in others. This laxness is reflected in the lack of control over purchases of commercial explosives and inadequate regulations regarding their storage and security. Most illegal bombings in the United States use stolen commercial explosives. Strong recommendations have been made to create more uniform laws in this area, but progress has been spotty.

The most devastating explosions in the United States (at the Murrah Building and first World Trade Center attack) were accomplished with fertilizers as the prime components (ammonium nitrate and nitrated urea, respectively). Because of the enormous cost and disruption to the agricultural community, it is difficult to place strict control on these bulk materials unless the perceived threat escalates considerably. However, the fertilizer industry has a volunteer program that requests sellers of these fertilizers to know their customers. Early evidence suggests that this approach has been effective, but sustainability and long-term followup is an obvious concern. If the threat of terrorist acts escalates, however, more stringent licensing procedures should be invoked for these materials and a limited list of other high-risk chemicals. As expected, the cost and inconvenience to legitimate users go up correspondingly.

TOXIC AND FLAMMABLE CHEMICALS AS TERRORIST WEAPONS

The report *Making the Nation Safer: The Role of Science and Technology in Countering Terrorism* addressed how current or new technology might help thwart or mitigate terrorist attacks using chemicals. Toxic chemicals have long been considered for warfare. The fear of chemical weapons engenders significant dread in most people and consequently fulfills a key goal of terrorists. Over the years, governments have studied ways to improve the effectiveness of these weapons, and much progress has been made, especially in toxicity and delivery techniques. In the hands of a terrorist in crowded places, such as enclosed buildings, stadiums, and subways, or possibly even distribution networks, such as sewers, the impact and effectiveness could be enormous in terms of both casualties and fear. Other potentially devastating distribution systems include the postal service, food distribution, and water supply networks. Most chemical warfare agents are relatively simple to synthesize from easily obtained chemical precursors (at least in the United States). Preventing terrorists from synthesizing small quantities of the most deadly chemical warfare agents is a daunting task.

The International Chemical Weapons Convention lists a number of chemicals and identifies specialized processing equipment that are banned or must be reported by the 160 signatory nations if they are used. In general, however, the quantities of the listed chemicals that must be reported are quite large compared to what a terrorist group might purchase or steal to make useful weapons. This convention is designed to constrain nations, not for suicide terrorists.

Another major concern relative to chemical terrorist weapons is the potential sabotage of chemical plants, manufacturing units, or large-volume storage vessels, or even more frightening, the deliberate release of toxic and flammable chemicals from tank cars in heavily populated areas or ships in busy harbors. *Making the Nation Safer* devotes significant attention to how technology might be used to mitigate many of the effects and problems from such chemical releases.

Sensor technology development and new sensor applications in this specific area could be a powerful approach. Sensors have the potential to thwart terrorists in the planning stage and before or during attempted attacks. They can also be used in forensic analysis. Specific applications for sensors are

• detection of abnormal air quality in buildings, subways, sewer pipes, and other closed areas
• detection of explosives in luggage
• detection of chemicals or nuclear materials during shipment
• early warning of contamination of food and water
• long-distance sensors to protect investigators
• mapping clouds of poisonous agents
• assisting physicians in assessing patient problems and condition
• determining level of contamination and when cleanup is complete

The principal recommendations are

• broad-based exploratory research to ascertain new sensor principles
• research to study how animals detect odors
• coordination of research and development on sensors and sensor networks with emphasis on systems in the field
• technology and verification programs to guide federal research investments and advise state and local authorities on the evolving state of the art

The remainder of the report covered findings and recommendations that dealt with the need for technology advances in

• filter systems for buildings that would have enough capacity to rapidly decontaminate or even prevent toxic materials from entering the entire air supply
• methods to neutralize toxic clouds
• methods to decontaminate areas and to dispose of contaminated materials
• robotics to protect personnel involved with cleanup
• sophisticated mining of databases to give early warning of toxic chemical or biological attacks
• improving the government's capability to protect food, water supplies, and pharmaceuticals
• better risk assessment technologies to determine the appropriate priority and effort to protect different potential targets
• develop an infrastructure of trained personnel and specialized equipment poised to assemble the best response approaches to different types of attacks

CHEMICAL INDUSTRY RESPONSE

Immediately after September 11, 2001, the chemical industry came under intense self-examination and governmental scrutiny. Senator Jon S. Corzine and his colleagues prepared a bill for the U.S. Congress to require chemical manufacturers to eventually shut down large plants near urban areas if the plants had processes or made chemicals that might explode and kill or injure people. The industry's strong negative response and plea for an opportunity to suggest approaches of their own helped defeat the bill.

Senator Corzine's bill had its origin in a law that requires about 15,000 companies to present hypothetical worst-case accident scenarios for toxic chemicals they produce. The industry succeeded in limiting public access to these scenarios, and today it is a crime if they are published.

Industry organized its response through the American Chemistry Council (ACC) and developed a mandatory security-based code of management for its members. The industry gave itself three years to implement this code. Many of the components of the Corzine bill were taken to heart, including a risk-based approach to identify the most likely terrorist targets and place priority on their protection. The actions being taken build on past experience and practices to prevent accidents and misuse of products.

The chemical industry has long viewed itself as a manufacturer of dangerous materials. Over the decades, often in response to disasters or customer misuse, the industry has developed many procedures to prevent accidents in the manufacture and use of its products. One of the most effective is the industry-wide code of conduct, called Responsible Care, dating from 1988. This program was created under the auspices of the ACC. Six principles form the basis of this code:

1. community awareness and emergency response
2. pollution prevention
3. process safety
4. distribution
5. employee health and safety
6. product stewardship

The code was designed to be flexible, continually challenging the member companies to go beyond the minimum requirements of regulations. Guiding principles that defined the ethic of the program were also created. Since establishment in 1988 a great record of accomplishments can be cited.

However, September 11, 2001, caused a new level of thinking in the industry and the federal government. All the excellent work to improve safety had been aimed at accidents, and accidents are preventable. Now deliberate sabotage must be rolled into the security equation. Moreover, the saboteurs are often willing to die during their acts.

Building on the success of Responsible Care, the industry created an initiative aimed at terrorism: the Responsible Care Security Code of Management Practices. The code aims to rapidly improve companies security performance using risk-based approaches to identify, assess, and address vulnerabilities; prevent or mitigate incidents; enhance training and response capabilities; and maintain and improve relationships with key stakeholders. The new code also recognizes that security is a shared relationship among suppliers, service providers, and government officials and agencies.

There are 13 management practices required of a company. They range through proof of leadership commitment, prioritization of vulnerabilities through risk assessment, cybersecurity, specific documentation requirements, training and drills, exchange of information among all stakeholders, evaluation of detected security threats and incidents, audits with third-party verification, and review of all processes when anything changes, for example, personnel, processes, and products.

One of the most striking features of this new code is that all members are required to fully implement it by 2005. Indications are that the three-year deadline will be met. As an example, the industry has already identified its 120 highest priority sites based on risk criteria, thus meeting the deadline of December 31, 2002. All these sites will meet the security enhancement requirements by the end of 2003. Another interesting new concept is the requirement for third-party verification of conformance and quality of a company's performance. The criteria for this verification are strict and thorough.

There are many other actions being taken especially for eliminating the risk itself. They include such activities as examining all processes and attempting to minimize quantities of the most dangerous in-process chemicals. While this has been a focus of the industry since the devastating Bhopal incident, where thousands were killed in India by release of methyl isocyanate from a large storage tank, it has received new impetus. The methyl isocyanate storage was only temporary, as the chemical was an intermediate for the products of the plant. Immediately after this incident, chemical companies examined all their processes and where possible eliminated intermediate storage of large quantities of dangerous materials. This has been a great contributor to the inherent safety of many processes, but much more needs to be done. A recent article in the American Chemical Society's publication *Chemical and Engineering News* talked about a strong movement now under way to design chemical processes from the ground up to be inherently safer and simpler to control. This, of course, is most pertinent to construction of new plants and is probably one area where new government licensing requirements will be focused.

POSSIBLE ACTIONS

Later this week, we will consider the broad scope of the National Research Council's involvement in terrorism studies. At this workshop, we are charged to find areas that can benefit from our joint sponsorship of public forums and studies. In my view, in chemical and explosives terrorism, we might consider such topics as

- new concepts and principles for sensor technology and capability
- practical new concepts for tracing precursor chemicals useful for chemical weapons or explosives
- the use of databases and data mining to detect suspicious activity
- interaction between our respective chemical industries and their associations to encourage sharing ideas of ways to interfere with terrorists
- the concept that future chemical plant construction incorporates specific features to make plants inherently safer and secure from sabotage
- the tension between civil rights versus effective terrorism prevention

The Role of the Russian Ministry of Internal Affairs in Combating Terrorism in Urban Conditions

*Sergey A. Starostin**
All-Russian Scientific Research Institute of the
Russian Ministry of Internal Affairs

"We are entering a unique era of terrorism that could make all of modern society its potential victim." These words, spoken more than 20 years ago by Joseph Alexander, head of the Institute of International Terrorism of the State University of New York, are being confirmed in full measure today.[1] The events of September 11, 2001, in the United States and the bombings of apartment buildings in September 1999 and seizure of hostages in October 2002 in Moscow have already firmly convinced everyone that for modern society, terrorism has become a global threat, along with other various dangers to which mankind is subjected at the start of the third millennium.

Indeed, modern terrorism is taking on new forms and features shaped by fast-moving processes under way in the high-technology sphere. Scientific and technical progress is giving rise to new varieties of terrorism. The appearance of such new concepts as biological, chemical, informational, radioelectronic, and environmental terrorism is no mere coincidence.

The globalization of terrorism is evident in that it is the topic of discussion at numerous annual international conferences, an example of which is ours here today. Allow me to thank its organizers for inviting representatives of the Russian Ministry of Internal Affairs (MVD) to take part.

It would be a mistake to think that modern terrorism in Russia in all its most radical manifestations is the result solely of the reform of the previous state socio-economic system and of the processes that have occurred in our country in recent years. Even in "stable" Soviet times, terrorist acts of rather broad impact were carried out in Russia. It is sufficient to recall the bombings in the Moscow subway

*Translated from the Russian by Kelly Robbins.

system in the winter of 1978. This was our first encounter with political terrorism, when the criminals aimed not only to attract attention to themselves but also to kill as many people as possible. The number of victims at that time was in the dozens.

The next stage of radical manifestations of extremism concerns the most recent phase of Russian history. Following is an incomplete list of crimes committed in Moscow alone in the past five years that are classified as terrorism according to our laws:

- 1998: bombings at the Tretyakovskaya subway station (three wounded) and at a synagogue
- 1999: car bombings at the U.S. embassy and the Russian Federal Security Service (FSB) (2 wounded); bombings in the lobby of the Intourist Hotel (11 wounded), at the MVD, and at the shopping mall at Manezh Square (1 killed, 40 wounded); bombings of two apartment buildings on Guryanov Street and Kashirskoe Shosse (more than 200 killed, including 21 children)
- 2000: bombing in the underground pedestrian passageway at Pushkin Square (7 killed, 53 wounded)
- 2001: bombing at the Belorusskaya subway station (10 killed)
- 2002: detonation of a 122-mm fragmentation mine shell at a McDonald's restaurant (1 killed, 7 wounded); seizure of hostages at the theater on Dubrovka Street (129 killed, of which 7 were foreign citizens)

To this list of terrorist acts we should also add the bombings in Buinaksk and Volgodonsk, the bombing of the government building in Grozny, and others. Clearly, this situation in Russia and in our major cities is directly linked with processes under way in the south, especially in the Chechen Republic. This region is also the focal point of the majority of crimes of a terrorist nature.

In predicting how the situation will develop, we should anticipate an increase in terrorism and certain directly associated crimes such as banditry. The increase in the number of serious and extremely serious crimes is a matter of considerable concern. The proportion of these crimes could reach 54.7 percent of all acts subject to criminal penalties. Insufficient sample size precludes us from making a reliable quantitative forecast for the crimes mentioned above. However, current growth trends point to the growing terrorist danger facing all citizens of the country (see Table 1).

During the forecast period, the unbreakable criminological linkage between terrorism and crimes related to the illegal trade in narcotics and powerful psychotropic substances is evident. If the main channels through which drugs flow are not blocked, the volume of drug-related crime will increase substantially. We can expect that the registered number of drug-related crimes will grow by 26.3 percent in 2003 as compared with the level in 2002.

Making a fundamental assessment of the growing crime threat, Russian Federation President Vladimir V. Putin said: "We are paying a heavy price both for

TABLE 1 Crime Forecast for 2003

		Growth (percent)	
	2001	2002	2003 (forecast)
		Worst-Case Scenario	
Banditry	−9.4	−13.1	26.5
Terrorism	142.2	10.1	30.6
		Moderate Scenario	
Banditry	−9.4	−12.5	11.6
Terrorism	142.2	15.3	19.0
		Best-Case Scenario	
Banditry	−9.4	−13.1	−3.2
Terrorism	142.2	10.1	7.5

the weakness of the state and for the inconsistency of our actions. Meanwhile, I would like to note and to emphasize that Russia will not make any deals with terrorists and will not be subjected to any sort of blackmail. International terrorism is becoming more brazen and operating in an increasingly savage manner. Terrorists are issuing threats to use means comparable to weapons of mass destruction. With a deep sense of responsibility, I would like to state that if anyone even attempts to use such means against our country, Russia will respond with measures adequate to meet the threat to the Russian Federation."[2]

The threat presented by terrorism to all of civilization has already been recognized at the international level, and there are no grounds on which to expect that this threat will weaken or diminish anytime soon.[3] Moreover, the intensification of the terrorist threat to Russia has given rise to the need to make well-founded changes in the national security strategy, specifically with regard to the possible use of the armed forces to eliminate hotbeds of international crime.[4]

The defining characteristic of the current operational situation in Russia is not only the reality that terrorist acts are being committed but also the constant threat that they will be carried out in the future. Here are a few examples. In the fall of 2002, Chechen fighters from the city of Urus-Martan and the village of Vedeno planned a terrorist act that was to be carried out in the city of Volgograd. The dam at the Volzhskaya State Regional Electric Power Station was selected as the target for sabotage. The terrorists planned to purchase explosives from Chechen servicemen in military units. The Chechen diaspora collected funds for this purpose. On August 26, 2002, internal affairs agencies received operational information on the planned terrorist act, which allowed them to prevent it from being carried out.

On October 28, 2002, after the seizure of hostages at the theater on Dubrovka Street, the district department of internal affairs received information that there were 24 men and 6 women (representatives of Arab countries) in Moscow illegally who were involved with the commission of the terrorist act.

It was also established that they intended to depart for the cities of Volgograd, Astrakhan, and Saratov in the near future to organize and carry out terrorist acts there as well.

The flow of such information is not diminishing so far in 2003. We respond immediately to all calls from citizens (up to 500 per month), and we investigate them all, including false reports. These investigations involve onsite work not only by personnel from the local district internal affairs agencies but also by specialists from the field engineering unit and canine teams to check for the possible presence of explosives, bombs, and poisonous substances in unattended or suspicious objects.

During the operations in 2002, we discovered 10.5 percent more crimes punishable under Statute 222 of the Russian Federation Criminal Code (illegal acquisition, distribution, sale, storage, shipment, or possession of weapons, ammunition, or explosive substances or devices) than during the same period of the previous year. In Moscow alone, about 1,000 firearms were taken out of illegal circulation, more than half of them rifles, as well as several hundred military grenades and more than 10 kg of explosives.

It should be noted that the increased criminal-terrorist threat throughout Russia has for the first time presented society with the question of how to minimize the consequences of terrorist acts for the civilian population. This is primarily a matter of prevention and immediate assistance to victims, deactivation of any devices or agents used, development of new means of protection, and education of the public in how to behave safely in terrorist threat situations.[5]

On the topic of preventing terrorism, it is impossible to overlook those important factors that in our view not only destabilize the operational situation in the country as a whole and in Moscow in particular but also give rise to crimes of a terrorist nature. The activities of extremist organizations and groups represent a serious factor in destabilizing the criminal situation in the country. This matter is especially urgent for our capital: There are more than 120 nationalities living in Moscow, people of the most varied political and religious convictions (more than 5,000 Chechens, more than 2,000 immigrants from Dagestan and Ingushetia).

Each day, about 3 million people pass through the capital. On average days, approximately 100,000–150,000 vehicles pass through state road inspection checkpoints on entering the city. Up to 165 long-distance trains arrive at the capital's nine railway stations each day, along with up to 1,950 local trains.

There are more than 300 associations and religious denominations actively operating in the city, and by no means are all of them devoted to pacifist aims. According to our data, more than 1,000 religious groups and cults are conducting their destructive activities in Moscow, preaching fanaticism based on distorted spiritual and ethical canons (the Satan Society, White Brotherhood, Aum Shinrikyo, Jehovah's Witnesses, the Castrati, and many others). It should be noted that a number of religious structures are largely financed by extremist-oriented foreign organizations.

Extremist organizations of a radical political orientation are also operating in the city, such as the People's National Party, Russian Master, the Freedom Party, numerous groups of soccer fanatics, and so forth. The dangers presented by right- and left-wing political extremism should not be underestimated, nor should those arising from the most aggressive form of religious extremism, Wahhabism. These dangers must be evaluated realistically and adequate measures taken in a timely manner to suppress illegal activities.

Here again, it is of primary importance to coordinate the efforts of law enforcement, other government agencies, and various public associations empowered to deal with this problem. Passed in July 2002, the Federal Law on Countering Extremist Activity established the legal and organizational foundations for this activity and delineated the responsibilities of the agencies charged with its implementation.

It must be noted that in the Russian Federation there is a division of functions in the effort to combat manifestations of terrorism. Countering political terrorism falls within the purview of the Federal Security Service, while suppressing criminal terrorism is the responsibility of the MVD.

The MVD is pursuing a number of preventive measures to fight terrorism. Among the most effective are targeted preventive search operations (such as Vortex-Antiterror) aimed at locating individuals belonging to criminal groups of an extremist or terrorist orientation, members of illegal armed groups and their accomplices, and members of Muslim organizations and religious centers that are promulgating Wahhabism.

Terrorism prevention efforts are under way daily and involve almost all the various service units of the MVD. Joint work is being carried out with Moscow's municipal services agencies to seal off garrets and basements of apartment buildings and to check out rented apartments and other facilities in such buildings. Special attention is being paid to protecting and providing operational coverage for the city's industrial sites and other facilities presenting a heightened danger.

An algorithm of actions aimed at preventing terrorist acts and other extremist manifestations in locations where large numbers of citizens gather during major cultural events has been developed and is being applied in practice. The safety program designed for Moscow sports facilities during 2003–2006 calls for the acquisition and installation of modern video observation and monitoring systems, radio and cable communications hardware, and other means for technical control and examination. The total cost of the necessary equipment is 100 million rubles ($3.28 million).

Units serving the Moscow subway system have also received orientation and training in antiterrorist operations. The fact that many millions of passengers use the system carries with it the danger of crime, including the possibility of terrorist acts. In view of the movements of an enormous number of people, many of whom are visitors to the capital, the crime situation in the subway system compels the subway system police unit to operate in a state of constant readiness.

The police road patrol service plays a special role in preventing terrorist acts in the capital. Its officers keep a 24-hour watch at state road inspection checkpoints and inspect the flows of cargo arriving in the capital.

MVD units provide antiterrorism protection to facilities of special importance, those vital to life and welfare, and those presenting a heightened degree of danger (including heating and power stations, dams, and water pumping stations, which have active chemically dangerous substances stored on site). Many of the facilities have installed video cameras that are monitored at guard stations by enterprise security personnel. Special police emergency call systems have been installed at these facilities. Some of the sites are equipped with fire alarm systems linked to centralized alarm centers at local district units of the MVD.

A wide-scale educational campaign has been launched to develop a sense of watchfulness among the population and instill basic habits of proper behavior during bomb threats. Police units are constantly providing the public and passengers with specially prepared reminders on what to do if they find unattended or suspicious objects. Similar training sessions have been organized for subway train operators and drivers from the various passenger transport enterprises. Created for terrorism prevention purposes, the antiterrorism automated search system facilitates the efficient exchange of information on the movements of persons of interest to us and the registration of members of extremist organizations.

The sharp increase in the number of terrorist incidents in 1999 served as a warning signal that strategies and tactics for countering the advance of terrorism were in need of review. Even then, three years ago, it was noted that there had been some unfavorable qualitative changes in the structure of this type of violent crime. In particular, the overall proportion of attempts on the lives or health of people increased, with a complementary decrease in the share of crimes targeting material objects. Crimes became bigger in scope, being characterized by large numbers of human victims, and terrorists became increasingly brutal and brazen. Moreover, terrorist societies and groups received an expanded amount of informational, tactical, and mutual resource support. Political and criminal terrorism coalesced against a backdrop of convergence and cooperation of illegal and legal structures of an extremist nature with nationalist, religious separatist, fundamentalist, and other organizations on the basis of their mutually beneficial interests.

Our prime task is to coordinate the antiterrorist activities of federal executive-branch agencies in their interactions with analogous agencies at the republic, oblast, and local levels and with enterprises, institutions, and organizations with the aim of increasing the efficiency of measures to discover, prevent, and suppress terrorist activities. In cooperation with other law enforcement agencies at the local and federal levels, the MVD is continuing to work actively towards further exposing the terrorist underground.

It should be noted that scientific research on the circumstances in which terrorist acts are carried out, the personalities of terrorists, and so forth, plays a special role in preventing crimes of a terrorist nature. By analyzing acts of terrorism that have taken place, it is possible to arrive at several particular features or, if you will, laws of operation (see Figures 1–5).

The diagrams graphically illustrate the facilities and individuals that should be the focus of top-priority preventive work, and this allows us to define the basic objectives this work should entail.

The well-known events at the theater center on Dubrovka Street have forced us to increase our efforts to rid the capital's economy of the "ethnic crime business." In 2002 we uncovered more than 500 enterprises under various forms of ownership that were, according to operational data, involved in

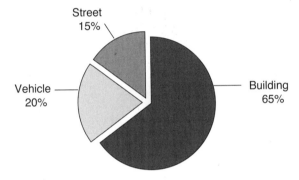

FIGURE 1 Distribution of terrorist acts committed in Russia by location.

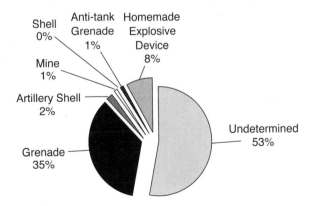

FIGURE 2 Distribution of bombings in Russia by type of explosive device used.

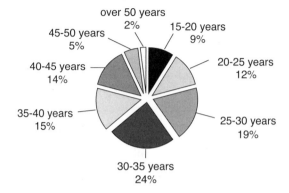

FIGURE 3 Distribution of terrorists by age.

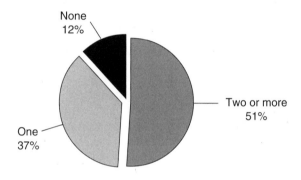

FIGURE 4 Distribution of terrorists by number of previous convictions.

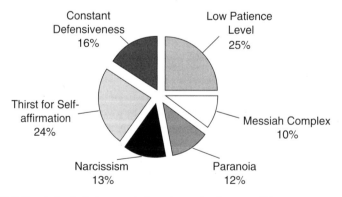

FIGURE 5 Psychological characteristics of terrorists' personalities.

providing financial or other support to criminal groups composed of individuals from the North Caucasus region and the Caucasus republics. Already in 2003 we have discovered more than 200 commercial entities in Moscow that are controlled by Chechen, Dagestani, Azerbaijani, Armenian, and Georgian organized crime groups.

The criminal groups mentioned above have a most negative effect on the operational situation in Moscow. In comparison with similar Slavic groups, these groups are the source of greater social and public danger. Relations within them are founded on familial and clan-based principles. Crimes in which they are involved are, as a rule, well organized, brutal, and unpredictable in nature. Furthermore, while criminal bombings carried out by Azerbaijani or Georgian organized crime groups are primarily a means of eliminating criminal business competitors, the situation with Chechen groups is different. In addition to the criminal component, we frequently see attempts to exert pressure on the political situation, to use terror to obtain changes in the federal government's position on settlement of the Chechen crisis.

There have been certain positive developments, specifically, in uncovering and cutting off flows of weapons, explosives, and narcotics into the capital. For example, on December 24, 2002, while investigating reports of the arrival in Moscow of Chechens aiming to carry out terrorist acts, our personnel in cooperation with colleagues from the FSB arrested two individuals from Chechnya and confiscated two suicide vests with explosives, military grenades, and a remote control device. On January 20, 2003, an ethnic crime group was arrested while bringing a large quantity of narcotics into Moscow. More than 40 kg of heroin was seized.

I would now like to say a few words about our views of what we must accomplish in our efforts to fight terrorism.

- A unified database on extremist groups and their leaders must be created.
- Heavier administrative and criminal penalties should be established for those who participate in street riots and promote extremist means of political struggle.
- The political process should be monitored not only in Moscow but also in the various republics and oblasts that make up the Russian Federation (including small cities where the socioeconomic and ethnopolitical situations are strained).
- Guided by the experience of Israel, Spain, and other countries, a modern antiterrorist infrastructure should be formed, including the secret services, the media, public and religious organizations, the educational system, and the migration service.
- It would be expedient to set harsher punishment for illegally dealing in weapons and explosives and committing crimes involving the use of firearms in order to ensure that judicial proceedings for such criminal cases are appropriate to the danger they present to society.

- In cooperation with the media, an information campaign should be organized to persuade the public to voluntarily surrender illegal weapons, explosives, and ammunition.
- The protection of dangerous facilities should be increased, perimeter barriers around them strengthened, and video monitoring, alarm, and control systems installed at their entrances and exits to facilitate immediate notification of the presence of weapons and explosives.
- A solution must be found to the question of creating centers in large cities to hold migrants who have been found to be in Russia illegally and who have been issued court orders for forcible removal from the Russian Federation. A mechanism for financing their deportations must also be worked out.
- Increased administrative penalties should be put in place for violations of passport and visa regulations in special status locations (republic and oblast capitals, regions where especially dangerous industrial facilities or atomic power plants are located, and so forth).
- All government agencies should increase their efforts to prevent and suppress commercial activities associated with the illegal trade in weapons, drugs, prostitution, and pornography; the illegal reproduction of information on computer disks or tapes; illegal operations involving foreign currency and antiques; and so forth, as all of these activities produce large profits that can be used to finance terrorists and extremists.
- Measures should be taken to identify enterprises and firms involved in organizing the illegal migration of foreign citizens. The activities of organizations and firms inviting foreign citizens from abroad should be monitored, especially if they involve citizens from countries that are militarily, politically, or economically unstable. Action should be taken to prevent the uncontrolled movement throughout the Russian Federation of individuals without identity papers and foreigners who refuse to leave the country when the authorized duration of their visit has expired.
- It would seem appropriate to increase the amount of funds available for rewarding citizens who assist internal affairs agencies in identifying and exposing individuals planning or committing terrorist acts and their accomplices.
- With the aim of controlling cargo shipments and preventing the possibility that weapons, explosives, and explosive devices might be transported to major cities along with agricultural or other products, special terminals equipped with monitoring equipment should be established at the city limits to inspect heavy freight vehicles (refrigerator trucks, semitrailers, and so forth).

The following changes should be made in laws and regulations by various levels of government in the Russian Federation:

- Questions regarding arrest procedures, grounds for arrest, and pre-arraignment detention terms for persons suspected of committing terrorist acts or serving as accomplices in such crimes should be considered. At present, individuals suspected of committing a crime can be detained for 48 hours, after which they must be formally charged and held or else released. Investigators spend most of this legally permitted period taking care of the various necessary procedural matters, such as preparing the arrest documents, securing a lawyer for the accused, and notifying the prosecutor's office. It is unrealistic to expect that in the remaining time investigators will be able to gather evidence and decide whether the person in custody is guilty or not guilty. Given the degree of danger that terrorism presents to the public, it would seem expedient to temporarily establish special arrest procedures and detention terms for individuals suspected of planning to commit or participate in terrorist acts.

• The MVD, FSB, and Central Bank of Russia should be given expanded powers to institute tighter controls on the activities of individuals and legal entities involved in commercial operations, including those in the wholesale trade business, as well as controls on the use of funds by public organizations and their leaders and activists if operational information indicates that they are involved in financing terrorist activities.

• Internal affairs agencies should be notified when notarized general vehicle licenses are issued.

NOTES

1. Terrorism in modern capitalist society. 1980. (2nd ed.). Moscow: Russian Academy of Sciences Institute of Scientific Information in the Social Sciences. p. 8.

2. See How to defeat terrorism. 2002. Ekspert 41, November 4.

3. On research in this field, see Terrorism—a general threat to security in the twenty-first century: An analytical report. 2001. Moscow: Center for Strategic Development. p. 20.

4. See Terror without borders? An answer will come. 2002. Rossiiskaya Gazeta 206, October 30.

5. The website *www.crdf.org* provides information on scientific research in the field of victimology.

The Three R's:
Lessons Learned from September 11, 2001

Robert Prieto*
Parsons Brinckerhoff Inc.

A year and a half has passed since the terrorist attack on New York City. Thousands died that day, and the lives of millions of others were directly affected.

We cannot bring those who died that day back to life. Nor can we stop all deliberate acts of destruction targeted to our cities and their infrastructure. But we can improve the ability of our built environment to resist, respond, and recover from uncontrollable forces of nature and man. If this paper helps ensure that neither the events of September 11, 2001, nor the lessons we should draw from it are forgotten, then it will be judged worthwhile. If not, history will write a different epitaph.

A UNIQUE PERSPECTIVE

I am a New Yorker, one who grew up and worked in the city throughout my entire career, as chairman of Parsons Brinckerhoff, New York's oldest engineering firm whose roots, reaching back to 1885, predate our work on New York City's first subway; as cochair of the Infrastructure Task Force established by the New York City Partnership in the aftermath of the attacks; and increasingly as a student of the history of great engineering "system" failures.

In essence, history has handed our profession an unusual challenge and an unmatched opportunity. How we respond will say much about the future of the heavily engineered environment we call our cities as well as much about our own profession.

EVENTS AND IMMEDIATE AFTERMATH

To fully appreciate the events that day, we must understand their rapidity and scale. Table 1 provides a chronology. Within 18 minutes, planes struck each of the two World Trade Center towers in New York. Eighteen minutes after United Airlines flight 175 struck the south tower, all bridges and tunnels into the New York City area were closed. Sixty-two minutes after the south tower was struck, it collapsed, killing those still trapped inside as well as first responders who arrived to deal with the impact of American Airlines flight 11 into the north tower. The Port Authority Trans Hudson (PATH) line station was partially crushed by the collapse of the south tower. Twenty-three minutes later, the north tower collapsed.

The collapse of the twin towers caused collateral damage of varying degrees to 29 million sq ft of office space in lower Manhattan; started fires in nearby structures; and caused major portions of the transportation, power, telecommuni-

TABLE 1 Chronology of Events of September 11, 2001

Time (EDT)	Event
8:46 a.m.	A hijacked passenger jet, American Airlines flight 11 from Boston, Massachusetts, crashes into the north tower of the World Trade Center, tearing a gaping hole and setting the building afire.
9:03 a.m.	A second hijacked airliner, United Airlines flight 175 from Boston, crashes into the south tower of the World Trade Center and explodes.
9:17 a.m.	The Federal Aviation Administration shuts down all New York City area airports.
9:21 a.m.	The Port Authority of New York and New Jersey orders all bridges and tunnels in the New York area closed.
9:40 a.m.	The FAA halts all flight operations at U.S. airports, the first time in U.S. history that air traffic nationwide has been halted.
9:43 a.m.	American Airlines flight 77 crashes into the Pentagon.
10:05 a.m.	The south tower of the World Trade Center collapses, plummeting into the streets below. A massive cloud of dust and debris forms and slowly drifts away from the building.
10:10 a.m.	A portion of the Pentagon collapses. United Airlines flight 93, also hijacked, crashes in Somerset County, Pennsylvania, southeast of Pittsburgh.
10:24 a.m.	The FAA reports all inbound transatlantic aircraft flying into the United States are being diverted to Canada.
10:28 a.m.	The World Trade Center's north tower collapses from the top down as if it were being peeled apart, releasing a tremendous cloud of debris and smoke.
11:02 a.m.	New York City Mayor Rudolph Giuliani urges New Yorkers to stay at home and orders an evacuation of the area south of Canal Street.
2:49 p.m.	Subway and bus service is partially restored in New York City.
4:10 p.m.	Building 7 of the World Trade Center complex is reported on fire.
5:20 p.m.	The 47-story Building 7 of the World Trade Center complex collapses. The evacuated building was damaged when the twin towers across the street collapsed earlier in the day. Other nearby buildings in the area remain ablaze.

cations, and other infrastructure to be stressed to failure simultaneously. Many of the lessons learned came from observing the relative response of these systems to the same originating event and failure environment.

A little more than two hours after the first plane struck, an evacuation of southern Manhattan was ordered. During the next several weeks, rescue efforts continued and critical infrastructure systems were restored pending permanent solutions.

The impacts were overwhelming:

- 2,801 people killed in New York
- 29 million sq ft damaged or destroyed
- New York City Emergency Operations Center destroyed
- 125,000 workers displaced
- section of New York City subway destroyed by beams from the World Trade Center
- PATH World Trade Center station partially collapsed, rendering one of three Hudson River crossings out of service
- 350,000 passengers initially displaced
- $1.9 billion in telecommunications infrastructure destroyed
- cell traffic to 10 cell sites interrupted
- two substations and local distribution system of power grid badly damaged
- local power grid badly damaged
- service disrupted for 12,000 electric customers, 270 steam customers, 1,400 gas customers

THE THREE R'S OF CRITICAL INFRASTRUCTURE

What are we to learn as engineers from the attacks of September 11, 2001, and beyond? What are we to teach to those who follow in our footsteps? How are we to define critical infrastructure in the future? These are but a few of the questions we must answer if we are to meet history's challenge.

This need to learn—and to teach—has caused me to return to the age-old fundamentals of education, namely the Three R's. However, in the twenty-first century's highly engineered environment and with our increased recognition of the threats this environment faces, the traditional Three R's of reading, 'riting, and 'rithmatic have been replaced by resist, respond, and recover, at least as they relate to critical infrastructure.

The *National Strategy for the Physical Protection of Critical Infrastructure and Key Assets*, released by the White House in February 2003, provides a national perspective on the lessons to be learned, while a more scientific perspective is provided by the National Research Council report entitled *Making the Nation Safer: The Role of Science and Technology in Countering Terrorism*, published in August 2002. This paper offers a slightly different perspective— one founded on our city's infrastructure systems.

BOX 1
Critical Infrastructure Defined

• Systems whose rapid failure would lead to a catastrophic loss of life
• Systems whose failure or significant degradation would lead to unacceptable economic consequences
• Systems whose rapid failure would significantly impact rescue and response efforts
• Systems whose significant degradation would significantly impact recovery efforts

NOTE: Rapid is relative to the consequences possible as opposed to an absolute timescale.

In Box 1, a definition of critical infrastructure builds upon and helps shape these Three R's. This definition sharpens the focus of the definition contained in H.R. 3162, the USA Patriot Act, wherein critical infrastructure is defined as "systems and assets, whether physical or virtual, so vital to the United States that the incapacity or destruction of such systems and assets would have a debilitating impact on security, national economic security, national public health or safety, or any combination of those matters."

An important point is that each element of infrastructure is not of the same critical importance. We must focus our efforts to ensure that limited resources are most appropriately applied. Let us now look at each of the Three R's in turn.

The First R—Resist

Critical infrastructure must be designed to resist attack and catastrophic failure. Immediately following the attacks and the subsequent collapse of the World Trade Center towers, there were those who called for high-profile buildings and other critical infrastructure to be designed to stop airplanes. This, simply put, is utter nonsense. Unless we are prepared to live in a heavily engineered environment more closely resembling the complex of caves in Afghanistan, we will not design buildings to stop planes. The challenge is to keep airplanes away from buildings and to root out those who challenge our way of life at the source.

Does that mean our profession is to do nothing? Far from it. Each engineering disaster, whether natural or manmade, has taught us lessons. Over time, these lessons are disseminated within a subset of our profession or within an industry segment. Some lessons are only understood with the fullness of time and often offer a deeper understanding of the real challenges we as engineers face. Short-term code modifications often satisfy the tendency to overreact in the short term but, as understanding develops, may fail to sufficiently react in the long term.

Our profession's tendency to specialize often constrains our ability to translate lessons learned across a broad range of disciplines and industry segments. Here, perhaps, lies a role for the National Academies—to know all that is being done, to learn from an incident, to consolidate this invaluable source of knowledge, and to ensure its timely distribution across the industries. Perhaps the return of the Renaissance ideals embodied in the master builders are once again in order.

In New York City on September 11, 2001, we saw the best of engineering, not the failure of it. We saw two proud structures swallow two maliciously guided planes that were fully loaded with fuel, and endure not only an impact beyond their design basis but also an ensuing fire. In the face of these attacks, these buildings did not simply allow themselves to be overwhelmed as the attackers most likely envisioned. Rather, they were the first of the many heroes to die that day, but only after they had bought the time for up to 25,000 people to leave and live. This is the true testament to the designers of the structures, and our recognition of their successful resistance to an overwhelming attack in no way diminishes the human tragedy associated with those who did not safely escape that day.

Our challenge as we move forward is to learn what we can from this tragedy and, as we have in the past, intelligently incorporate these lessons into our endeavors of the future. We must be comprehensive in our understanding, thorough in our consolidation of lessons learned, and broader in our distribution, especially for the lessons that transcend specialties and industries.

Not all damage on September 11 was to high-profile buildings in New York. In dollars, the damage to surrounding infrastructure—transportation, electricity, and telephone—exceeds that of the buildings. The very open role of infrastructure to tie developments together in some ways limits its ability to resist deliberate attack. Infrastructure's limited ability to resist provides a sufficient segue to the second of the Three R's of critical infrastructure.

The Second R—Respond

The attacks of September 11, 2001, destroyed the operability of large portions of the transportation, electricity, and telephone networks servicing lower Manhattan and impacted, more broadly, entire system operation. In the immediate aftermath of the attacks, transit system operators modified system operation to stop passenger flow into the affected area and to remove trains already in the area. That immediate action prevented any loss of life to transit passengers or workers despite the subsequent destruction of portions of the transit system from falling debris. On the heels of that immediate response came an even more daunting challenge: to reconfigure the original transportation system to meet the needs of the 850 businesses and 125,000 workers physically displaced when 29 million sq ft of office space was damaged or destroyed and provide for a reasonable restoration of service to the more than 350,000 passengers to lower Manhattan who had their commuting patterns disrupted. Many valuable lessons for the highly engineered environment that cities represent can be learned, including the following:

- The link between infrastructure and development is crucial.
- "Core capacity" of infrastructure systems is essential.
- Deferred maintenance represents a real cost and a real risk.
- Operational and emergency response training is an integral element of critical infrastructure response.
- Today's highly engineered environment requires a first responder team that goes beyond the traditional triad of fire, police, and emergency services.

Let us consider each lesson in turn:

Lesson 1—The link between infrastructure and development is crucial.

Infrastructure and development (in other words, the built environment) are intricately linked, often in ways we fail to fully appreciate. Each is the sine qua non of the other. However, as is often the case with all that we engineer, we can best appreciate the strengths, weaknesses, and functionality only in their failure or application in response to some new paradigm.

September 11 highlighted the interrelationships of infrastructure and development. In the localized failure of the built environment, or development (the collapse of the World Trade Center towers), we witnessed a localized destruction of the attendant infrastructure (subway lines 1 and 9, the local power grid, PATH station, and so forth). In the reconfiguration of regional development (an estimated 29,000 employees working outside New York City as a result of September 11 and another 29,000 temporarily backfilled in other existing metropolitan-area space), we modified our regional transportation network (mandatory high-occupancy vehicle [HOV], increased ferry service, increased transit ridership at other river crossings, and so on). Similar analogs exist for utility and telecommunications networks affected on September 11. However, this ability to reconfigure the infrastructure systems in response to a new development paradigm draws heavily from what we find in Lesson 2.

Lesson 2—Core capacity of infrastructure systems is essential.

In early 2001, I had the opportunity to attempt to explain the importance of some planned New York City transportation improvements to members of the political arena. These improvements were about enhancing the core capacity of a well-developed transportation network in order to improve overall system reliability, availability, and performance. Core capacity is the degree of interconnectivity of the various elements of the system as well as the number of alternative paths available—its flexibility and redundancy.

These additions to core capacity strengthened the overall system, going well beyond the benefits associated with new system connections from some new point A to new point B. My case for strengthening a complex system, inherently tying together the most complex and engineered urban environment in the world, was nearly lost. Traditional project evaluation models focused on new riders from new connections between points A and B. But, in complex systems, the dislocations that can be caused by even a partial loss of overall system capacity and capability can be much more profound. Similarly, the improved reliability, availability, and performance created by adding core capacity to a complex system can pay dividends not often easily seen.

Such was the case for the regional transit system in the aftermath of September 11, 2001. The core capacity of these systems provided the flexibility to deal with commuting patterns literally modified overnight with lines and stations outside the immediately affected area, seeing changed passenger volumes exceeding those often associated with new point A-to-B connections. It was gratifying to receive the call from the political arena several days later stating that they now understood core capacity.

Each of the infrastructure systems impacted by September 11 responded more or less quickly depending on the core capacity inherently incorporated in the system as well as the concentration of critical infrastructure in the damaged area. Older systems tended to be more "built out," while many newer systems were still heavily focused on building new A-to-B connections and as such had not yet achieved the level of core capacity of some of the more mature systems. This suggests that core capacity needs to be a criterion as we plan and implement the new infrastructure the twenty-first century will undoubtedly require.

Complex systems need a new model. We must recognize that dislocations can be profound. We must also recognize that improved reliability, availability, and performance pay hidden dividends. Core capacity is not just about the extent of the system or the number of alternate system paths. It is also about the intrinsic quality of the system at the point in time when it is stressed. This brings us to the third lesson learned.

Lesson 3—Deferred maintenance represents a real cost and a real risk.

The history of engineering is marked by exciting breakthroughs, great works of master builders, and outstanding service to our nation's and the world's population. Regretfully, it is also marked by systemic degradation of some of our greatest achievements. As a society, and perhaps even in some parts of our profession, we do not see sustained maintenance as important as the creation of the next new grand work. Whatever the reason—its routine nature, the ability to hopefully do it tomorrow, the lack of technical complexity, or just plain lack of "sex appeal"—we are collectively guilty of allowing some of our most complex systems to fall into disrepair and to have their level of reliability, availability, and operational and safety performance degraded. We have seen this most notably in failing rail systems in England and the United States, but the impacts of deferred maintenance affect every element of infrastructure.

To a large measure, the ability of New York City's transit system to respond and to take full advantage of the core capacity inherent in its system has its roots at the time of the system's nadir. Out of crisis emerged a commitment to fund, reorganize, rebuild, improve, and maintain to a well-defined standard. This, too, stands as one of the lessons to recognize as we engineer and operate our increasingly complex infrastructure systems. The strength of a well-maintained system is clearly seen in the aftermath. Other elements of infrastructure with higher backlogs of deferred maintenance are struggling to keep up, and for many the challenges are in the years immediately ahead.

The condition of the system—how well it is maintained—is critical to sustain its ability to respond. The backlog of deferred maintenance should be viewed as an element of systems risk. On September 11, 2001, and in its aftermath, systems in a state of good repair fared better in both the response and recovery phases. This ability to respond often to other than design-basis events is key to the integrity of new security and safety systems.

Lesson 4—Operational and emergency response training is an integral element of critical infrastructure response.

In the same way we factor constructability reviews into our design process and maintainability considerations into our construction details, so must we address operational training as an element of our engineering of critical infrastructure. The events of September 11, 2001, show many areas of exceptional performance, but this serves to only underscore the importance of operational training. The operational training for the events of the twenty-first century changed after September 11. New scenarios need to be considered. New threats in the form of weapons of mass destruction, higher risk of collateral physical and economic damage, and more extended response time frames need to be addressed. First responder training (actions, interactions, communications, decision making) needs to be integrated with infrastructure system operational training.

Simple items such as establishing evacuation routes and off-property staging areas must be clearly provided by the infrastructure of our built environment, but also must be clearly integrated in first responder protocols.

Scenario training must be evolutionary as new threats emerge. Emerging response plans must be reviewed regularly and revamped as needed. Unusual incident reporting must be similarly kept up to date and relevant. Training to handle a growing range of threat scenarios must be kept current.

On September 11 we saw the impact of having the Emergency Operation Center (EOC) in proximity to a high-profile target. We also saw the importance of having safe, redundant capability and comprehensive integration with other relevant EOCs. Quick response is essential, and the importance of interoperability of first responders has not received as much attention in the past as might be warranted now. But we must not stop there. We must also understand how the first responder team has evolved in light of our increasingly engineered environment.

Lesson 5—Today's highly engineered environment requires a first responder team that goes beyond the traditional triad of fire, police, and emergency services.

In early 2001, at the World Economic Forum (WEF) in Davos, Switzerland, one of the WEF governors was attempting to mobilize construction equipment to assist in rescue and recovery for victims of an earthquake in India. Engineers and constructors were not viewed as traditional members of the emergency response team and the barriers to "doing the right thing" were immense. Out of that frustration grew the WEF Disaster Response Network.

On September 11, 2001, we witnessed the engineering and construction industry voluntarily reach out and provide the technical and construction expertise for one of the greatest disasters in a highly engineered environment. All necessary protocols were not firmly in place and response training had never fully factored this dimension in. Yet, this "fourth responder" will be even more critical as the twenty-first century unfolds.

Response protocols in our engineered urban environment will increasingly need to proactively incorporate this fourth responder. New, dedicated first responder training facilities reflecting the unique nature of highly engineered environments and their infrastructure need to be deployed, and legislation needs to be provided to remove the onerous risks that accrue to engineer volunteers, who are often not covered by Good Samaritan statutes.

If we learn—and remember—each of these five lessons well, we will greatly enhance our ability to respond. But our ability to resist and respond in our critical infrastructure must also be matched by the third R, our ability to recover.

The Third R—Recover

We design to resist, to avoid catastrophic failure in our critical infrastructure, to delay the failure as long as possible if it is not preventable, and to minimize loss of life, collateral damage, and degraded system performance. Having built in as much resistance as makes sense from a risk-weighted and operational and economic perspective, we enhance our ability to respond. We provide core capacity; we focus on reliability, availability, and performance. We reconfigure inherently resilient systems for both the short and the long term.

But, for our critical infrastructure, that is not enough. We must recover the capacity and service that were destroyed. We must restore the engineered fabric, making it better than it was, if possible. We must engineer for recovery. From an engineering standpoint, this can mean many things:

- providing for accessibility to the sites of critical infrastructure
- ensuring availability of specialized construction equipment, contracts, and materials
- developing a well-documented system with clear interface points
- preplanning and rehearsing response and recovery scenarios for high-probability events (earthquake, hurricane, flood in areas so prone)

However, to truly respond in a highly engineered environment, even more is required. A vision must exist. Whether that involves the notional concept of the master builder of the past or the well-developed consensus builder recent history has required is irrelevant. Each aspect of our engineered environment must be understood not only in terms of its past and present but perhaps more importantly in terms of its future. How it will evolve. How resistance, response, and recovery will be built in as the system expands. How it fits in that vision of the future. What role it provides as part of a larger engineered environment. It is only with this vision in hand that a clear, unambiguous, and deliberate recovery effort can begin.

THE CHALLENGE AHEAD

The challenge ahead for our cities and their critical infrastructure is best viewed from the perspective of the Three R's—resist, respond, recover. To successfully meet this challenge we must

- understand the uniqueness of cities
- develop a systems perspective
- recognize the open nature of infrastructure
- engage the full range of talent available worldwide in the government, academic, and private sectors

OTHER RELATED DOCUMENTS

Gilbert, P. H., J. Isenberg, G. B. Baecher, L. T. Papay, L. G. Spielvogel, J. B. Woodard, E. V. Badolato. 2003. International issues for cities—countering terrorist threat. Journal of Infrastructure Systems (March).

National Research Council. 2002. Making the nation safer: The role of science and technology in countering terrorism. Washington, D.C.: The National Academies Press. (*http://www.nap.edu/books/0309084814/html/*)

Prieto, R. 2002. A 911 call to the engineering profession. The Bridge 32(Spring). Washington, D.C.: National Academy of Engineering. (*http://www.nae.edu/nae/naehome.nsf/weblinks/CGOZ-58NLJM?OpenDocument*)

Prieto, R. 2002. The Three R's: lessons learned from September 11th, presented at the Royal Academy of Engineering, London, October 28, 2002.

The White House. 2003. National strategy for the physical protection of critical infrastructure and key assets. February. Washington, D.C.: U.S. Government Printing Office. (*http://www.whitehouse.gov/pcipb/physical_strategy.pdf*)

The Role of the Russian Ministry of Emergency Situations and Executive Branch Agencies of the City of Moscow in Dealing with Emergency Situations Arising from Acts of Terrorism

*Aleksandr M. Yeliseev**
Moscow Main Administration for Civil Defense and Emergency Situations

The problems of ensuring the security of people and territory are a top priority for executive- and legislative-branch agencies of the Russian Federation. The major radiation accident at the Chernobyl Atomic Power Station in 1986 and the destructive Spitak earthquake in 1988 demonstrated the need for creating a Russian system for preventing and eliminating the consequences of emergency situations. The Ministry for Civil Defense, Emergency Situations, and Elimination of the Consequences of Natural Disasters (MChS) became the central component in this system. Territorial subunits of the MChS are among the executive-branch agencies of the various republics and oblasts that make up the Russian Federation, and they act at the local level to implement state policy with regard to protecting people and territory from emergency situations.

Moscow has historically represented the spiritual center of the Russian land. It is Russia's largest industrial center, making a substantial contribution to the country's overall economic indicators. Our city is the country's most important transport hub, on which the operation of the entire Russian transportation system is dependent. It represents the most important concentration of financial and information flows, which has a significant impact on the development of the state as a whole. Moscow is the center of scientific and cultural life, the focal point of a significant part of our national heritage, and a unique world-class historical and architectural center. All of these factors determine the level of the threat to the vital interests of citizens, social groups, and the city as a whole.

---

*Translated from the Russian by Kelly Robbins.

The following types of threats are most typical: criminal, terrorist, social, political, infrastructural, natural, industrial, environmental, informational, and psychological. These threats are of a complex and interrelated nature, with the majority being transnational in scale. These circumstances are characteristic of almost all the world's major megacities; therefore, they call for a great deal of attention to be devoted by the city leadership to problems of ensuring the security of urban facilities and residents of the capital.

Here, we proceed from the belief that ensuring the security of the population against emergency situations resulting from terrorism, natural and industrial disasters, and other causes is a difficult and complex task, and carrying it out successfully can be done only with the active involvement of all city departments, agencies, and organizations. Therefore, the Moscow City System for Preventing and Eliminating the Consequences of Emergency Situations was created in 1996, functionally linking the city's various district and departmental services units. City policy for ensuring the security of the population and the urban infrastructure is implemented through the Commissions on Emergency Situations, which have been established in each agency and department of the city administration and which are headed by leaders at the corresponding level. This operating principle facilitates management of the actions of city units in preventing emergencies as well as responding to threats and responding to emergencies once they have occurred. It is also helpful in coordinating the actions of the various services and organizing and efficiently carrying out emergency rescue operations.

In connection with the implementation of a special law passed by the city of Moscow, work is under way citywide to implement a comprehensive targeted program for improving the Moscow city system for preventing and eliminating the consequences of emergency situations. The program was developed on the initiative of the Moscow City Government and the MChS and was supported by the deputies of the Moscow City Duma. The basic goals of the program include

- implementing a set of measures aimed at preventing emergency situations, including the establishment of an effective system for monitoring and predicting accidents, catastrophes, and natural disasters
- modernizing the management and communications system through the widespread use of the latest information technologies
- improving the speed and efficiency of emergency response by creating a highly mobile and technically well equipped rescue service and by developing aviation technologies for use in emergency rescue operations
- improving the citywide system for educating the population on the appropriate actions to be taken during emergency situations

However, in recent years terrorism has been one of the main threats to public security. It presents a special danger to major cities and political, economic, and cultural centers. Terrorist acts are taking on ever-increasing scale and becoming more and more diverse both in form and in the goals for which they are carried out.

Since 1998, Moscow has been subjected to terrorist attacks on more than one occasion. We remember the bombings of apartment buildings on Guryanov Street and Kashirskoe Shosse, the shopping mall at Manezh Square, the underground passageway at the Pushkinskaya metro station, and the seizure of hostages during the performance of the musical *Nord-Ost*, in which more than 3,000 people were victims, of whom about 600 were killed.

These events have shown that terrorist acts are ever more frequently moving from the realm of potential threats to that of real emergency situations. In our view it is the world community's failure to respond appropriately to the terrorist acts committed in Moscow in the fall of 1999 that led to the tragic events of September 11, 2001, in the United States. Those events demonstrated once again that terrorism has no nationality but rather is international in nature, and not a single state is secure against it.

Expert assessments highlight the broad scope of this phenomenon, and many believe that at present in the various countries of the world there are about 100 major terrorist organizations, which maintain contacts among themselves. Therefore, the problem goes beyond the bounds of individual states. Furthermore, in recent years terrorism has acquired the capability of using the achievements of science and technology to further its criminal aims.

We have great understanding for the position of the New York City authorities, as we ourselves were on the scene only minutes after the bombings of the Moscow apartment buildings in 1999. Under the leadership of Moscow Mayor Yury M. Luzhkov and Russian Emergency Situations Minister Sergei K. Shoigu, we organized efforts to deal with the consequences of these explosions. We provided detailed reports on these incidents to the European community at an international conference in Vienna in 2000.

Antiterrorism activities in Moscow are conducted at all levels of the city government. This work is coordinated by an antiterrorism commission operating under the leadership of the city's mayor, and includes the following activities:

- improving laws related to the struggle against terrorism
- increasing the effectiveness of preventive measures
- ensuring the secure operations of industrial facilities and sites where large numbers of people gather

I would like to say that we have done a certain amount of work to ensure the security of residents and of the capital in general, primarily with regard to the creation of laws and regulations addressing these matters.

The city has recently enacted a Law on Protecting the Population and Territory of the City of Moscow from Emergency Situations of Natural and Industrial Origin. A strategy for the security of Moscow has also been adopted, outlining in systematic form the views of the city's leadership on ensuring the safety of its residents. In the process of developing this strategy, the programs Moscow Radiation Security and Moscow Chemical Security were also created and adopted to deal with matters related to protecting potentially dangerous facilities against terrorism. In the past few years, Moscow has passed more than 100 regulations governing matters related to the city's security, and we are prepared to acquaint representatives of the international community with them.

Executive-branch agencies are devoting special attention to monitoring and controlling the activities of all officials involved in implementing preventive measures against emergency situations. In 2002 alone, the State Inspectorate for Protecting the Population and Territory from Emergency Situations conducted checks at more than 10,000 enterprises, organizations, and institutions. Those guilty of violating urban security regulations face administrative penalties and are prosecuted through the civilian court system.

City policy regarding new construction is pursued rather effectively. Moscow has established a system of measures that prohibits the construction or reconstruction of any industrial buildings, housing, or other public facilities that do not include design features intended to prevent possible emergency situations, including potential terrorist acts.

The city has created the Center for Monitoring and Forecasting Emergency Situations, for which the main objectives are the prevention and early detection of emergencies. The components of this system include stationary and mobile Lidar units, which use laser, infrared, and visual observation methods to detect fires and atmospheric emissions of harmful substances.

In accounting for the large amounts of special cargo (gasoline, reagents for refrigeration systems, and so forth) that pass through Moscow and other world cities, cargo that also represents a potential threat of the commission of terrorist acts, we have tightened controls on the transport of such materials by road and rail within the city limits. The city's law enforcement agencies are paying special attention to the safety of capital residents in locations where large numbers of people gather, such as markets, fairs, and the sites of large cultural events and sports competitions.

The quality of efforts to prevent and eliminate the consequences of emergency situations depends primarily on the level of preparedness of the leadership, specialists, and city residents. This matter is being addressed by providing training to almost all categories of city residents at special educational institutions, enterprises, and places of residence. For example, in 2002, about 30,000 people received special training at educational centers and more than 2 million blue- and white-collar personnel received training at their worksites.

Training games represent the most effective form of preparation for individuals in positions of leadership. Such games allow participants to practice dealing with matters such as procedures for notification and assembly of senior officials, technologies for application in emergency rescue operations and other urgent activities, organization of assistance to city service providers in eliminating the consequences of emergency situations, comprehensive provision of aid and services to the affected population, and a number of other citywide undertakings.

Earlier this year, a special tactical training exercise was conducted at a Moscow subway station to focus on coordinating the activities of city services in eliminating the consequences of a possible terrorist act involving the use of dangerous chemical substances. During the training exercise, a number of practical measures were developed with the aim of improving the efficiency of emergency rescue efforts under such conditions, and these measures have now been submitted to the Moscow City Government for review.

Efforts to train young people occupy an important place in our work. Last year, in cooperation with the Moscow Educational Committee, we began training students from the capital's higher educational institutions to serve as reserve rescue personnel. A class entitled "Principles of Everyday Safety" has also been introduced for students in all grades in elementary and secondary schools. The number of participants in "Safety School" competitions is constantly on the rise. Each year, more and more secondary school students participate in "Young Rescuer" summer camps.

Regarding measures to prevent emergencies, we must not forget that the city must also be prepared to eliminate their consequences. The main element of this system is the Center for Crisis Situation Management, which is designed to gather and process information about emergency situations, inform the population, and make well-founded decisions on how to handle such situations.

At present, plans call for the creation of a Unified Monitoring and Dispatch Center for the city of Moscow on the basis of the facilities of the Moscow City Crisis Situation Management Center and the Force Management Center of the State Fire Service Administration of MChS. This new center, which would be reachable by dialing 01, would facilitate the efficient collection and processing of emergency reports, analyze an enormous amount of information under extremely time-critical conditions, and coordinate the actions of all dispatch services included in the city's unified dispatch system.

The current combined daily volume for the two centers mentioned above is approximately 6,000 calls. After the switch to the single telephone number 01, it is predicted that the number of calls alone will rise to 18,000 per day. This will require a large set of organizational and technical changes to be made, taking into account foreign experience in operating rescue services using single telephone numbers such as 112 and 911.

Creating, training, and developing forces for eliminating the consequences of emergency situations is of enormous significance in the functioning of the system. To this end, the Moscow City Search and Rescue Service has been created in the capital. Also operating in cooperation with us in the city are various MChS rescue units and a number of commercial entities. If a major emergency occurs, plans call for augmenting the rescue service by calling in specialists and equipment from other city organizations.

Since the city search and rescue service was established, rescuers have carried out about 60,000 rescue operations and have saved more than 25,000 people. In 2002 alone, Moscow firefighters handled about 7,000 fires. The timely and skillful actions of personnel from the city's medical service have saved the lives of thousands of Muscovites involved in emergency situations and accidents.

Unfortunately, Muscovites have been forced to confront inhuman acts of terrorism in practice. We profoundly share the pain and suffering of other nations affected by emergency situations of any kind. Therefore, the government of Moscow is devoting a great deal of attention to humanitarian operations, including those of international scope. We are providing humanitarian aid to the suffering population in various regions of Russia and in other countries, including Kosovo, Afghanistan, Korea, Bolivia, the Balkans, Germany, the Czech Republic, and others.

Overall, we may conclude that the government of Moscow has a great focus on international cooperation in combating terrorism and crime and eliminating the consequences of terrorist acts and natural and industrial disasters. In recent years, stable contacts have been established among counterpart police and emergency services agencies at the municipal level as part of the comprehensive cooperation between Moscow and foreign cities, including those in Europe. Close cooperation is under way with the cities of Vienna, Berlin, Madrid, Dublin, Helsinki, and others in the form of information sharing, exchanges and training of specialists, and joint training exercises.

In May 2002, on the initiative of Moscow Mayor Yury M. Luzhkov, a meeting of police officials from European countries was convened to promote better coordination in the struggle against terrorism. Moreover, an international meeting on matters of security in major cities is to be held in Moscow in June 2003.

In conclusion, I would like to say that the system that has been created in Moscow for preventing and eliminating the consequences of emergency situations stands ready to cooperate closely in the twenty-first century with any who treasure the ideals of humanism and defense of the most important human right, the right to life.

CYBERTERRORISM

A Perspective on Cybersecurity Research in the United States

*Wm. A. Wulf**
National Academy of Engineering

Anita K. Jones
University of Virginia

This paper is a perspective on—an opinion about—the state of cybersecurity research in the United States. It is not a thorough enumeration of the ongoing research, but rather a critique of the overall state of that research. The essential conclusion of this critique is that although the nation is at great risk from cyberterrorism, we have virtually no research base on which to build secure systems. Moreover, only a tiny cadre of researchers are thinking deeply about long-term solutions to the problem of cybersecurity.

If the problem were merely a matter of implementing techniques that are known to be adequate, this might not be a serious issue. The truth is that we do not know how to build secure information systems. The only model widely used for cybersecurity is the "perimeter defense" model, which is demonstrably fragile. To be sure, many immediate problems of cybersecurity can be handled by implementing or enforcing known "best practices," such as patching software to correct each new, successful attack. Solving the fundamental problem will require long-term, innovative basic research, and at the moment we have very few people capable of doing that research.

HOW VULNERABLE IS THE UNITED STATES?

Although we began by asserting the vulnerability of the United States to cyberterrorism (and, indeed, cybercrime), in truth no one knows how vulnerable we really are. We are probably more vulnerable than we would like to be, and

*This paper is derived from a similar paper by the authors in the National Academy of Engineering publication *The Bridge*, Spring 2002, 32(1):41–45.

maybe a lot more vulnerable than we can survive. We know that financial cyber-systems have been attacked, but the extent of damage has generally not been disclosed to preserve their image of integrity. Military systems have also been attacked, but the most serious attacks have also not been disclosed for security reasons. (It has been reported, however, that more than 60 percent of U.S. military computers have been compromised.) We know that national defense computers and networks use the same software and hardware as the public, and thus are subject to the same kinds of attacks. These military systems are, of course, an attractive target for sophisticated state-sponsored intruders who want to undermine our military preparedness. We also know that the country's infrastructure—power, pipelines, water distribution, and so forth—is increasingly controlled by computers that communicate via networks, including the Internet, and thus are potential targets.

The U.S. legal system exacerbates the risk of cyberattack because it prevents the exchange of information among private corporations about attacks, thus preventing one company from learning from the experiences of others. In anticipation of Y2K problems, Congress passed special legislation enabling corporations to exchange information (with limited liability). However, no such legislation has been passed to permit the exchange of cybersecurity information. Other laws—laws to protect civil liberties, for example—prohibit the exchange of information among some government agencies. Although this is an admirable goal, it does make cybersecurity more difficult to achieve.

The bottom line is that no one knows exactly how vulnerable we are. We can obtain an idea of the magnitude of the problem, however, from public information. The 1997 Presidential Commission on Critical Infrastructure Protection, with access to classified and proprietary information, focused on cybersecurity. Although the commission's charter included **all** critical infrastructure—power, water, communications, financial, and so forth—they chose to focus on just **one**, our cyberinfrastructure. In its report, the commission found that "all our infrastructures [are] increasingly dependent on information and communications systems... [that] dependence is the source of rising vulnerabilities, and therefore, it is where we concentrated our efforts." In other words, all forms of infrastructure are so vulnerable to cyberattack that the commission decided to virtually ignore other vulnerabilities. Information technology has become crucial to every aspect of modern life, and a serious attack could cripple any system, from an emergency military deployment to health care delivery to the generation of electrical power.

Publicly reported attacks have been relatively unsophisticated and, although annoying, have not had dire consequences. The unreported attacks have been more serious, but the details have not been made known to the public—or, in some cases, not even to the responsible public officials. Potential attack scenarios are even worse, but the probability that they will happen is simply not known.

Our critical systems have many vulnerabilities, ranging from errors in software to trusted but disgruntled employees to low-bid developers outside the

United States. But the problem goes much deeper. In many cases, attackers have found clever ways to combine two or more legitimate features of a system in ways the designers had not foreseen. In these cases, undesirable behavior results from correctly implemented software. In addition, software vendors have found that the public is not willing to pay for security. Buyers do not choose more secure products over less secure ones, especially if they must pay a premium for them, so venders have not invested in security. The overriding fundamental source of vulnerability is that we do not have a deep understanding of the problem or its solution, and little if any research is being done to develop that understanding.

HOW PREPARED ARE WE TO RESPOND?

There are different answers for the short term and the long term, and to some extent there are different answers for the military, the private sector, financial institutions, and other communities. Unfortunately, the only short-term solution is to patch systems as we discover bugs in them. To be effective, this requires that every member of a vast army of system administrators and users be vigilant. Alas, the evidence shows that such widespread diligence is extraordinarily hard to achieve.

Of equal importance, the Internet is essentially a monoculture—almost all of the computers connected to it are IBM compatible. Because they use a single operating system and set of applications, a would-be attacker has to find only **one** vulnerability in any part of the system to attack the vast majority of computers connected to the network. That is why attacks all seem to spread rapidly.

In the long term, we will need a deep research base on cybersecurity. Unfortunately, one of the principal findings of the Presidential Commission on Critical Infrastructure Protection was that the current research base is not adequate to support infrastructure protection. For historical reasons, no U.S. federal funding agency has assumed responsibility for supporting basic research in this area—not the Defense Advanced Research Projects Agency, not the National Science Foundation, not the U.S. Department of Energy, and not the National Security Agency.

As a result, only relatively small, sporadic research projects have been funded, and the underlying assumptions on cybersecurity that were established in the 1960s mainframe environment have not been questioned. When funds are scarce, researchers become very conservative, and bold challenges to the conventional wisdom are not likely to pass peer review. Incrementalism has become the norm; thus, no long-term cybersecurity solution has been developed, or even thoroughly investigated.

Also, few researchers elect cybersecurity as a topic. It has been estimated that only seven Ph.D. students each year choose to work in the cybersecurity area.

WHAT NEEDS TO BE DONE?

Four critical needs must be met to improve cybersecurity:

1. the need for a new model to replace the perimeter defense model
2. the need for a new definition of cybersecurity
3. the need for an active defense
4. the need for coordinated activities within cybercommunities, the legal system, and regulatory systems

The Need for a New Model

Most research on cybersecurity has been based on a perimeter defense model. This model states that the object to protect is "inside" the system, the attacker is outside the system, and the system must therefore keep the attacker from breeching the system's perimeter. It is interesting that this model is so deeply entrenched in our thinking about cybersecurity that our terminology reflects it: We have firewalls to keep outside attackers from penetrating our defenses; we build intrusion detection software to determine whether an outsider has foiled our perimeter defense; we build a DMZ (demilitarized zone) to allow both insiders and outsiders to access certain restricted facilities; etc. This perimeter defense model of computer security—sometimes called the Maginot Line model—has been used since the first mainframe operating systems were built in the 1960s. Unfortunately, it is dangerously, even fatally, flawed.

First, like the Maginot Line, it is fragile. In World War II, France fell in 35 days because of its reliance on this model. No matter how formidable the defenses, an attacker can circumvent them and, once inside, can compromise the entire system.

Second, the model fails to recognize that many security flaws are "designed in." In other words, a system may fail by performing exactly as specified. In 1993 the Naval Research Laboratory conducted an analysis of some 50 security flaws and found that 22 of them were designed into the requirements or specifications for supposedly correct system behavior.

Third, a perimeter defense cannot protect against attacks from inside. If all of our defenses are directed outward, we remain vulnerable to the legitimate insider. An FBI study of attacks on financial systems determined that insider attacks were twice as frequent as outsider ones and that each insider attack was 50 times more costly than the average outsider attack.

Fourth, major damage can be done without penetrating a system. This was demonstrated by the distributed denial-of-service attacks on Yahoo and other Internet sites two years ago. Simply by flooding the system with false requests for service, these sites were rendered incapable of responding to legitimate requests. Such attacks need not be against Internet sites; we can be grateful that so far denial-of-service attacks have not been directed against 911 services in a major city, for example.

Fifth, the Maginot Line model has never worked. Every system designed with a Maginot Line-type notion of security has been compromised, including the systems the authors built in the 1970s. After 40 years of trying to develop a foolproof system, it is time we realized that we are not likely to succeed.

Sixth and finally, the perimeter defense model cannot work for deep theoretical reasons. In short, to build a truly secure system, one would have to prove a theorem that no bad thing can ever happen, where *bad thing* is not completely defined. The experience with cryptographic protocols is interesting in this regard. These protocols are relatively small pieces of program whose function is critical to maintaining the perimeter defense model in networked systems. Because of their criticality, a number of these protocols have been "proven correct," only to be subsequently broken by someone with a different notion of bad behavior than was presumed in the proof. For these reasons, replacing the perimeter defense model of computer security is essential to the long-term solution to cybersecurity.

The Need for a Better Definition of Security

The second critical need for cybersecurity is to redefine *security*. The military definition of security emphasizes protecting access to sensitive information. This is the basis of the layered (confidential, secret, top secret) and compartmentalized (code word) classification of information.

The somewhat broader definition of security used in the computing research community includes two other notions: integrity and denial of service. Integrity implies that an attacker cannot modify information in the system. In some cases, for instance, medical records, integrity is much more important than secrecy. We may not like it if other people see our medical records, but we may die if someone alters our allergy profile.

Denial of service means that the attacker does not access or modify information but denies users a service provided by it. This relatively unsophisticated form of attack can be used against phone systems, for example, 911, financial systems, and, of course, Internet hosts. Because more than 90 percent of military communications, and almost 100 percent of law enforcement and other first responder communications are sent via the public switched telephone network, attackers could seriously disrupt a military activity or response to a terrorist incident by simply tying up the phone lines at appropriate bases or municipal crisis control centers.

Practical definitions of security must be more complex than confidentiality, integrity, and denial of service and must be tailored for each kind of entity; that is, different systems are needed for credit cards, medical records, tanks, flight plans, student examinations, and so forth. The notion of restricting access to a credit card to individuals with, say, secret clearance is nonsensical. Other factors, such as the timing (or at least the temporal order) of operations, correlative operations on related objects, and so on, are essential concepts for real-world security. (It used to be said that the best way to anticipate major U.S. military operations was to count the number of pizza deliveries to the Pentagon.)

The military concept of sensitive but unclassified information also has a counterpart in the cyberworld. Indeed, the line between sensitive and nonsensitive information is often blurred in cyberspace. In principle, one must consider how any piece of information might be combined with any other pieces of information to compromise a system. With the vast amount of information available on the Internet and the speed of modern computers, it has become all but impossible to anticipate how information will be combined or what inferences can be drawn from such combinations.

The Need for an Active Defense

The third critical need for cybersecurity is for an active defense. Not all experts agree, but based on our experience during the past 30 years, we have concluded that a passive defense alone will not work. It is unlikely that a system can be built that anticipates all possible uses, misuses, and vulnerabilities. Thus, effective cybersecurity must include some kind of active response—a threat or a cost higher than the attacker is willing to pay—to complement the passive defense.

Developing an active defense will be difficult because identifying the source of an attack is difficult. The practical and legal implications of active defenses have not been determined, and the opportunities for mistakes are legion. The international implications are especially troublesome. It is difficult, usually impossible, to pinpoint the physical location of an attacker. If it is in another country, a countermeasure by a U.S. government computer might even be considered an act of war.

Resolving these legal and related issues will require a thoughtful approach and careful international diplomacy. We desperately need long-term basic scholarship in this area, and we need to start now.

The Need for Coordinated Activities by Legal and Other Societal Mechanisms

Any plan of action must also involve a dialogue on legal issues, the fourth critical need for cybersecurity. In the United States, the coupling between the legal system and cybersecurity (and cybercrime) is only beginning to emerge. From our technically based perspective, two kinds of issues should be addressed soon: (1) issues raised in cyberspace that do not have counterparts in the physical world and (2) issues raised by place-based assumptions in current law.

The first category includes many issues from new forms of intellectual property, for example, databases, to new forms of crime, for example, spamming. Issues of particular interest to this discussion are rights and limitations on active countermeasures to intrusions—indeed, determining what constitutes an intrusion.

The second category, issues raised by place-based assumptions in current law, includes many basic questions. How does the concept of jurisdiction apply in cyberspace? For tax purposes, for example, sales taxes, where does a cyberspace transaction take place? Where do you draw the line between national security and law enforcement? How do you apply the concept of *posse comitatus*?[1]

Not all of these issues are immediately and obviously related to cybersecurity. But cyberspace protection is a "wedge issue" that will force us to rethink some fundamental ideas about the role of government, the relationship between the public and private sectors, the balance between rights of privacy and public safety, and the definition of security.

CONCLUSION

The security of our information infrastructure and other critical infrastructures will be a systems problem, as well as a significant research challenge. A particular government agency must take on the mission of revitalizing research in cybersecurity with the following objectives:

- development of wholly new methods of ensuring information system security
- development of a larger research community in cybersecurity
- education of computer system and computer science majors in cybersecurity at the undergraduate level, which would eventually improve the state of the practice in industry

Achieving these goals will require a guarantee of sustained support over a long period as an incentive to researchers to pursue projects in this area.

In the past few months, members of the U.S. House of Representatives Committee on Science have held hearings on the state of research on cybersecurity and have introduced three acts that would provide initial funding for basic research through the National Science Foundation and the National Institute of Standards and Technology.[2] Although these initiatives are heartening, their full impact will not be felt for a decade or more. Historically, policy makers have not continued to support research with such long horizons. However, in the aftermath of September 11, 2001, we are hopeful that Congress is now ready to provide stable, long-term funding for this high-risk research.

NOTES

1. *Posse Comitatus* is an 1880s-era law that prohibits the federal military from functioning in the territory of the United States.

2. See H.R. 3316 Computer security enhancement and research act of 2001, H.R. 3394 Cyber security research and development act, and H.R. 3400 Networking and information technology research advancement act. For the text of written testimony by Wm. A. Wulf, see the NAE web site, *www.nae.edu* under "Site Highlights."

Analysis of the Threat of Cyberattacks to Major Transportation Control Systems in Russia

Mikhail B. Ignatyev
St. Petersburg State University of Aerospace Instrumentation

INTRODUCTION

Russia is a large and cold country for which the transportation infrastructure is of vital significance. Russia has a developed system of railroads; powerful systems for gas, oil, and electricity distribution; developed air, sea, and river transport systems; and a significant road transport system, although the latter is in need of intensive work. An intermodal shipping system[1] is being created, and this requires a highly developed informational infrastructure. Every cargo shipment must be accompanied by a packet of documents, and delays in preparing these documents often lead to delays in shipping, especially when cargo is transferred from one mode of transportation to another at junctures between the sea, rail, and road transport systems.

As with the means of transportation themselves—planes, trucks, or ships—the cargo being carried may also be used for terrorist purposes. This is illustrated by the terrorist act of September 11, 2001, in New York City, as well as other incidents.[2]

Large computer systems are used to manage transport flows. Criminal elements use these computer systems to steal cargo in especially large volumes. They steal large freight containers and even entire trains of such freight cars, gas and oil from pipelines, ships and their cargo, and large trucks on the roads. Customs rules are violated, and large amounts of contraband are circulated. Major transport control systems have become a battlefield for criminal elements and governmental authorities. To protect information and ward off cyberattacks, all known means of protection are being utilized, but there are also special points to consider.

First, computerized transportation control systems are directly linked to specific cargoes. Information about the cargoes and their shipment routes and schedules are of interest to criminal groups and therefore requires protection.

Second, a supplemental information system is needed to track the movement of cargoes, and this is especially important during emergencies. A number of projects could be proposed in this regard, including a cybernetic container, cybernetic pipeline, robotic system for use in gas pipelines, and system for the external control of various modes of transport—planes, automobiles, and ships.

Third, to ensure that correct decisions are made in rapidly changing situations associated with the battle against terrorism, interactive modeling of emergency situations is needed on the basis of three-dimensional graphics and animation, multiagent systems, and virtual world technologies.

Fourth, a cyberspace immune system must be created based on the analogy of biological immune systems, with special cyberagents playing the role of the white cells.

Fifth, an external control system must be created in which the top level is integrated into controls at the lowest level in order to prevent emergencies.

A CYBERSPACE IMMUNE SYSTEM

Construction of a cyberspace immune system is a matter of global interest. In the first stage of the formation of cyberspace, no thought was given to information protection, while in the second stage, passive protection methods, such as steganography and cryptographic systems, began to be implemented. The third stage is now beginning, and it has become obvious that passive methods will not resolve the problem. It is necessary to look to the analogy of biological systems, which over the millennia have developed immune systems to protect against penetration by disease-causing microbes and substances.[3]

Among plants and animals, resistance to bacterial and viral infections on an individual and species basis is ensured by a complex and multifaceted protection system inherent in each organism. In the battle between protective forces and infectious agents, the advantage often lies with the latter, as microorganisms multiply rapidly, creating populations numbering in the many millions, including mutant forms with more aggressive properties than those present in the initial strain. To protect themselves, it is likely that at a certain evolutionary stage, vertebrates developed a system of adaptive immunity (antibody formation). This is an organism's most powerful line of defense, particularly against repeated contacts with infectious agents. The capability or lack of capability to produce antibodies is an inherited characteristic. The genetic regulation of antibody biosynthesis has several specific features. For instance, the formation of an antibody molecule by one polypeptide chain is controlled by two different genes. One of them controls the formation of the part of the chain involved in constructing the active center, with the construction of this part being different for antibodies having different specificities. Another gene controls the formation of the part of the chain that is constructed the same in all antibodies related to a given class of immunoglobulins. The degree of natural resistance to disease possessed by a given type of animal is determined by many factors, which in total reflect the special characteristics of both the animal and the disease pathogen.

The creation of a cyberspace immune system is possible by creating a multi-agent system. Some of the agents would perform useful work in transmitting information and could be identified with responsible principles (these agents could be analogous to red blood cells). Other agents would perform active police functions, detecting and rendering them harmless (these agents would be like antibodies). A third group of agents and other information structures could be identified as alien and harmful to the operation of the information system, and they would be removed from cyberspace. To construct a cyberspace immune system, it will be necessary to look at the architecture of the Internet and other global systems.

VIRTUAL WORLDS AND CYBERTERRORISM

Current Situation

• Society is undergoing a massive and often uncontrolled process of virtualization, resulting in virtual enterprises, work, universities, museums, economies, government, anatomy, and so forth.

• There is no single theory of virtual worlds, but rather various and often mutually exclusive views of philosophers, cultural specialists, psychologists, sociologists, and computer specialists.

• Hardware and software involved in the formation and support of computerized virtual worlds are developing rapidly without prior consideration of their capacities and the consequences of their use.

• Certain features of virtual worlds, such as initiation, interactivity, presence, resonance, reflexivity, and classification as information management systems allow us to assert that the concept of protection cannot be reduced to modern methods of protecting the base technologies that form the foundation supporting virtual worlds, but rather must take their special features into account.

• The most important characteristic of virtual worlds is their direct impact on the individual and, as a result, on society—the totality of the real world—which gives rise to the need to protect not only the infrastructure of a given object but also the life and health of the individual. Furthermore, by integrating biological and electronic elements (biocybernetic interface), the problems of protecting virtual worlds go beyond the limits of cyberterrorism and are associated with other forms of terrorism—biological, chemical, electromagnetic, radiological, and so forth.

Goals of Work

The main goal should be research and development of methods and models for forming, managing, and interacting with computer-created virtual worlds with the aim of improving the efficiency (safety, reliability) of the operations of various types of human-machine systems, including those related to transportation.

The fundamental problem involved in creating virtual worlds is the definition and formalization of mechanisms for establishing and managing these worlds as well as facilitating interactions with them in terms of sensory motor parameters and other human characteristics. This is because virtual worlds are based on a set of human sensations experienced upon entering a given virtual environment and interacting with objects in it using various characteristics—physical, psychological, physiological, and so forth—that are either similar to or substantially different from those involved in the user's daily life and activities.

Research and development efforts are proposed in the following areas:

- virtual worlds as a focus of protection
- virtual worlds as a means of protection
- virtual worlds as a means of modeling situations and training specialists in how to combat cyberterrorism

Proposed Approaches

The process of addressing these tasks and the role of virtual worlds in this process may be described as follows:

- a class of functional tasks in the topical area
- functionally significant states of consciousness (psychological conditions) for each task described in terms of modalities (visual, auditory, and so forth)
- the virtual world as an integral representation of states of consciousness
- the information management channels of virtual worlds, which perform functional tasks and support the virtual world, with dynamic distribution of sensory motor resources among the various tasks being handled at a given time
- the integrated systems of virtual worlds, involved with receiving and transmitting (interaction), information computing (processing), and management
- a number of unified device and software modules for the creation and support of virtual worlds

The creation of virtual worlds will make it possible to resolve certain typical management problems, for example,

- organizing the information management field "user-application" (representation of information plus management) with the possibility of managing the volume and content of information exchanged between them (response rate, periodicity, content, formats, and transmission channels)

• recommending behavior in working with an application according to the following model: recorded stage in virtual multimedia scene corresponding to effective behavior → scene corresponding to user's current decisions → comparison and correction of discrepancies

• determining conditions for initiation of functionally significant state of consciousness of a given type and, on this basis, forming or predicting a person's behavior in various situations (for example, by sending a selection of initiation conditions)

The proposed and traditional approaches are presented in Table 1.

Virtual worlds should be considered both in the broad sense of the struggle against cyberterrorism and their use for civilian purposes (dual-use technologies) and in the narrow sense of their possible use in specific topical areas, for

TABLE 1 Traditional and Virtually Based Management Systems

Traditional Management Systems	Management Systems Based on Virtual Worlds
Systems-oriented architecture is divided into complexes according to functional tasks.	Open function-oriented modular architecture is divided into complexes according to typical concepts of perceptive human resources and related operations necessary to handle functional tasks, with dynamic distribution of resources among the tasks.
Integrated processing of all incoming information and interaction of separate subsystems are driven mainly by the operator; that is, a person decides on an action to be taken after receiving and processing a variety of multiparametric information.	Two-level management: the top level is represented by the user, who determines the basic management objectives; the second level receives the user's command, analyzes it under specific application conditions, and selects and performs the appropriate function, taking into account available resources; that is, the user goes from coordinating system operations and categorizing information to giving the management system commands that it dynamically redistributes as it handles the command.
As a rule, separate management systems are created for new applications.	Virtual worlds for specific applications are formed on the basis of the tasks at hand using a number of unified standard device and software modules appropriate to the level of operations of the base virtual world.

example, in external control of transportation systems in emergency situations, with a potential second application in the area of intermodal shipping. In the latter case, one of the main objectives would be the development of virtual reality-based models of the seizure of a plane, ship, or vehicle by terrorists.

Basic Stages of Study

1. study of internal and external mechanisms for creating and managing virtual worlds with the aim of analyzing possible points at which they could be subject to outside effects and the consequences of such effects

2. study of the role of virtual worlds in the process by which individuals carry out tasks in a particular topical area: "fragment of reality plus tasks at hand plus human action" (primarily sensory motor, cognitive, and linguistic) to determine mechanisms for protection against outside effects

3. construction of a generalized model of virtual worlds, including models of internal and external mechanisms for creation and management, basic characteristics and their management and classification, and user representations and behavior

4. construction of a model for the protection of virtual worlds that would facilitate adaptive (level of automation of interaction is determined by the user's condition, the user's preferred means of receiving information, limitations on technical resources, and so forth) and bilateral (with mixed initiative) interaction between the individual user and the application

5. testing of models using the example of the creation of protected systems in the fields of transportation, education, and science

6. creation of electronic means for the training of specialists in this field

EXTERNAL CONTROL OF MEANS OF TRANSPORTATION IN EMERGENCY SITUATIONS

The events of recent years show that means of transportation—planes, ships, and motor vehicles—are increasingly being used as tools in the commission of terrorist acts. Means of transportation are controlled by people, and the current security concept is based on the assumption that these people value their own lives and will therefore operate their vehicles so that they themselves will not suffer and will not find themselves in any dangerous situations. However, terrorist acts are committed by people who are prepared to sacrifice their lives for the sake of ideas, and such people are becoming increasingly common because of the growth of social inequality and the exacerbation of the world situation. This forces us to reconsider the very concept of transportation security. These conditions gave rise to the idea of external control of means of transportation. The essence of this idea is as follows: In emergencies, the control capability of the pilot, captain, or driver would be shut off (as they might be under the control of malefactors), and external control of the vehicle would be implemented from a special center, thus preventing the vehicle from being used as a weapon.[4]

The technical means for instituting external control would be provided by the presence of onboard computer systems, which already perform a large volume of functions in the operation of various types of vehicles. Aviation computer systems handle complex tasks related to navigation, control, diagnostics, overall aircraft operations, communications, and so forth. Computer systems aboard ships also take care of many tasks and have made it possible to reduce crew sizes significantly. New generations of automobiles are also equipped with computer systems, which help to conserve fuel and improve safety. However, implementing external controls is a complex problem involving the resolution of many technical, psychological, and legal issues.

It should be noted that the development of means of transportation is proceeding at a rapid pace. Transportation systems do a great deal of environmental damage to the planet, many people are killed in transportation accidents, and it is becoming obvious that the entire concept of transportation development needs to be reviewed and linked to the concept of security. All means of transportation should have external control capability, which not only will make it possible to improve security but also will facilitate the resolution of problems related to traffic jams, intermodal shipping, and so forth. To resolve these problems, we need a computer model of the entire transportation space, populated with representatives of all means of transportation in the form of agents that would accurately reflect the location of each vehicle and its characteristics, destinations, and capabilities. In essence, this calls for the construction of a multiuser virtual world. This is no simple task, but in our times it is an achievable goal and can be tackled in stages, region by region, so that in the future it would grow to encompass the entire planet. With the help of this multiuser virtual world, it would be possible to test various options for resolving transportation problems and select the best ones for the current situation. As an example, we have considered the multiuser virtual transportation world of St. Petersburg, which has a multitude of problems.[5]

Resolution of the problem of external control of means of transportation in emergencies involves the following elements:

- detection of an emergency situation on an aircraft
- decision to implement external control
- removal of control capabilities from cabin and institution of external control—a problem of onboard equipment
- operation of dispatch center where external control commands are processed
- placement of aircraft in multiuser virtual-world mode for flight coordination
- landing of aircraft in external control mode

Plans call for participation in this project by the leading scientific research, design, engineering, and flight-testing organizations in the Russian aviation sector. These organizations specialize in designing, operating, and testing heavy, light, civilian, and military aircraft; onboard systems for automated and manual flight control; ground-based flight control systems; onboard and ground-based radio communications systems; and others. They have great creative potential and experience and have done much previous scientific and engineering work in aircraft design, testing, and operation; design and operation of onboard equipment and software for use aboard civilian and military aircraft; systematic development of failure-resistant and fail-safe onboard equipment, such as ergatic (man-machine) systems; development and operation of imitation and seminatural model displays; certification of aircraft, equipment, and software; and operation of flight control systems. Based on this concept, a number of technical features could be developed for the stage-by-stage implementation of the project, with the goal of the first stage being the execution of a test flight of a heavy passenger plane in external control mode. The problem must be resolved with the involvement of leading foreign firms and organizations.

CONCLUSION

The appearance of international terrorism on a broad scale represents a challenge to all mankind. Problems involving the improvement of security may be resolved only through the joint efforts of many countries.

NOTES

1. Chernenko, V. I., and M. B. Ignatyev. 1996. Multimodal transportation in northwest Russia for sustainable development. Proceedings of the Conference on Sustainable Interregional Transport in Europe, Kouvola, Finland, June 10–12.

2. Wilkinson, P., and B. M. Jenkins. 1999. Aviation terrorism and security. London: Frank Cass Publishers. See also Ignatyev, M. B., N. Simatos, and S. Sivasundaram. 1996. Aircraft as adaptive nonlinear systems which must be in the adaptational maximum zone for safety. Proceedings of the First International Conference on Nonlinear Problems in Aviation and Aerospace, Daytona Beach, FL.

3. Ignatyev, M. B., L. A. Mironovsky, Yu. M. Smirnov, and G. S. Britov. 1973. Management of computing processes. M. B. Ignatyev, ed. Leningrad: Leningrad State University Publishing House, 296 pp. See also Ignatyev, M. B., A. V. Nikitin, and L. G. Osovetsky. 1988. A bioinformational analogy for building a base interface for software and the INTERFACE-DNA-PC mobile technological environment. In Issues of Programming Technology. Leningrad: Leningrad Institute of Aviation Instrument Building of the USSR Academy of Sciences.

4. Ignatyev, M., N. Simatos, and S. Sivasundaram. 1996. Aircraft as adaptive nonlinear systems which must be in the adaptational maximum zone for safety. Proceedings of the First International Conference on Nonlinear Problems in Aviation and Aerospace, Daytona Beach, FL.

5. Ignatyev, M., A. Nikitin, and N. Reshetnikova. 1999. Virtual educational, scientific, and industrial environments. In Proceedings of the International Conference on the Internet, Society, and the Individual, St. Petersburg.

Cyberattacks as an Amplifier in Terrorist Strategy

Lewis M. Branscomb
Harvard University

In modern industrial societies, information technology may be exploited by terrorists as either a target or a weapon or both. Information technology (IT) is also essential in arranging defenses against terror attack. This multifaceted character of IT is unique among the technologies of concern to the counterterrorist.

As a target, not only the telecommunications and data network infrastructures might be subject to a cyberattack, but so might all of the other areas of critical infrastructure whose efficient functioning depends on computer controls, data management, and digital communications. Of particular concern are the Systems Control and Data Acquisition (SCADA) systems that are rapidly replacing operating engineers as the control elements in networked industrial applications. The electric power distribution industry is a particularly sensitive but not unique example. SCADA software is built outside the United States; it is difficult to prove that no trapdoors were implemented in the software. Furthermore, while more advanced power companies use encrypted communications through buried optical fiber to communicate among the SCADA computers, in some cases, unprotected Internet communications were still used after September 11, 2001.

As a weapon, IT is very familiar, for hackers have demonstrated how information systems may be used to defeat themselves since the beginning of the Internet. Most familiar are the viruses, worms, and Trojan horses; less familiar but more destructive are the sophisticated attacks that may allow the attacker to gain control of the software system (key-zero state).

A cyberattack on a nation's communications and data network systems may be very disruptive and exact large penalties in inconvenience and in burdensome economic cost. Disruption, if repeated, of energy, telecoms, or transportation and finance can exact high economic cost and public distress. There are attacks that could create more serious damage to communications, but they are probably more difficult for terrorists to accomplish. Examples might include

- cumulative delayed action attacks on critical infrastructures (Trojan horses) or backdoor traps in software or hardware, such as were mentioned by Dr. Ignatyev
- attacks that benefit from a corrupted insider, especially one with access to systems management
- attacks on soft but important targets such as the Internet; one example is attacks on root name servers, but since these files are replicated on other name servers, all must be successfully attacked

The National Academies study *Making the Nation Safer: The Role of Science and Technology in Countering Terrorism* concluded that most communications systems, while vulnerable to attack, are also resilient and can in most cases be brought back into service in a relatively short time.[1] Thus, cyberwarfare is not considered a weapon of mass destruction.

However, cybertechnology is accessible to terrorists; it is ubiquitous in target systems, critical to their proper functioning, and attacks can be deployed covertly from anywhere. Indeed, IT systems are also critical in all phases of counterterrorism:

- intelligence
- detection of imminent attacks
- response and damage mitigation when attack occurs
- forensic analysis and recovery

Thus, a cyberattack may be designed to inhibit all of these defensive functions, increasing the risk of attack and aggravating the consequences by inhibiting response and damage mitigation. In this way, a cyberattack may be used to amplify the effect of a more conventional attack using explosives or chemical, biological, or nuclear weapons.

The most serious threat from a cyberattack may be the use of the cyberattack to amplify a physical attack. A cyberattack may accomplish this in a variety of ways, for example,

- interference with emergency services and command/control communications
- unauthenticated false messages directing inappropriate actions; false information creating confusion and panic
- attacks on local critical infrastructure on which response and recovery depend

In each of these examples, the period of effectiveness of the attack need only be for a short time, perhaps a few hours or less, which may be significantly shorter than the time for recovery of the communications system in question.

There is another weapon that shares this characteristic: the portable device delivering an electromagnetic pulse (EMP) sufficiently strong to damage the operating condition of electronics systems such as computers, digital telephone switches, and the like, but not strong enough to permanently damage the hardware.

It follows that emergency operations centers (EOCs), such as those in all major cities, should be protected against both cyber- and EMP attacks on their information systems. We should be prepared for the likelihood that a well-planned terrorist attack might begin with an attack that removes the EOC from effectiveness for a few hours, during which time a major physical (or biological or chemical) attack occurs.

The National Academies study referenced above provided a variety of recommendations, some of which require changes to communications hardware, intended to reduce the effectiveness of cyberattacks. Among them are the following:

- ensure secure and interconnected communications among first responders and crisis managers
- develop and apply methods for high-reliability authentication of security messages
- develop ways to ensure that critical networks degrade slowly and reversibly when attacked
- devise systems for acquiring a snapshot of system state and preserve the most critical data in critical large systems under attack, to allow them to be recovered in most important respects as quickly as possible

Some longer-range research tasks were to

- develop telecommunications system software so that limited service will continue when in a volume-saturated state
- design self-adaptive networks that reconfigure automatically when attacked
- address the security needs of mobile wireless communications
- create better decision support tools for crisis managers
- address the security flaws in operating systems and network software

Underlying these practical research objectives is the need, at least in the United States, for expanded investments in basic research and advanced research education to address the general lack of strong security in computer operating systems and network software.

The lack of a full effort in computer security research is a consequence of the perception in the commercial world that the research performed in the 1970s and 1980s addressed commercial security concerns to an adequate degree. Consequently, the weak market for very high security resulted in a lack of investment and training in security research and development. Wm. A. Wulf addresses this issue in his paper.

NOTE

1. Making the nation safer: The role of science and technology in countering terrorism. 2002. National Research Council, Washington, D.C. Available online in PDF at: *http://books.nap.edu/ html/stct/index.html*. Hard copies may be ordered from National Academies Press at: (888) 624-8373 or *www.nap.edu*.

Cybercrime and Cyberterrorism

*Mikhail P. Sychev**
N.E. Bauman Moscow State Technical University

The world community has entered the age of the information boom. Modern civilization is directly dependent on new telecommunications technologies, which are used in almost all spheres of human activity. The development of information technologies, with the irrevocable changes they have brought in the ways people live and interact, has also displayed a negative side by reducing society's confidence in the inalienable right to the protection of privacy. Each of us is becoming increasingly dependent on the information circulating in global computer networks, on its reliability, protection, and security.

The Internet began to be created in the 1970s. In 1998, 143 million people had access to it, and by 2001 the number of users had reached 700 million. The Internet first appeared in Russia in August 1990. The country is experiencing a computer boom, and although it lags significantly behind developed foreign countries, the Russian segment of the Internet already has about 6 million users.

The development of information and network technologies has led to the appearance of so-called cybercrime. Although the term *cybercrime* is not yet established in Russian law, the concept has become firmly established in practice. The category of cybercrime could include unauthorized access to computer information; the creation, use, and distribution of malicious computer programs (including via the Internet); disruption of the normal operations of computers or information networks; illegal seizure of information resources; illegal sale and distribution of special-purpose radioelectronic devices; forgery of documents with the help of computer technologies; distribution of unlicensed computer software; financial machinations over the Internet; and several other crimes. The

---

*Translated from the Russian by Kelly Robbins.

common characteristics of such crimes include the following: As a rule they have no physical manifestations, and they are distinguished by a high degree of latency, that is, they occur undetected, which according to expert assessments reaches 85 to 90 percent in Russia.

Cybercriminals are using various types of attacks that allow them to penetrate corporate networks, seize control over them, or block exchanges of information. They also use computer viruses, including network worms, which modify or delete data or block the operation of computer systems; logic bombs, which are activated under certain conditions; or Trojan horses, which send various data from an infected computer to their "owners" over the Internet.

The weapons of cybercriminals are constantly being improved, and their tools for mounting information attacks are becoming increasingly refined. In the future, we can expect to see new nontraditional types of network attacks and computer crimes.

Today, such new concepts as information security and, more precisely, network security have entered our lives. For example, the first known virus transmitted over the Internet, HAPPY-99, appeared in January 1999. It is believed (although not officially proven) that this virus, which affected the entire global network, appeared first in Russia and was created to obtain access to the passwords of customers of many Western banks.

The U.S.-based Computer Security Institute has reported that in 1999 about 90 percent of major firms and governmental organizations surveyed had discovered security violations of their computer systems. Furthermore, 70 percent of these firms and organizations noted that these violations were the result of intentional actions by criminal elements working over the Internet. According to the results of a poll of 273 organizations, it was determined that their financial losses totaled more than $265 million, or an average of about $1 million per organization. The survey also found that attacks by hackers against major companies increased by 79 percent from July to December 2001.

In April 2001 a Russian hacker broke into the Internet server of a company in the U.S. city of McLean, Virginia, that provides online banking services. He demanded to be paid not to distribute the confidential data and to destroy them instead. According to information from leading research firms, the worldwide volume of damage from malicious programs totaled about $14.5 million in 2002. But, as many companies often hide the real extent of the damage, it could easily be double that figure.

In October 2002, American intelligence services reported on the most serious attack on root DNS (Domain Name System) servers in the history of the Internet. According to information from the National Infrastructure Protection Center of the U.S. Federal Bureau of Investigations, during the attack, 7 of the 13 servers managing global Internet traffic stopped responding to user requests, and the operation of two other servers was intermittently interrupted. The root servers had been targeted to receive an enormous number of incorrect requests, and as a result, they were forced to handle a volume 30–40 times higher than normal. There were no serious disruptions to the Internet only because the duration of the attack was short, just one hour. However, if a longer attack were to occur or a greater number of root servers were to fail, the normal operation of the Internet could be disrupted. Among the computers most affected by the root server attack were those at the Information Center of the U.S. Department of Defense. Outside the United States, root servers failed in Tokyo and Stockholm. As the Russian group SecurityLab learned, the attack on the DNS servers was carried out by the Russian hacker ech0, a former member of the Nerf Security Group. This was not the first act of sabotage by the Nerf Security Group against the United States. In September 2002 they broke into the website of the U.S. Department of State, an attack that was initially thought to be a terrorist act on the part of Osama bin Laden.

In March 2003 a U.S. hacker temporarily managed to "occupy" the website of the official Iraqi news agency INA, placing calls for the overthrow of Saddam Hussein on one of its pages. Computer hackers thought to be from Brazil gained access to Cuban websites and posted comments directed against U.S. President George W. Bush and the possible war against Iraq.

Also in March 2003 an unknown hacker pretending to be Finnish Prime Minister Paavo Lipponen used his electronic mail address to inform the president of Russia of Finland's intention to take back Karelia, sending copies of this message to the international media and various diplomatic posts. A note at the bottom of the message indicated that its contents were not to be taken seriously.

Hackers are sometimes considered modern technical hooligans. By joining together in groups, hackers are becoming more dangerous and could bring down not only isolated websites but also entire zones of the Internet. Organized crime groups are increasingly using the capabilities of the Internet to carry out swindling operations in e-commerce and the credit and financial sphere and to provide information support for drug trafficking. Also becoming increasingly widespread are extortion attempts in the registration of domain names coinciding with the names of well-known political and governmental figures and major firms and companies. A sharp increase is forecast in the number of such crimes owing to the increasing numbers of Internet users.

A particular concern is that global computer networks present unique new opportunities for facilitating the laundering of proceeds from criminal activity. This phenomenon is manifested in the creation and operation of so-called virtual banks. The main problem is that such banks operate with very little control or oversight, and it is not always clear where crimes involving them are committed. The virtual blackmail industry is also broadly developed on the Internet, and blackmail often subsequently leads to racketeering. Online casinos are generally chosen as targets for such crimes, since as a rule they bring in substantial profits for their owners. On the Internet, everything happens just as it does in "real" life. A group of hackers attacks a casino site during its most profitable hours and issues an ultimatum to the management. If they refuse to pay, the hackers will begin attacking with enviable persistence, and in the end, the online casino owners usually submit.

Cybercrime is growing exponentially, as illustrated by data from the CERT Coordination Center (see Figure 1). It would be possible to attempt to predict that already in 2003 the number of incidents involving computer security violations will exceed 170,000, essentially equal to the number of incidents recorded by CERT for the entire information collection period beginning in 1988.

Meanwhile, according to CERT data, the number of computer system bugs also continues to increase (see Figure 2). It is predicted that almost 7,200 such bugs will be found during 2003. Attacks on computer systems have become so frequent that after the widespread circulation of the LoveBug virus, the Pentagon decided to adopt a special InfoCon virus threat scale analogous to the DefCon scale for military threats or ThreatCon for terrorist threat. In the opinion of military experts, this will help to coordinate efforts in an emergency.

The world community is fully conscious of the level of potential consequences from the threat of cyberterrorism, and as a result, representatives of European Community member states as well as the United States, Canada, and Japan signed the International Convention on Cybercrime in November 2001. This convention defines cybercrime as crimes committed in the information en-

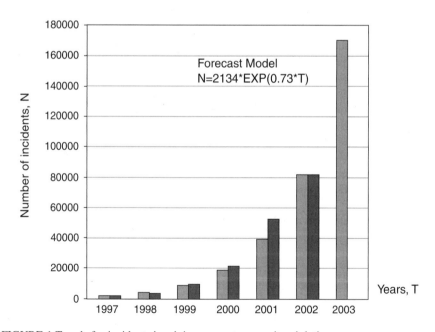

FIGURE 1 Trends for incidents involving computer security violations.

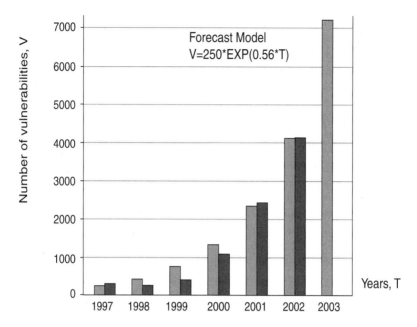

FIGURE 2 Trends for the number of computer system bugs.

vironment, against information resources, or with the help of information technologies.

With the aim of intensifying the struggle against cybercrime, the convention calls for close cooperation among law enforcement agencies in the various countries and assigns them very broad powers. However, in the opinion of several experts, the individual articles of the convention in fact assign too many powers to these agencies. As a result, certain difficulties could arise in getting states with more liberal laws to adhere to it.

Obviously, the situation in Russia is not yet so tense because its computer networks are far less developed, but soon it will escalate significantly, and we are well aware of the realities of the modern cybercriminal world. The first hackers appeared in Russia in 1994. The first and most famous Russian hacker was Vladimir Levin. He managed to penetrate the seemingly impervious security system of the American company Citibank. In 2002, Russia already registered 3,371 computer information-related crimes, with more than 90 percent of these being crimes related to unauthorized access to information resources, or so-called computer break-ins. American intelligence services caught up with Levin in 1994, and he spent five years in an American prison.[1] However, under Russian legislation Levin was not guilty, for at that time Russia had no laws covering computer crimes.

The Criminal Code of the Russian Federation now includes articles establishing penalties for types of crimes that were previously not described. Chapter 28 of the code, Crimes in the Computer Information Sphere, consists of three articles outlining the penalties for unlawful access to computer information (Article 272); creation, use, and dissemination of malicious computer programs (Article 273); and violation of rules for the operation of computers, computer systems, and networks (Article 274). It should be noted that these articles of the criminal code do work. For example, in 2001 alone, the number of crimes registered under articles 272–274 increased by almost 150 percent over the level recorded in 2000.

Cybercrime is not limited only to crimes committed over the Internet. It is increasingly impacting all types of crimes committed in spheres where information, information resources, and computers represent targets, means, or tools for crime. If crimes are planned and committed with the aim of violating public security, frightening the population, or pressuring the authorities to act in a particular way, then their intent, execution, and results are in full accord with the definition of terrorist acts and are typical manifestations of a fundamentally new type of terrorism—cyberterrorism.

In accordance with the general definition, terrorism is the intentional or targeted use of violence or threat of violence to force society, the state, or the government to meet the political, economic, religious, or ideological objectives of a terrorist organization. A terrorist act entails an emotional impact on public opinion, engenders sentiments of fear and panic in society, leads to the loss of trust in the authorities, and ultimately causes political instability. Terrorism is a political crime directed against the interests of the public and the security of the state, society, and individual citizens.

Unfortunately, the general concept and specific elements of cyberterrorism are not fully covered in either the Russian Criminal Code or Russian Federation Law No. 130-FZ on Combating Terrorism (July 25, 1998), even with the amendments and additions made after the events of October 2002 in Moscow.

There are various interpretations of the term *cyberterrorism*. It is often difficult to make a clear distinction between cybercrime and cyberterrorism. Nevertheless, cyberterrorism differs from other criminal forms of action in cyberspace primarily in its goals, which are those common to political terrorism in general. The cyberterrorist differs substantially from the hacker, computer hooligan, or computer thief, whose actions are motivated by greed or hooliganism. The main tactics of cyberterrorism include ensuring that this form of cybercrime has dangerous consequences, is well known by the population, has broad public resonance, and creates an atmosphere that threatens repetition of the act without identifying a particular target. Cyberterrorism is oriented toward using various forms and methods of knocking out the information infrastructure of a state or using the information infrastructure to create a situation producing catastrophic consequences for society and the state.

It must be noted that this form of terrorism has its own special characteristics. It creates a particular concern that extremist groups, separatist forces, and proponents of ideas contrary to universal human values are striving to make intensive use of modern cutting-edge information technologies to promote their ideologies and achieve their goals. As a result, we can already speak of cyberterrorism as presenting a real threat of a new form of terrorist activity to individual countries and to the world community in general.

Given the current growing number of acts of international terrorism, which presents a danger to people's lives and welfare, threatens the peace and security of all states, and undermines trust in the state authorities, it is vitally important to provide protection against this type of criminal activity. Therefore, a heightened level of international cooperation is now needed for scientific research on preventing and suppressing acts of cyberterrorism.

Most importantly, scientific research is needed to develop a unified conceptual framework. Further review and corrections are also needed regarding laws, regulations, and other legal documents on this type of crime, including those governing international activities. Research work aimed at creating modern technologies for detecting and preventing network attacks and neutralizing criminal actions against information resources is of the highest significance. Of course, all of this is impossible without improvements in the multitiered system for training personnel in the information security field.

Finally, another important scientific problem faced by the international community is that of developing the scientific and methodological foundations for joint research projects on countering cybercrime and cyberterrorism.

NOTE

1. Editor's note: In fact, although Levin was identified as the perpetrator of the attack against Citibank in 1994, he was not arrested until March 1995 and was finally convicted and sentenced in February 1998.

Protecting Bank Networks from Acts of Computer Terrorism

Boris I. Skorodumov[*]
Institute of Banking Affairs of the Association of Russian Banks

The rapid adoption of information technologies by various Russian banks and the development of trends toward distributed data processing using modern computer hardware are accompanied by the appearance of new or modified problems that represent the negative side effects of technological progress. Much attention is being paid to issues of information security in the developing e-business sector. This is an important issue for Russia as we move toward joining the World Trade Organization (WTO), which is highly likely after our country's banks introduce international financial accounting standards and comply with certain additional conditions in 2003. Russian banks are highly automated and are developing their networks and their presence on the Internet (*www.cbr.ru*). This progress, however, is accompanied by the exacerbation of security problems and specifically by the phenomena of cyberterrorism and cybercrime.

The targeted city program "Electronic Moscow," announced on December 24, 2002, indicates that the introduction of modern information technologies has led to the appearance of new types of crimes such as computer crime and computer terrorism—unlawful interference with the operation of computers, systems, and networks or the theft, acquisition, or extortion of computer information (*www.iis.ru*). Cyberterrorism and cybercrime are new forms of criminal activity using computers and telecommunications. According to data from ex-

[*]Boris I. Skorodumov is a candidate of technical sciences; assistant professor, Department of Information Security of Bank Systems, Moscow Engineering Physics Institute; chair of the Information Security Subcommittee of the National Association of Funds Market Participants (NAUFOR); deputy director of the Institute of Banking Affairs of the Association of Russian Banks. Translated from the Russian by Kelly Robbins.

perts from the Council of Europe, credit card cases alone result in annual losses of about $400 million. Losses from viruses total about $12 billion, while violation of property rights causes $250 billion in damages.

The number of crimes in the information technology (IT) sphere committed against governmental information systems is constantly on the increase. According to data from the Central Intelligence Agency, Internet sites of central U.S. government agencies were attacked 750,000 times in the past three years. Other sources indicate that the number of such attacks could be 1 million. In 2001 the networks of the U.S. Space Command alone were attacked 30,000 times. From 1998 through 2001, the number of such attacks increased fivefold.

According to data for 2002 published in the quarterly report of the U.S. Computer Security Institute (CSI), 223 of 503 organizations surveyed suffered financial losses totaling $455,848,000 as a result of various types of information threats being carried out against them. For example, while in 1997, 21 organizations suffered losses of $20,048,000 from theft of proprietary information, in 2002 these losses amounted to $170,827,000. The annual CSI/FBI Computer Crime and Security Survey is conducted as a public service by the CSI with the participation of the Computer Intrusion Squad of the FBI's San Francisco office. Its purpose is to increase the level of security awareness and help in determining the scope of computer crime in the United States (*www.gocsi.com*).

According to data on high-tech crimes from the Moscow Main Administration for Internal Affairs, its personnel discovered about 3,000 pornographic websites in the period from March through December 2002 alone, with the profits from each site averaging $30,000. Some of this money was going to support the activities of extremist and terrorist groups. The number of cyberattacks against enterprises, organizations, and citizens is growing at a stable pace. According to information from the Main Administration for Special Technical Measures of the Russian Ministry of Internal Affairs, in 2001 the number of computer-related crimes committed in Russia increased by almost 150 percent compared with 2000 (*www.mvdinform.ru*).

It should be noted that in our country today the overwhelming majority of banks are commercial or nonstate owned, and their automated systems contain almost no information involving state secrecy. In addition, the limited-access information that circulates in such automated bank systems in most cases includes no state secrets whatsoever. Russia currently has no general official information security recommendations or requirements for such systems, for example, in the form of any set standards. Only old requirements for security organizations remain in effect. Bank security is primarily provided with the help of technical means of protection. If such means prove inadequate to ensure the absolute security of cash, valuables, and important papers, armed guards are posted at main offices and major branches.

Technical means of protection include reinforced buildings, vaults, and safes; fire and security alarm systems; sprinkler systems; and the use of firearms and communications systems. Newly constructed banks may open only after they have telephone service, the appropriate technical reinforcements and structures (vaults) for storing cash and other valuables, and the necessary fire, security, and panic alert systems. In Russia, information security problems were studied and addressed in a timely fashion only for the protection of state secrets in military, governmental, or other state-related automated systems. Thus, over time, a situation developed in which very specific commercial sector problems went unresolved because of the absence of such a sector. At present, this presents a substantial obstacle to the development of secure information technologies in the Russian commercial market, for instance, in banks, which are being formed and integrated into the world trade system.

A response might be to recommend that the information security requirements for state-automated systems continue to be used in order to address the problems of protecting commercial information in banks. For example, we could take advantage of the latest technical advances of authoritative state organizations, which recently issued materials on the protection of confidential information not involving state secrets.

To deal with this problem objectively, it would be appropriate to look at the commonalities or differences in processes involved in defining parameters for and ensuring the security of information in automated systems. I propose analyzing this problem using the example of automated banking systems, which involve the storage of huge amounts of valuable information and entail a corresponding number of security problems. There are also other reasons for doing so. In particular, the Doctrine for the Information Security of the Russian Federation, which was affirmed by Russian President Vladimir V. Putin, emphasizes that "computer crimes associated with the penetration of the computer systems and networks of banks and other lending organizations represent a serious threat to the normal functioning of the economy as a whole." It should be noted that information security requirements have been formulated and are being applied in the Russian Central Bank system. For instance, these requirements are covered in Order No. 02-144, dated April 3, 1997, and titled "On the Institution of Temporary Requirements for Ensuring the Security of Electronic Payment Processing Technologies within the Russian Central Bank System."

These regulations do not apply to Russian commercial banks, which handle such problems at their own discretion and according to their own capabilities. These issues are dealt with differently abroad. For instance, in Germany and France, commercial banks have specially developed methodological materials for use as guidance in handling information security matters.

Russian commercial banks could use publicly accessible Russian Central Bank documents on information protection. However, it is not that simple. It should be kept in mind that the fundamental goals of government-run and private banks are diametrically opposed, as clearly stated in the relevant legislation. Article 1 of the Federal Law on Banks and Banking Activities states: "A lending organization is a legal entity that, *having profit as the main goal of its activities* and operating on the basis of a special permit (license) from the Central Bank of the Russian Federation (the Bank of Russia), has the right to carry out banking operations as stipulated under this Federal Law." Article 3 of the Federal Law on the Central Bank of Russia states: *"Earning a profit is not the goal of the activities of the Bank of Russia."* These different goals give rise to different ways of achieving them, although the components and means used could be similar. Let me clarify this thesis: A commercial bank, like any other market organization, is essentially a highly risky enterprise. Therefore, Western markets have highly developed theories and practical mechanisms for the management of risks, including those that are computer related. Risks are constantly monitored and analyzed. In accordance with the recently adopted Russian Law on Technical Regulations, "risk is the likelihood by which some harm will occur . . . ," that is, the collective characterization of whether some security threat might be realized. Such characterizations may be highlighted in various Western sources of statistical data, for example, in the annual CSI/FBI survey. Besides risk characterizations, it also includes examples of financial losses suffered, including by banks. Our country currently lacks adequate information of this sort (*www.mvdinform.ru*).

Materials from the Global Association of Risk Professionals (GARP) focus on the following requirements for risk identification and assessment:

- Risk assessment must take into account internal and external risk factors and must be made at all levels of an organization.
- An organization must identify risks both within its control (manageable risks) and those beyond its control.
- All materially significant risks that could have a negative effect on the achievement of the organization's goals must be identified and assessed on a continuous basis.

GARP was founded in 1996 and has more than 15,000 members. Its Russian branch was established in 1998.

The new Russian Law on Technical Regulation also gives rise to a new formulation of the concept of security, which the law does not limit to the diffuse synonym *protectedness* as it appeared in older government documents. This law states that "security is a condition in which intolerable risk of harm is absent. . . ." Furthermore, its Article 7 states that "technical regulations taking into account the degree of risk of harm establish minimum necessary requirements for ensuring

- radiation security
- biological security
- explosives security
- mechanical security

- fire security
- industrial security
- thermal security
- chemical security
- electrical security
- nuclear and radiological security
- electromagnetic compatibility with regard to ensuring the secure operation of equipment
- consistency of measurements"

Before 2003, documents issued by Russian state organizations on information security did not include the word *risk*.

Denial of service (DoS) attacks could serve as a prime example of the new threats presented by cyberterrorism. Three years ago, six U.S. Internet companies suffered losses totaling $624 million as a result of DoS attacks lasting only two hours. Following this incident, widespread calls for change were made:

- Establish inter-network screens to record spoofing attempts.
- Work out a plan with your Internet provider to determine the source of the DoS attack.
- Create your own rapid response group.
- Develop your own comprehensive plan for preventing and dealing with the consequences of attacks.

Russian Internet banks have begun to suffer similar attacks, although they have been carefully concealed from public knowledge.

All of this calls for the adoption of a common (market economy-wide) approach to resolving the information security problems of commercial organizations, especially banks—in other words, a risk management approach. Because economic and market factors are of top priority for commercial banks, it is very important for automated banking systems that everything be done to reduce or eliminate risks of financial losses and to ensure that profits are made for the owner and users given the existing real (assessed) threat conditions. In particular, this would include minimization of the typical banking risks, such as losses incurred by mistakenly sent payments, falsification of payment documents, and so forth.

We must also address the concepts of ownership of information resources. Ownership entails rights to control, use, and dispose of a given piece of property as well as the opportunity to exercise these rights effectively in real life. Information systems resources and the information itself are someone's property. Therefore, the security of a commercial automated banking system should be regarded as a matter of ensuring the exercise of the owner's rights with regard to the resources included in the system. The exercise of the owner's rights is associated with the ability to manage the resources effectively and, as part of this management, to ensure that their use is limited to only authorized individuals.

The protection of information in automated banking systems involves a number of special points that must be taken into account, as they have a great impact on information security technology. In addition, other characteristics of commercial automated banking systems explain the need for creating specialized information security requirements (standards) for commercial bank networks.

The adoption of information technologies by banks, the development of trends favoring distributed data processing using modern computer hardware, the creation of information and telecommunications systems for various purposes, and the need for information exchanges among these systems have shaped the efforts of the world community in categorizing and prioritizing the fundamental requirements and characteristics of such systems, including in the area of information security. This matter is particularly urgent for so-called open general-use systems that handle confidential information not involving state secrecy, which are experiencing very rapid growth in our country. The term *open* means that all devices and processes in the system (computer network) work together in accord with a certain range of standards and are therefore open to interaction with other systems (computer networks). This sort of approach entails the need to link into a unified system a wide variety of hardware and software used in computer systems or networks by all sorts of commercial organizations with no single manager or owner. In particular, this also has an effect on mechanisms for cryptographic protection of information or protection against unauthorized access to information. During 2003, Russia is implementing the basic international standard ISO 15408 for information security criteria. The use of the ISO 15408 standard will make it possible to initiate work to improve domestic information security standards and bring them into line with existing international practices in this field of knowledge and technology. The new criteria have been adapted to the needs of mutual recognition of the results of information security assessments on an international scale and are intended for use as a basis for such assessments. The criteria were approved as a standard by the International Organization for Standardization in May 1999.

The common criteria make it possible to compare the results of independent information security assessments. This is done by advancing and implementing a multitude of general functional security requirements and assurances for information technology hardware and systems in the process of evaluating information security and corresponding tolerable risks.

The main advantages of the common criteria include the comprehensive nature of its information security requirements, flexibility of application, and openness to subsequent development in line with the latest scientific and technical achievements. The common criteria were developed so as to meet the demands of all three user groups (consumers, developers, and evaluators) for studies of the security properties of information technology hardware or systems, called *evaluated products* in common criteria terminology. This standard can provide useful guidance in developing hardware and systems with information security functions as well as in procuring commercial products and systems with such functions. The common criteria may be applied to other aspects of information technology security besides those mentioned above. This standard is mainly focused on threats resulting from human actions, malicious or otherwise, but it may also be applied to threats not caused by human actions. Specialized requirements for the credit and financial sphere are likely to be formulated in the future.

The traditional concept of security with regard to information involving state secrets entails an assessment of three characteristics: accessibility, integrity, and confidentiality. However, this is a somewhat narrow view of the problem. For commercial banks, the legal standing of banking information is a pressing matter that has become increasingly important in recent years, along with the creation of a legal and regulatory base governing property security in our country, especially when it involves the interactions of automated systems owned by various legal entities. The legal standing of information may be defined as a characteristic of security information that makes it possible to ensure the legal force of documents or information processes in accordance with the legal regime for information resources established under Russian law.

This last point is particularly important given the need to ensure strict accounting of all information services, which is the economic basis for the operation of any information system and serves to facilitate tight regulation and control of access to information using system resources. It is often necessary to ensure strict notarization (legal accountability) of information, which is essential in resolving conflicts between clients and providers of information services.

In addition to the features of commercial automated banking systems, the following could be noted:

- specific threat and intruder model
- possibility of ensuring against information risks
- wide variety of commercial organizations
- need to determine the value of information
- expediency of dynamic protection and monitoring systems
- application of openly created means of protection

On February 20, 2003, the Association of Russian Banks (ARB) and the National Association of Funds Market Participants (NAUFOR) signed a memorandum creating the Association of Participants in Confidential (Secure) Electronic Document Exchange in Russia. This association is open to organizations adhering to the fundamental principles of confidential electronic document exchange as set forth in the memorandum, the main goal of which is the creation of a collective-use center for financial authentication. This authentication center will be created taking into account foreign experience and the characteristics particular to Russia.

Now, during the year when the ISO 15408 standard is being introduced, it would be convenient to establish requirements for commercial or banking sector security, focusing on the special aspects involved in ensuring the security of commercial information not involving state secrecy.

Computer Security Training for Professional Specialists and Other Personnel Associated with Preventing and Responding to Computer Attacks

Anatoly A. Malyuk, Nikolai S. Pogozhin, and Aleksey I. Tolstoy*
Moscow Engineering Physics Institute

INTRODUCTION

The level of knowledge and skills required in the area of information security is among the basic factors determining the effectiveness of efforts to counter computer attacks on real targets. Therefore, the training of specialists in this field may be considered one of the most important organizational-technical means of ensuring information security. As noted in the Doctrine for Information Security in the Russian Federation, "the development of a system for training personnel involved in ensuring information security" is among the top-priority measures to be taken in implementing state policy for ensuring Russia's information security. The training system for information security personnel, for which the foundations have already been created, is one of the most important elements of information security as a whole. This report reviews the characteristics of the information security personnel training system in Russia, defines the basic areas of educational activity, and highlights the most promising of them, which are associated with continuing education. The report also discusses the basic problems that need to be resolved in order to ensure that the necessary level of training is provided for specialists and other personnel at facilities where information technologies could be subject to computer attacks.

*Translated from the Russian by Kelly Robbins.

THE TRAINING SYSTEM FOR INFORMATION SECURITY PERSONNEL IN RUSSIA

Russia has laid the foundations for a state system for training personnel in information security. This system is composed of the following elements:

Training Providers

- higher educational institutions (more than 80) having licenses to educate students in one of seven specialties included in the state classified listing of specialties and areas of training for degreed specialists
- regional training and scientific centers (22), based at leading higher educational institutions in the various regions of Russia and designed to address problems of providing training for specialists in a specific region
- continuing education training centers (as a rule, not state run; established in almost all regions of Russia, so it is difficult to determine their numbers), created by organizations actively operating in the information protection services market and licensed to conduct their training activities by local governmental authorities responsible for education

Participants

- university students and other course participants being trained at higher educational institutions, regional training and scientific centers, and continuing education training centers
- instructors at the various educational institutions and centers
- administrative personnel organizing and facilitating the training process

Educational and Methodological Resource Support

- state educational standards for higher professional education in the seven specialties included in the information security classification
- educational plans for training specialists in the specific specialties
- educational programs for specific training courses in the seven specialties
- educational programs for continuing education or retraining courses aimed at allowing participants to obtain additional qualifications
- textbooks, educational and methodological handbooks, and practical laboratory training exercises
- informational materials supporting the training process

Management Subsystem

- Russian Federation Ministry of Education, which issues licenses for educational activities conducted by higher educational institutions

• executive-branch entities at the regional level responsible for education and the licensing of educational activities associated with continuing education

• educational methodology associations—public organizations composed of representatives of educational institutions that train specialists in the information security field, as well as organizations and departments that employ such specialists (These associations monitor the educational activities of the various institutions and centers to ensure that students are provided with the necessary training at a level meeting the requirements established by the State Educational Standards.)

The two basic types of educational activities being carried out within the system for training information security personnel are as follows:

1. training of degreed specialists: specialist (seven specialties; title: mathematician or information protection specialist; training duration: five or five and a half years); bachelor's degree (four years); master's degree (six years)

2. continuing education: qualification improvement (72 or more training hours); additional qualification (up to 500 training hours); complete retraining (more than 500 training hours)

An evaluation of the need for information security specialists to deal with the problems of countering computer attacks indicates that the first type of training is not meeting all objectives for the following reasons:

• the long duration of training for specialists (up to six years to complete training). The training system that has been created is just getting under way in Russia. It will show its full capabilities once the first six-year training cycle is complete.

• the insufficient number of specialists being graduated. Given the number of higher educational institutions that graduate information security specialists (about 80) and the average number of specialists per year graduating from such institutions (about 20), the average number of specialists graduating each year is estimated at about 1,600. According to several estimates, state institutions alone need to hire about 1,500 such specialists per year, and this does not take into account the needs of the large number of private enterprises and organizations.

• the inertia of the educational process associated with the long-term stability of educational programs and plans (lasting about one training cycle). During this time, the subject matter requirements could change significantly.

• problems of professional orientation for incoming students owing to the difficulty of instituting strict principles for the selection of personnel to be trained in information security specialties. The existing educational system is oriented toward the training of young people, beginning from the first year in university (age 17–18). Even if a strict system of selection were to be put in place not only on the basis of knowledge but also taking into account psycho-physiological characteristics (and this is very doubtful), effective selection will not be ensured, as during the training period (up to six years) the given parameters could change substantially. Furthermore, young people's life goals are also subject to significant changes. As a result, specialists graduating from these higher educational institutions could either not work in their area of specialization or could carry out functions antithetical to the goals of information security protection.

• difficulty of organizing targeted training for specialists to meet the needs of specific enterprises. Unfortunately, at present it is difficult for any enterprise to define the skills and knowledge that information security specialists will need when they graduate four to six years from now.

This type of educational activity represents only one segment of the training requirements. Information security specialists are commonly employed in the development and creation of complex information protection systems requiring a broad range of knowledge and skills.

In contrast to the training of degreed specialists, continuing education has a number of substantial advantages. These include

• short duration of training (72–500 hours)
• flexibility and possibility of changing educational programs
• ease of implementing targeted training geared to the interests of specific enterprises
• possibility of meeting quantitative needs for trained specialists

Therefore, we might expect that this form of educational activity will find broader application in the training of professional specialists and other personnel involved in combating computer attacks. This activity is oriented toward the utilization of specific information technologies and information protection systems. It would be useful to review the particular features of continuing education in greater detail.

Continuing Education in Information Security

When we account for the problems that arise during the educational process, it is possible to define the special characteristics of continuing education in information security by answering the following questions: "Who should be trained, what should be taught, and how and where should training take place?" "How should the training be managed?" "How should learning be evaluated?" We shall now attempt to answer these questions.

The answer to the question "Who should be trained?" is associated with the selection of the contingent of students. It is appropriate to follow the principle of a differentiated approach aimed at determining the categories of students working at specific enterprises. These categories could include the following:

- information technology specialists working in units responsible for the operation of hardware and software
- specialists who use information technologies in units involved in carrying out an enterprise's primary mission
- information protection specialists working in information security units
- information security administrators responsible for monitoring the level of information protection
- physical security specialists. Modern physical protection systems are complex automated control systems consisting of devices (microprocessors, video equipment, other special hardware, computers, communications channels and systems) and software (systems software and applications) operated by security service personnel. An automated system of this sort processes "sensitive" information, the loss or distortion of which could reduce the operational effectiveness of the entire physical protection system and, as a result, could help terrorists accomplish their objectives.
- unit managers
- senior management

It should be noted that training managers at all levels is a requisite component of personnel training. Knowledge of the basic objectives involved in countering cyberterrorism and of ways of accomplishing these objectives is a mandatory condition for effective decision making both at the stage of creating an information security system and at the stage of responding to a critical situation.

Another point is that functional responsibilities involved with the management of information technologies and those involved with the management of information security subsystems must be divided among various specialists. Because of this requirement, those receiving training should be divided into different groups.

The question "What should be taught?" may be answered through the selection of training programs. The special nature of the professional knowledge and skills of information security specialists combined with the possibility of using such dual-use knowledge and skills for contrary purposes allows us to formulate the following principles that should provide guidance in the selection of training programs:

- Offer a differentiated approach to training, that is, different training programs for different categories of students.

- A specialist should have only the knowledge and skills he is supposed to have. Extra knowledge and skills could lead the specialist to develop ambitions that could lead to his carrying out unauthorized operations on his own initiative or under the influence of an outsider. The consequences could be catastrophic. Consequently, extra knowledge and skills among information security specialists could be harmful, and this must be kept in mind in designing training programs. Representatives of the enterprises whose employees are being sent for training must therefore play an important role in the program design process. This will help to ensure that the continuing education programs are targeted to the specific needs of the enterprises.

- Establish authorized access to the educational content. Given the nature of the knowledge and skills possessed by information security specialists, this sort of knowledge should be conveyed only to those who need it. Students are selected solely by the enterprises sending personnel for training. This also helps to ensure the targeted nature of extended training programs.

- Ensure the information security of the training system. This principle follows from the preceding one. The training system must ensure the accessibility, confidentiality, and integrality of information needed for the educational process (primarily with regard to the material covered in training).

Answering the question "How should training take place?" makes it possible to define the technological requirements involved in implementing continuing education programs. Most training centers in Russia generally use traditional educational technologies (lectures, seminars, practical exercises), which require that students take time off from work to participate. The development of the system for training information security personnel is oriented toward the use of modern information and educational technologies. This makes it important for the educational system to introduce distance-learning technologies such as virtual training courses, electronic textbooks, and remote testing. This should increase efficiency and reduce training costs because of a reduction in the amount of time required for training (trainees spend less time away from their worksites).

The answer to the question "Where should training take place?" is already determined in the given case. At present, it can be stated that the necessary facilities for the information security training system have already been established, as described above. The further development of these facilities entails the resolution of such problems as how to improve methods for their management, how to ensure the information security of the training process, and how to develop their material and financial infrastructure.

Improving and developing the personnel training system in the information security sphere requires a response to the question "How should training be managed?" Here, it is necessary to look at the prospects for the development of the training system itself, taking into account the key points involved in implementation of the Federal Targeted Program for the Development of a Unified Educational Information Environment (2001–2005), which was enacted by Resolution 630 of the Government of the Russian Federation dated August 28, 2001. This program calls for the "creation of conditions for a phased transition to a new level of education on the basis of information technologies. . . ." Therefore, the system for personnel training in information security must be viewed as part of the unified educational sector of Russia, understood as "the totality of organizational measures, informational and methodological resources, and modern educational and information technologies that ensure the high quality of education in all regions of Russia and the effective utilization of the country's scientific and pedagogical potential." Consequently, management of the modern personnel training system for the information security sphere must take into account the following points:

• standardized educational and methodological resources
• existing infrastructure of system facilities
• availability of modern information and educational technologies in the system
• existence of a tri-level system for the management of education in Russia (Ministry of Education or Regional Administrative Agency—Educational Methodology Association—Educational Institution or Training Center)
• need to protect information presented in course content

It therefore follows that the system for training information security personnel must look like a corporate training system meeting the need to provide training for specialists within defined limits, for example, the need to ensure information security, and this must be taken into account in managing such a system.

The answer to the question "How should learning be evaluated?" carries with it additional changes in the management of the system for training information security personnel. The nature of the knowledge and skills possessed by information security specialists gives rise to the need for adherence to the following principles in evaluating the level of learning among students:

• standardized approach to the certification of specialists completing multiyear courses at higher educational institutions
• differentiated approach to certification of specialists completing continuing education courses

This involves

• testing of knowledge at the end of a specific course of study completed at an educational institution or center

- certification of a given level of knowledge and skills by an independent certification center
- certification of knowledge and skills meeting current job requirements at the student's worksite (could be conducted by a unit or senior staff at the worksite in cooperation with training or certification centers)

Implementing the measures outlined above entails subsequent changes in the system for managing personnel training in the information security sector:

- improvement of the testing system
- creation of the two types of certification systems described above

The requirements of the system for training information security personnel, taking into account the field of continuing education, are based on the experience of the Moscow Engineering Physics Institute (MIFI).

TRAINING OF INFORMATION SECURITY SPECIALISTS IN THE DEPARTMENT OF INFORMATION SECURITY AT MIFI

MIFI has been involved in educational activities in the information security field since 1991. Degree programs are offered for specialists in the fields of comprehensive protection of information technologies and comprehensive information security for automated systems. Graduates of these programs are qualified as information protection specialists, and the course of study takes five and a half years to complete.

Continuing education is provided in the form of qualification enhancement courses. The educational programs are different for the various categories of students and are coordinated in advance with the organization sending students to be trained, taking into account their individual requirements. MIFI's leading partners (clients for educational services) in the realm of continuing education for information security personnel are the Central Bank of the Russian Federation and the Savings Bank of the Russian Federation. The educational technologies used are both traditional (with students taking time off work) and modern, involving elements of distance-learning technologies (with students spending only part of their training time offsite). Between February 1995 and December 2002, more than 2,500 specialists from all regions of Russia have been trained.

Examples of the continuing education training programs being conducted by MIFI in 2003 are presented in Table 1.

COMMUNICATIONS ACTIVITIES

Experience and information on teaching methodologies in the information security field are shared at conferences at various levels. The following confer-

TABLE 1 MIFI Continuing Education Programs

No.	Program	Training duration, hours/days
	Training Cycle 1: Security of Bank Information Technologies	
1.1	Security of network technologies	88/11
1.2	Protected corporate bank networks	40/5
1.3	Information security of bank e-mail systems	40/5
1.4	Security of bank intranets and virtual private networks	40/5
1.5	Cisco Systems solutions for protecting corporate information networks	40/5
1.6	Systems for detecting attacks on corporate bank networks	24/3
1.7	Monitoring network security	40/5
1.8	Anti-virus protection for information technologies	24/3
	Training Cycle 2: Administration of Information Technology Security	
2.1	Information technology administrators	40/5
2.2	Administering corporate virtual private networks using FPSU-IP screening routers	40/5
2.3	Information security in a Microsoft Windows NT environment	40/5
2.4	Information security in a Microsoft Windows 2000 environment	40/5
2.5	Information security in an OC Sun Solaris environment	40/5
2.6	Data security mechanisms and policies in SQL	24/3
2.7	Data security mechanisms and policies in Oracle	24/3

ences are held annually under the aegis of the Ministry of Education of the Russian Federation:

• Problems of Information Security in the Higher Education System (January, Moscow, MIFI)
• Information Security (including international participants; June, Taganrog, State Radiotechnical University)
• Methods and Technical Means of Ensuring Information Security (October, St. Petersburg, State Technical University)

At the international level, efforts to develop systems for training information security personnel in various countries are coordinated by Working Group 11.8 (Information Security Education), which is part of Technical Committee 11 (Security and Protection in Information Processing Systems) of the International Federation for Information Processing. The World Conference on Information Security Education (WISE) is held every other year with the support and direct participation of this organization. The third such conference, WISE-3, will be held in the United States (Monterey, California), June 26–28, 2003, and WISE-4 is scheduled to take place at MIFI in Moscow in May 2005.

Information Assurance Education in the United States

Anita K. Jones
University of Virginia

To discuss education and training in information assurance, we first need to specify what the student is being prepared to be able to do. The range of material covered in courses in information assurance is broad because students are educated or trained for a number of quite different jobs or careers. They include the following:

- information system (or Internet) administration
- cyberattack response
- information system design
- cybersecurity research
- security service provisioning
- cryptography system implementation and administration

And, of course, different courses treat the material at different depths of understanding.

We use the term *information assurance* to describe the content area that others may call "information system security" or "cybersecurity." Training will be discussed after we have discussed education at the university level.

UNIVERSITY PROGRAMS IN INFORMATION ASSURANCE

In the United States, the federal government does not determine what is taught by schools and universities. Our Constitution gives the individual states jurisdiction over education. At the university level, there are about 1,000 universities and colleges. Fewer than one-half are research universities that offer graduate degrees. Some universities are public (or state) universities and are partially funded by tax revenue collected by the state in which they reside. Others are completely private.

It is the faculty in each university or college who determine the courses that are taught and the content material of each course. U.S. universities offer three levels of programs. At the undergraduate level, typically there is no degree program specifically focusing on information assurance. It is considered more important for the undergraduate student to receive a broad education. Several hundred universities do teach some sort of information assurance courses at the undergraduate level. A small number of those teach only courses in cryptography.

In the United States, most information assurance courses can be found in the curriculum for computer science. Sometimes material on information assurance is taught as just one module within a course on more expansive topics such as networks, operating systems, or databases. In other cases, there are complete courses, or even a sequence of courses, in information assurance. The subject of cryptography is often treated by itself with courses either in computer science or in mathematics. In the United States the subject of physical security is rarely—if at all—taught in a university.

At the graduate level, some universities offer master's degrees. For example, Carnegie-Mellon University offers a master's degree in information security technology and management. Most students take industrial positions after graduation. Entire degree programs in information assurance are relatively rare at the master's degree level. At the Ph.D. level, about 900 doctorate degrees are awarded each year in computer science and engineering. I estimate that no more than 5 to 10 of those degrees are in information assurance. As a result, the United States is producing very few Ph.D. students who are capable of performing research in information assurance. Consequently, the capability of the United States to field new research programs in information assurance is limited by a lack of qualified personnel.

GOVERNMENT ENCOURAGEMENT OF INFORMATION ASSURANCE EDUCATION

The U.S. government encourages increased education in information assurance at the university level, but this is simply encouragement, not direction. First, the federal government offers scholarships to students who study information assurance. In one program, called the Federal Cyber Service Scholarships for Service, the government pays for two years of education, and in return the student works for the U.S. government in the area of security administration for two years after graduation. In 2003, 200 Cyber Service scholarship students will graduate from either undergraduate or graduate programs. In addition to this program, there are several other government-funded scholarship programs, as well as some programs that fund university faculty to develop and teach new courses in information assurance.

A second kind of encouragement from the federal government is in the form of a certification program for Centers of Academic Excellence in Information Assurance Education. The purpose of this relatively new certification program is to encourage the teaching of more courses and the awarding of more specialized degrees in this field. The objective is to increase the number of professionals who are expert in information assurance.

This certification program is sponsored by the National Security Agency. Universities that decide to seek certification submit documentation describing both research and educational activities in information assurance. This documentation describes the content of the courses and research programs. It cites the research papers published by faculty in the literature, as well as programs for outreach (teaching students via the Internet or outside the grounds of the university). The government reviews the submitted documentation. Currently, more than 45 colleges and universities are certified as Centers of Academic Excellence in Information Assurance Education, including the University of Virginia. This program is described at *http://www.nsa.gov/ia/academia/ caeiae.cfm?MenuID=10.1.1.2.*

The third kind of federal government encouragement is in the form of increased funding for research. In 2002, Congress authorized additional funds for new cybersecurity research centers and undergraduate program development grants.

In the United States the term *education* refers to courses taken in organized degree programs. For our purposes, education is found in colleges and universities. In addition, there is a need to train professionals who are already expert in some aspect of the information systems but who are unfamiliar with cybersecurity. Similarly, some professionals may need to refresh what they know about cybersecurity because the field changes so rapidly. Occasionally, such training courses are taught in university outreach programs, that is, in nondegree programs. More often, training is offered by community colleges, private industry, or professional associations, especially in the context of technical conferences.

As such, education and training in information assurance in the United States is not centrally designed, defined, or funded. And the material offered as part of university education or for professional training is defined by those who offer the specific courses. As a result, there are no nationwide standards for information assurance education.

NATIONAL STRATEGY

In February 2003 the U.S. President issued a document entitled *The National Strategy to Secure Cyberspace*. It states three strategic objectives:

1. prevent cyberattacks against U.S. infrastructures
2. reduce national vulnerability to cyberattacks
3. minimize damage and recovery time from cyberattacks

This document does direct some government agencies to take specific actions. However, the document recognizes that except for government networks and computers, most of the cyberinfrastructure of the United States is owned and operated by private industry. The federal government does not have the authority to give explicit operational direction to that industry on how to protect the cyber infrastructure that is offered to the public for use and the cyber infrastructure that underpins industry's ability to conduct business. So, much of the strategy in the document encourages, rather than directs, industry to be aware of the problem and to protect itself. This document is publicly available and can be found on the Internet at *http://www.whitehouse.gov/pcipb*.

In summary, cybersecurity is recognized as a very serious issue in the United States. While a wide variety of education courses are offered, many believe that too few professionals with expertise in information assurance are being graduated from our universities. More graduates are needed at all levels.

Many also believe that (both inside the government and inside private industry) more thought needs to be given to cybersecurity threats to U.S. information systems, as well as threats to other infrastructures that might be amplified using cyberattacks. The strategy for protecting cyber infrastructure requires a public and private partnership between government and the private sector. Many of the actions to be taken to reduce vulnerability and to minimize damage from cyberattacks will be taken by private industry. Other actions can only be taken through international cooperation. All such actions require the involvement of trained professionals with strong knowledge and skills in assuring cybersecurity.

Technical Protection of Electronic Documents in Computer Systems

Valery A. Konyavsky
Scientific Research Institute of Problems of Computer Technology and Information
Russian Ministry of Communications and Information

Information results from the reflection of the movement of material objects in living systems.[1] It circulates in company with similar organisms in the form of data and reports. Data are formed as a result of the reflection by these organisms of material objects, including reports. Reports are formed as organisms for the transmission of data to other organisms. They contain the totality of data being transmitted and represent a selection of signs with the help of which data may be transmitted to and received by another organism.

The transformation of data into reports and reports into data is carried out by individuals using algorithms for coding and decoding the set of symbols received into the elements comprising its "information" model of the world. Thus, information in the form of data is born in the minds of individuals (and only there) and cannot be protected through technical means.

Until recently, the problems of technical protection were reduced to the protection of computers from unauthorized access, the limitation of access to data, and network protection. Paradoxically, at none of these stages was there any discussion of what exactly we were protecting. It is obvious that if a plant produces teapots and a factory makes boots, then they will be potential targets for crime. Computer systems do not produce information. They process certain reports and elaborate others. But what does the information system produce? What should be protected? If we agree that it does not produce information, then it remains to be determined exactly what it does produce.

The results of information systems operations include spam (informational trash) and electronic documents. What is not deemed a document is just a useless scrap of paper. Structured and combined together, electronic documents repre-

125

sent information resources, which have value when—and only when—they are complete, authentic, accessible, and current.

For a report to be an electronic document, it must include a number of attributes attesting to its compliance with special requirements of high-tech end products deemed by society to have legal weight. It must adhere to technical and technological requirements for document creation and transmission, points that must also be documented by various generally recognized means.

Again, information systems produce electronic documents, a process that involves elements such as

- computers
- data (other electronic documents)
- network (telecommunications) resources
- information technologies

One important information security-related event that has occurred in the last decade is the appearance and development of the concept of device security. The main ideas of device security include the following:[2]

- recognition of the multiplicative protection paradigm and, as a result, equal attention to implementation of control procedures at all stages of information systems operations (the protection of the entire system is no greater than the protection of its weakest link)
- "materialist" resolution of the fundamental question of information security: "What first—hardware or software?"
- consistent rejection of software-oriented control methods as obviously unreliable (attempts to use software to monitor the correctness of other software is equivalent to attempting to resolve the unsolvable question of self-applicability—"Munchausen Syndrome") and the shifting of the most critical control procedures to the device level (Archimedes' principle), in accordance with which "support points" must be created to carry out device-based control procedures
- maximum possible separation of condition-stable (software) and condition-variable (data) elements of control operations (divide-and-conquer principle)

The need to protect information technologies has only recently been recognized. Up to now, the public has defined an electronic document as a file signed with an electronic signature. This is incorrect. Here are two illustrations—a coded message and a piece of currency. Neither has a signature or a seal, but they are documents nonetheless. Why do we accept them as documents? Only because (and this is enough) we trust the technologies by which they were produced. If the commander of a military unit receives a coded message with orders from his command from the hands of the code officer, he has every reason to accept the text he has received as a document (order). And if he finds that same text lying on his desk without knowing how it got there, then it is time to investigate the matter. Such investigations involve methods little known in broader circles. Matters are different with regard to the currency. Few of us ever receive bills directly from the printing plant. More often, the ways in which bills come into our possession are not completely known. Our behavior is also different—when we receive bills at a local branch of the state savings bank, as a rule we count them quickly, but if we receive them as change from a trader at the market, we might examine them more carefully for evidence they may be counterfeit.

Technologies for electronic exchanges must meet certified standards, and this compliance must be monitored. The various stages of the information exchange process involve people (operators, users) and information technologies—technical (personal computers, servers) and programmatic (operating systems, preprocessor output programs). Information is created by people, then transformed into data, and then entered into automated systems in the form of electronic documents, which together with other such documents represent information resources. Computers exchange data over communications channels. During the operation of automated systems, data (electronic documents) are transformed in accord with information technologies being applied. Therefore, we may identify the following seven components of technical security:

1. authentication of participants involved in information exchange
2. protection of hardware from unauthorized access
3. delineation of access to documents, personal computer resources, and networks
4. protection of electronic documents
5. protection of data in communications channels
6. protection of information technologies
7. delineation of access to datastreams

In working with the last component, protection is required not only for data in communications channels but also for the channels themselves. In fact, at present it is impossible to create a system of any large scale on these channels—it is expensive, ineffective, and unprofitable. It is almost impossible to make full use of a given channel. Existing channels are operating at barely 10 percent of capacity, which suggests the obvious conclusion, namely, the organization of virtual private networks using existing channels. This requires datastream tunneling; that is, data in various virtual private networks created over common channels must be isolated. Access to these data must be restricted.

Taken together in their entirety, points 1, 2, 3, and 5 and, in part, 7 also compose the focus of information protection as it is traditionally understood. It is obvious that this focus is actually much broader, including at least points 4 and 6. This fully explains the lack of significant successes in traditional approaches to resolving these problems in practice.

Having clarified this,[2] following are a few requirements for implementing the various levels of protection. As a house is built of bricks or other structural components, an information system is likewise built from various premanufactured elements, with only a small applied component being created from scratch, as a rule (although this newly created component is the most important, as it determines the functionality of the system). It is appropriate to recall the multiplicative protection paradigm, particularly that the level of information security of a system is no higher than that of its weakest link. For us this means that when using premade components we must select them so as to ensure that the protection level for each one is no lower than that required for the system as a whole. This applies to the protection of both information technologies and electronic documents. Lack of protection for either means that efforts in other areas are wasted.

AUTHENTICATION OF PARTICIPANTS IN INFORMATION EXCHANGE

Operator identification/authentication (IA) must be performed on a device basis at each stage in the operating system loading process. IA databases must be stored in the energy-independent memory of the information security system so that access to them via a personal computer would be impossible; that is, the energy-independent memory must be located outside the personal computer's address space. The control software must be stored in the controller's memory and protected against unauthorized modifications. The integrity of the control software must be ensured through the technology built into the information security system controller. Identification must be performed using an alienable information carrier.

As with operator IA, device-based procedures for remote user IA are necessary. Authentication may be handled through various means, including by electronic signature. A requirement for "intensified authentication" is becoming mandatory, that is, periodic repetition of the procedure during the work session at various time intervals short enough to prevent an ill-intentioned individual from doing significant damage if protection measures are thwarted.

PROTECTION OF HARDWARE FROM UNAUTHORIZED ACCESS

Means of protecting computers from unauthorized access may be divided into two categories: electronic locks and device modules for authorized loading. The main difference between them is the way in which integrity control is implemented. Electronic locks operate on a device basis to carry out user IA procedures, but they must resort to the use of external software to perform integrity control procedures. Device modules perform all the functions of electronic locks as well as integrity control and administration functions. As a result, these modules not only provide user IA but also handle the authorized loading of the operating system, a most important function in the construction of an isolated programming environment. Device modules handle a significantly wider range of functions than electronic locks, and they require device-based performance (not using operating system resources) of complex functions such as file system selection, reading of real data, and so forth. In addition, by integrating control functions into the hardware, device modules also offer greater reliability of results.

- **Control of technical integrity of personal computers and servers.** Control of the integrity of personal computer components must be carried out by the information security system controller before the operating system is loaded. All resources that might be used must be monitored, including

  - central processor
  - system BIOS (Basic Input/Output System)
  - supplemental BIOS
  - interrupt vectors INT 13 and INT 40
  - CMOS, including floppy disks, hard disks, and CD-ROMs

The integrity of the technical components of servers must be ensured through intensified network authorization procedures. These procedures must be carried out at the point at which the computer being verified logs on to the network and again at time intervals previously determined by the security administrator. Enhanced authentication must be implemented using the recommended type of random number generator device. The performance of the device must be monitored with a system of recommended tests.

- **Control of operating system integrity.** Control of the integrity of system components and files must be carried out by the controller before loading of the operating system, which is done through the mechanism of real data reading. Since the electronic document exchange process may involve the use of various operating systems, the controller's built-in software must handle the most popular file systems. The integrity of a given software package must be guaranteed by the technology of the data security system controllers. The controllers' devices must protect the software from unauthorized modifications. The well-known (published) hash function must be used to monitor integrity, and its standard value must be stored in the energy-independent memory of the controller protected on a device basis from access from the computer.

- **Control of applications software and data.** The integrity of applications software and data may be monitored by the data security system on a device or software basis if its integrity was registered on a device basis at the preceding stage. The well-known (published) hash function must be used to monitor integrity, and its standard value must be authenticated with the help of a remote technical data carrier (identifier).

LIMITATION OF ACCESS TO DOCUMENTS,
COMPUTER RESOURCES, AND NETWORKS

Modern operating systems increasingly include built-in access limitation capabilities. As a rule, these capabilities utilize particular features of specific file systems and are based on attributes closely linked to one of the application program interface (API) levels of the operating system. This inevitably leads to problems, including at least the following:

• **Linkage to features of specific file systems.** As a rule, modern operating systems use not one but several file systems, both new and old. It usually happens that an operating system's built-in access limitations work with a new file system but might not with an old one, as they make use of substantially different features in the new file system. This circumstance is usually not directly addressed in the system documentation, which could lead the user to become confused. Let us imagine that a computer with a new operating system is running software developed for the previous version, which is oriented toward the features of an older file system. The user rightly assumes that the established security mechanisms, certified and intended for this operating system, will perform their functions, while in reality they will be turned off. In real life, such cases may be encountered fairly often. Why rewrite an application just because you have changed operating systems? Especially when the goal is to ensure the compatibility of old file systems and link them to new operating systems!

• **Linkage to the API of the operating system.** As a rule, operating systems now change frequently, once every year or year and a half. It is not impossible for them to change even more often. Some of these changes involve changes in the API, for example, the replacement of Win 9x with WinNT. Since the access limitation attributes are a reflection of the API, a move to an updated version of an operating system requires the reworking of security system add-ons, retraining of personnel, and so forth. Thus, we might posit the following general requirement: The subsystem for access limitation must be built on the operating system and be independent of the file system. Of course, the set of attributes must be sufficient for the purposes of describing the security policy, and the description must not be in operating system API terms but rather in terms that are customarily used by security administrators.

ELECTRONIC DOCUMENT SECURITY

The life cycle of the electronic document occurs in three spheres of existence, located concentrically one within the other: the electronic environment of numerical processes, the analogous environment of subjects and objects, and the social environment of cognitive subjects. The outermost layer is formed by the multitude of cognitive subjects of the social environment, which forms the sector of activity for the document that dictates the rules of information exchange for its subject members, including requirements for interactive technology. If these rules and requirements are met, the report is deemed a document, while the information it contains is deemed by the sector as a (juridical) fact, a formal basis for initiating, changing, or terminating specific relations between subjects in the society.

The requirements of the sector of effectiveness may be divided into two categories: semantic, which are applicable to the representation of the meaning of the information, and technological, which dictate the formation of the document. The semantic aspects are the prerogative of the social environment and therefore are not considered in this paper and are deemed to be fulfilled. Given this condition, in order for a report to be recognized as a document, the parameters of the technologies used in its creation, transformation, transmission, and storage must fall within the bounds of allowable deviations from a certain standard prescribed by the sector for document-based electronic interaction. Only in this case do we have the legal grounds for considering that the requirements are met, for example, with regard to ensuring the integrity, confidentiality, and authenticity of the document.

The traditional analog document is created once in object form—a sheet of paper with a surface of designs or letters. The physical parameters of the object are stable with regard to external effects, and any changes made are relatively easy to detect. Over the course of its entire life cycle, the object document is not transformed into a different object. At any moment, the analog document is concentrated in a single point in space, so opportunities for unauthorized access are limited. The selection of available traditional information technologies is narrow, so the requirements for standard technology are obvious in their omission. Electronic documents are another matter. The ease and simplicity of modifying them are based on the very environment in which they exist—copying and replacement operations are fundamental even in Turing machines. The electronic document is transformed many times during its life cycle, and physical indications of its distortion are difficult to find. Here, requirements for the correlations of technologies and standards are extremely significant. Therefore, protecting the electronic exchange of information involves two classes of tasks: ensuring that the document remains equivalent to the original electronic document or standard over the course of its life cycle and ensuring that the electronic technologies used remain equivalent to the standards prescribed by the sector of effectiveness.

In the electronic environment it makes no sense to interpret information as data, sense, knowledge, or fact. Random numbers are also poetry to a computer—a multitude of binary bits, from which comes order, a sequence of 0's and 1's. Any two multitudes reflect the same information if the given relation of order is maintained—there are a multitude of isomorphs.[3] Thus, a binary-limited sequence can always be transformed into a number, and in the electronic environment, information is a number. A number does not change over time and space but is always fixed and static. When stored on a memory disk, a number is reflected by a "painting" of the disk surface with magnetic domains of various orientations. It is said that a computer's memory stores data, understood as the fixed form of existence of electronic information: data are numbers.

The purpose of any sort of protection is to ensure the stability (fixation) of the given properties of the protected object in all points of its life cycle. The degree of protection of an object is determined by comparing the standard (the object at an initial point in space and time) with the result (the object at the moment of observation). In our case, at the point of observation (when the electronic document is received) there is only very limited contextual information about the standard (content of the initial electronic document), although we have full information on the result (the document as observed). This means that the electronic document must contain attributes attesting to its compliance with technical and technological requirements, particularly the immutability of the information at all stages of document creation and transmission. One such attribute might be authentication security codes.[2]

- **Protection of documents during creation.** An authentication security code must be produced on a device basis during the creation of a document. Before code production begins, the isolation of the software environment must be ensured. There must be no opportunity for copying the document onto an external storage disk before the security code is produced. If a document is created by an operator, the code must indicate the operator's identity. If a document is created by the software component of the automated system, the code must indicate which software component it was.
- **Protection of documents during transmission.** Protection of the document during its transmission over external (open) communications channels must be implemented through the application of certified cryptographic tools, including those involving electronic digital signatures, for every document transmitted. Another option is also possible, in which a packet of documents is signed with an electronic digital signature, and each document is verified with another analog of a handwritten signature, for example, an authentication security code.
- **Protection of documents during processing, storage, and execution.** During these stages, document protection is ensured with the use of authentication security codes, which are required at the start and finish of each stage. These codes must be produced on a device basis and be linked to the processing procedure (the stage of information technology). For an incoming document with an authentication security code (ASC) and electronic digital signature, ASC_2 is produced and only then is the digital signature removed. Furthermore, at the next stage (n), ASC_{n+1} is produced and ASC_{n-1} is removed. Thus, at any moment, the document is protected by two codes—ASC_n and ASC_{n+1}. Authentication security codes must be produced and verified for any document placed in the operating

memory of a computer in which software environment isolation has been established and maintained. ASC_{n-1} is removed after ASC_{n+1} is put in place.

• **Protection of documents during access from the external environment.** When a document is being accessed from the external environment, its protection involves two mechanisms that have already been described above, namely, identification/authentication of remote users and limitation of access to documents, computer resources, and networks.

PROTECTION OF DATA IN COMMUNICATIONS CHANNELS

Channel coders have traditionally been used to protect data in communications channels, and there are no alternatives. Two points must be kept in mind: (1) certification and (2) channels transmit not only data but also control signals.

PROTECTION OF INFORMATION TECHNOLOGIES

Electronic documents in automated systems are not only stored but also processed. A computer represents memory and computation. When a document is processed, some data disappear and others appear, but the information remains the same. The numbers change but the information does not, as the isomorphism is maintained between the multitudes of binary signals in the old and new formats. In the electronic environment, there must be in principle some new form of existence for information accompanying the process of data transformation—information cannot disappear between the start and conclusion of the process. We must therefore assume that information exists in a dynamic form, in the form of a process.

A process is by definition dynamic, involving the changing of something over time, while information must be constant. To avoid a contradiction, a dynamic process must have some time-fixed or static feature. Such a feature exists: the fixation of the description of the process in time, no matter what point in space (a computer) or moment in time the process was observed. In fact, the specific process of information processing in a computer is determined by a fixed algorithm, procedure, or protocol. Assuming there are two forms for representing information in the electronic environment—static, in the form of an object, and dynamic, in the form of a process—we can therefore also assume that there are two fundamentally different classes of elements in the electronic environment. As soon as the first class is defined as numbers, the second class may logically be termed functions (transformations, representations). At the start of a function, we have numbers (data), while at the end, we see new numbers (data). At any moment in time and any point in space, the function remains a function. The function (or in related terms, the representation, algorithm, transformation) is unchanged.

In passive form (storage), an electronic document is a fixed object in an analog environment (memory device), while in an active form, an electronic document exists as a fixed process in an electronic environment. Accordingly, let us identify two components involved in protection: protection of data (numbers), or the electronic document itself as a physical object, and the protection of processes (functions), representing the active form of existence of the electronic document. Information (data) is defined as a multitude with a specified relation of order. Protection of functions (algorithms) means protection of the computing environment in unvarying form with regard to the information or data processed in it. Electronic technology also represents an ordered multitude (of operations or processes) and therefore can be formally recognized as information technology. The internal unity of the components of protection is revealed: It is protection of information data and protection of information technology. Thus, the status of the document includes not only the identity of the document itself (its compliance with a standard) but also the compliance of the information technologies used with standard requirements.

Despite the obvious similarity, mechanisms for the protection of the electronic document as an object (number, data) and as a process (function, computing environment) are radically different. In contrast to the situation with protection of an electronic document, with protection of information technology, the characteristics of the required technology standard are reliably known, but there is limited information about the compliance with these requirements by the technology actually used, that is, the result. The electronic document itself, or more accurately its attributes, is the only object that could carry information about the actual technology (such as sequence of operations). As before, one such attribute would be the authentication security code. The equivalence of technologies could be established more accurately with a greater number of functional operations linked through this security code. The mechanisms would not differ from those used in protecting electronic documents. Furthermore, the presence of a particular authentication security code could be considered to signify the presence of a corresponding operation in the technological process, and the value of the code could also indicate the integrity of data at a given stage in the technological process.

LIMITATION OF ACCESS TO DATASTREAMS

As a rule, routers with a virtual private network builder function are used to limit access to datastreams. This function may be carried out reliably only with the help of cryptographic tools. In such situations, special attention must be paid to the key system and the reliability of key storage. Naturally, requirements for access policy in the differentiation of datastreams are completely different from those in the limitation of access to files and catalogs. In the latter, only the simplest mechanism is possible—access is either permitted or forbidden.

Complying with the requirements discussed above ensures a sufficient level of protection for electronic documents as the most important type of reports processed in information systems.

NOTES

1. Streltsov, A. A. 2002. Ensuring Russia's information security: Theoretical and methodological foundations. Moscow: Moscow Center for Continuing Mathematical Education, 296.

2. Konyavsky, V. A. 1999. Information security management using the Akkord network security device. Moscow: Radio and Communications Publishers, 325.

3. Gadasin, V. A., and V. A. Konyavsky. 2001. From document to electronic document: Systems fundamentals. Moscow: RFK-Image Lab, 192.

Certain Aspects Regarding the Development of Conditions Favorable to Cyberterrorism and the Main Areas of Cooperation in the Struggle Against It

Igor A. Sokolov* and Vladimir I. Budzko
Russian Academy of Sciences Institute for Informatics Problems

The concept of cybernetic terrorism is interpreted rather broadly. In order to work out the necessary approaches for preventing threats of unauthorized penetration of systems—intrusion and infliction of damage—we believe it is appropriate to consider the problem from the standpoint of ensuring computer security. In doing so, it is simplest to classify the various types of intruders according to the goals of their actions, for example,

- obtaining access to secret data
- altering data that affect the completion of processes (within a particular automated system or outside it, but under its control) in which the perpetrator has an interest
- vandalism
- informational impacts, for which specific individuals or groups behave according to the perpetrator's wishes

The capabilities offered by modern information technologies for data storage and transmission may also be used for the hidden exchange of information to provide support for illicit activities. Thus, there are two main types of illegal activities in the computer sphere:

1. unauthorized penetration or intrusion into a computer system
2. hidden transmission of data via legal channels

*Translated from the Russian by Kelly Robbins.

Let us look first at external intrusion, that is, unauthorized penetration by perpetrators through devices to which they have free access. We will devote separate attention to threats from personnel within a given system on the supposition that the necessary organizational and other security measures have been put in place.

In the early 1980s, intrusion received a certain amount of attention in systems where state and corporate secrets were stored. Here, the focus was primarily on limiting the access of end users to information stored in a system. The question of security for physical data carriers was handled rather simply, mainly through organizational measures.

Information security was based on the principle of creating conditions in which the user has no physical opportunity to make any changes in the software programs—nonprogrammability. It was implemented by means of so-called dumb terminals and classical operating systems (IBM, DEC, and others), the architecture of which involved the separation of programs and data and the physical protection of systems software from applied programs and other elements. Furthermore, communications technologies were systems oriented and did not permit outsiders to log on. Exchange protocols for the telecommunications components did not allow perpetrators to penetrate the network.

The level of security provided by the architectural characteristics of computers and communications devices was sharply reduced with the appearance and accelerated introduction of new technologies, of which the following deserve special attention:

- personal computers, especially IBMs using Microsoft operating systems
- local networks with personal computer (PC) workstations
- the transmission control protocol/Internet protocol (TCP/IP) family of protocols and the creation of the Internet on their basis

A keen struggle began among the various means of protection and attack. The first applications for PCs were for home use. Within a few years, PCs began to be used in almost all spheres of human activity. IBM-compatible PCs using Microsoft software established a dominating position. With their simplicity of use and relatively low cost, they made it substantially easier and less expensive to create small systems for various applications than did computers with different architectures. The local nature of their installation made it easy to handle security matters.

This initial period saw the appearance of the first danger signals—computer viruses. At first, the intrusions were destructive in nature. The thesis was advanced that "he who takes careful precautions will not be affected." Therefore, most of the efforts were focused on the correct use of antivirus software and the proper way to use diskettes. From a security standpoint, it is unforgivable that very little attention was devoted to the operating system architecture and floppy disk technology serving as the catalyst for the development of intrusion tools. In the development of the architecture to date, almost no fundamental and reliable barriers have been put in place against virus attacks.

In the first stage, virus attacks composed the technology for intrusion. Modern antivirus packages (for example, the Kaspersky antivirus programs) essentially reflect the level of the current intrusion intellect on the whole. When we give high marks to the quality of current antivirus programs, we tacitly give the same high marks to this malicious intellect.

The appearance of local computer network technology laid the foundation for a new stage in the use of PCs. Users were given a qualitatively new interface, convenient and easy to use, which they quickly preferred over previous systems based on dumb terminals. The practical implementation of "paperless information technology" in an organization's work became a reality. Ethernet gradually became the dominant local network architecture.

The well-protected architectures offered by such manufacturers as IBM and DEC in their mainframe and personal computers were gradually pushed aside. The market supported cheap hardware, and its components became the de facto standard. At the same time, local networks created new channels for intrusion. Their use opened up opportunities for inflicting damages on a substantially larger scale than possible in attacks against a single-user PC. It is very important to note that software carries the majority of the load in organizing the exchange of data over local networks. If there is an intrusion into any PC on the network, the network driver and its network map can be altered, which at a minimum will bring down the entire network.

So-called software agents began to be widely used in local networks to carry out certain functions. These agents are loaded into client PCs in the process of performing a particular function. This approach gained widespread use in the implementation of software for electronic libraries, for which CD-ROMs were used as basic information carriers. Software agents also began to be used in diagnostic and monitoring systems. They appear automatically on specific workstations. For example, electronic libraries that perform essential service functions involved in working with data include an internal search system and other programs that are loaded automatically during disk initialization.

The placement of such a library on a server requires that the appropriate programs be transferred to a client machine. During the transfer process, someone could catch such a program and attach an intrusion program to it. One way of doing this, although it would not be easy, would be to intercept all Ethernet messages on a client machine through a network card configured to receive all MAC addresses. Including codes necessary for intrusion in a program being transferred would ultimately make it possible to gain unauthorized access to another workstation.

Another example of intrusion is the use of WinWord text editor macros. As macros are built-in programs, the addition of intrusion programs in the "body" of macros makes it possible to distribute them along with text documents and launch them when the text editor begins processing. There are many examples in which WinWord has been used in virus attacks.

Perpetrators have found even broader opportunities in the Internet environment. The dominant position of the TCP/IP family of protocols and their inherent capabilities have given rise to a new wave of various types of attacks with even more destructive consequences. Experience amassed in previous stages and the scientific-technical potential involved in carrying out intrusions has been put to full use.

A stable trend has been established by which the number of Internet intrusions has been doubling each year. This means that the amount of damage done has at least doubled as well. The scope of virus attacks is such that the network space of several countries at once can be affected.

At the same time, the Internet continues to play an increasingly important role as an international information repository and the least expensive means of communications. It is essentially one of the most important engines of world technological progress. It is very important to note that it has become the main daily working tool and information source in a number of fields. One example would be research and analytical activity using accessible electronic information resources via Internet Open Source Solutions, something a growing number of firms and organizations are doing.

In the environment described above, creating an IBM PC-MS-Ethernet-Internet system capable of ensuring the necessary level of security requires the involvement of the necessary number of high-class specialists in the information technology field and the acquisition of expensive security software and devices. The cost of these security technologies for a system built on this platform and requiring a high level of protection equals up to half the cost of the entire system itself. Operating and maintaining the security technologies entail substantial additional costs.

The more well-known outside intrusions that occur, the greater the demand for the products of companies that specialize in creating technologies for information security at various levels and with various purposes, producing methodological materials, and providing security consulting services. This business is developing successfully.

A system that is sufficiently protected from the outside remains vulnerable to intrusions launched from within through the capabilities of service personnel (operators, administrators, systems programmers, security officers, and so forth). A lack of on-staff capabilities in security software development must be rectified by using additional specialized software products from firms that specialize in providing enhanced protection in a Microsoft environment and by instituting additional heightened (and therefore expensive) organizational security measures.

Certain successes have been achieved in the development of technologies for intrusion detection, particularly in the Internet environment. There have been many more successes in detecting intrusions than in preventing such intrusions. Each time it has released the latest version of its operating system, Microsoft has announced the substantial expansion of the program's built-in security features, but each time it has turned out that these new features do not save average users, who lack the system enhancement capabilities of organizations. The well-known problems of ensuring security in modern automated systems in an IBM PC-MS-Ethernet-Internet environment are also applicable to a significant extent to cases involving the use of the UNIX operating system and RISC (reduced instruction set computer) processors.

New security solutions for virtual private networks (VPNs) have been widely developed in the past few years. The use of VPNs provides substantially increased protection against system intrusions over the Internet but does not resolve the problem within the system itself. VPN technology cannot be used for access to various general-access servers, search systems, portals, other information resources, or electronic mail. Furthermore, as the service provider plays a fundamental role in the organization of a VPN, this requires that these providers be highly responsible and that users place a great deal of trust in them.

Therefore, the first conclusion that can be drawn is that the IBM PC-MS-Ethernet-Internet environment, which is the most widespread today and is used in creating automated information support tools for various functional purposes, is poorly protected against intrusions. Efforts to stop the growth in the number of intrusions have not been successful. This situation is advantageous for firms specializing in the sale of consulting services and the production of supplemental means of protection, such as firewall systems, security shields, and monitoring systems. But it also increasingly complicates the lives of end users. The fundamental reason for this state of affairs lies in the inherent characteristics of the systems architectures. At the same time, the IBM PC-MS-Ethernet-Internet environment still represents the dominant foundation for existing and newly created automated information support systems.

The new technology of dense wavelength division multiplexing (DWDM), in which all types of channels are collocated on one fiber, has seen very rapid development in recent years. Each subchannel has a carrying capacity of 10 GBps, and there are 256 subchannels in each channel. Efforts are continuing to increase the number and carrying capacity of the subchannels. The use of DWDM technology makes it more efficient to use IP as the basic exchange protocol, and this explains the gradual shift away from lower-level protocols such as asynchronous transfer mode (ATM), frame relay (FR), and others.

The use of DWDM in developing the Internet will facilitate a substantial expansion in the volume and content of services provided, including IP-telephony, IP-video, video conferencing, and so forth. These and other types of services will make up an ever-increasing share of overall Internet use. DWDM offers expanded capabilities for making systems disaster resistant, which is defined as the ability of a critical application to maintain vitally important data and software resources and continue performing its functions (possibly with certain limitations) under conditions of overall system degradation caused by the massive destruction of system components or entire hardware complexes and linkages between them as a result of natural disasters, industrial accidents and catastrophes, or the intentional actions of individuals or groups. This function is also conveniently carried out over the Internet, as in such circumstances it is simpler and less expensive to resolve the problem of rerouting communications channels.

Finally, the use of DWDM makes it possible to advance efforts to implement distributed parallel computing (grid program [peer-to-peer computing]). The Internet is advantageous in this regard as well. Dealing with issues of providing security for data processing and transmission in cutting-edge distributed computing architectures is of fundamental importance if these architectures are to be broadly disseminated and used. The basic security components must provide a mechanism for authentication, access limitation, and confidentiality of communications among elements of the network. Ensuring the integrity of data and processes during failures and catastrophes should also be viewed as an important element of ensuring security. In addition, any system operating in an IP VPN environment must have a subsystem for security management that is designed to ensure the reliable and uninterrupted functioning of the base system in the event of threats or other actions, protect the technological process as a unified whole, and provide monitoring and audit capabilities.

Therefore, our second conclusion is that the Internet will develop and be used on an increasing scale in various spheres of human activity. However, if the IBM PC-MS-Ethernet-Internet architecture maintains its dominance, we will also see an increase in damages from intrusions and especially from intrusions for terrorist purposes.

This leads to our third conclusion, namely, that the danger of computer terrorism can be reduced only by using new systems technology solutions for the design of operating systems, collective use systems, and telecommunications protocols. The following could be suggested as areas for joint research with our American colleagues:

• definition of design principles and implementation mechanisms for ensuring the security of the LINUX operating system and preventing intrusions into individual computers and collective use systems, including the construction of such systems on narrow client principles
• definition of areas for improvement and development of recommendations on changing the IP protocol
• study of questions related to the construction of virtual private networks that are reliable in preventing intrusions
• study of questions related to the implementation of distributed parallel computing (GRID system)

It would also be appropriate to join forces to prepare the necessary methodological materials explaining the practical expediency of intrusion-resistant architectures to stimulate market interest in the shift to using hardware and software that could form the basis for the creation of reliably protected systems. Finally, it would be expedient to work together on preparing well-honed recommendations on the creation of a standardized set of laws on cyberterrorism.

PAPERS PRESENTED TO THE NRC AND RAS COMMITTEES

Problems of Combating Terrorism and Possible Areas for Russian-American Scientific Cooperation to Resolve Them

*Valentin A. Sobolev**
Security Council of the Russian Federation

Allow me to express my gratitude for being invited to speak at such an impressive meeting of scientists from the United States and the Russian Federation. It is important to note that all of us have been brought here by a desire to expand cooperation in the search for ways of enhancing the effectiveness of the struggle against terrorism.

The Security Council of the Russian Federation, chaired by Russian President Vladimir V. Putin, is devoting considerable efforts to resolving problems associated with the fight against terrorism. Russia actively supports the measures against international terrorism being taken by the world community, with the United Nations and its Security Council playing the central coordinating role. Our country has made an important contribution to strengthening the international antiterrorist coalition and consistently pursues a policy of creating a global system to counter these new challenges and threats on the basis of international law. Russia is a party to 11 international conventions associated with combating various forms of terrorism. The United Nations is doing a great deal of work on draft documents proposed by India regarding the comprehensive struggle against terrorism and by the Russian Federation concerning nuclear terrorism.

One of our top-priority efforts involves building antiterrorist cooperation within the framework of various regional structures. For example, Russia has participated very actively in organizing the activities of the Antiterrorist Center of the Commonwealth of Independent States (CIS) and in establishing a branch of this center in Central Asia. With Russia's support, the Council of Foreign Affairs Ministers of the Shanghai Cooperation Organization at its November

---

*Translated from the Russian by Kelly Robbins.

2002 meeting, passed resolutions supporting the creation of a Regional Antiterrorist Structure under the auspices of the Shanghai organization. Following up on this resolution, on January 10, 2003, the president of the Russian Federation signed the Federal Law on Ratifying the Shanghai Convention on Combating Terrorism, Separatism, and Extremism. Matters concerning the fight against terrorism also lie at the focus of the work of the Committee of Secretaries of Security Councils of Collective Security Treaty Countries[2] (with observers from other CIS member states) and of efforts undertaken by the "Slavic Four" (Belarus, Poland, Russia, and Ukraine) and the "Caucasus Four" (Azerbaijan, Armenia, Georgia, and Russia).

Another principal focus of our efforts has been Russia's participation in the antiterrorist coalition and the expansion of its cooperation in this area with the United States. This meeting of the joint committee of the Russian Academy of Sciences and the U.S. National Academies represents another good example of this sort of collaboration.

Terrorism has been known as a political and social phenomenon for some time. However, it is only now, with the development of processes of globalization and urbanization, qualitative changes in the societal infrastructure, and the accompanying widespread introduction of modern information technologies that terrorism has become a factor capable of affecting the fate of civilized development.

The terrorist acts committed in recent years in Russian cities, the actions of September 11, 2001, in New York City, the bloody events in Indonesia and the Philippines, the seizure of the concert hall in Moscow in October 2002, and the loss of life at the administrative complex in the city of Grozny have shown the entire world what a dangerous and vicious enemy we are dealing with. These events have convinced all right-minded people that international terrorism is a real force and an ominous threat to the future of all humanity. The danger is multiplying as it takes on the organizational features of a new sort of peculiar "international" and uses religious rhetoric to attract the support of fanatics of all varieties.

We are faced with a situation in which no single country in the world, not even the most powerful, can guarantee the protection of its citizens from the terrorist threat. This has led to the appearance of some new items on the agenda under the new world order, namely, the need for a profound analysis of the processes that are under way and for the creation of a united front of like-minded states to counter this plague of the twenty-first century.

It is very important that scientists from the U.S. and Russian national academies have become involved in the analysis of these processes and have already been collaborating successfully for a year. This is just one instance in which representatives of the scientific communities of our countries have joined forces to search for effective solutions to the problem of ensuring the national securities of our respective countries and of all humanity. This is a sign of the new times and the new political realities.

In this effort we proceed on the belief that the struggle against terrorism has many aspects. Among the most important of these are questions concerning how to fight terrorism in urban environments and how to deal with the threat of computer terrorism. As experience has shown, the concentration of a significant part of the population in cities and the vulnerability of the infrastructure of the world's major cities (composed of a complex system of facilities that support the population's daily needs and activities, including public services, industry, and the information infrastructure) create the preconditions for their becoming targets for terrorist acts.

Protecting the population and these facilities from terrorist acts is a very complex task, especially as the tools and methods used in terrorist activity are becoming increasingly refined. Terrorists are ever more frequently utilizing the latest developments from the world of science and technology. As a result, high-tech terrorism has given rise to a new reality in which particular groups or even individuals could gain access to materials that if used would produce consequences comparable to the impact of weapons of mass destruction.

A great danger of urban terrorism is associated with the possible use of radioactive, chemical, and biological means against the population. The difficulty of combating this sort of terrorism is illustrated by the recent threats to infect the population with anthrax, the pathogen for which was spread through the mail in the United States. Even though preparations to respond to a possible biological attack began in the United States in the mid-1990s, a network of diagnostic laboratories was created to rapidly detect pathogens and notify the various intelligence services, and broad-scale training exercises were conducted, all of these efforts proved to be insufficient to protect society against this case of biological terrorism. The system put in place to ensure public security in Japan could not protect the residents of Tokyo from the chemical attack carried out by the Aum Shinrikyo sect in that city's subway system.

At the same time, we note the growing threat of the appearance of cyberterrorism, the rise of which is associated with two factors. First, modern societies are becoming, in a practical manner, dependent on the stable operation of information and telecommunications systems. These systems are used in virtually all spheres of our lives, including in the operations of organizations in the credit and financial sector, small business, transportation, and government. Second, we might say that as these systems are constantly being improved, the means of disrupting their operations are also undergoing the same intensive process. If the threat of cyberterrorism were to be carried out, it could substantially reduce the government's ability to operate and cause irreparable losses associated with human casualties.

Cyberterrorism, which is making an increasingly notable appearance in overall crime statistics, provides fertile grounds for the activities of terrorists. For instance, in the last three years the number of recorded crimes committed in Russia with the use of modern information technologies increased by more than

150 times, while there was a 100-fold increase in the number of crimes involving the creation, use, and distribution of malicious programs. Similar problems also exist in the United States, where American specialists have noted the sharply increased number of hacking attacks in recent years, with the damages caused by hackers to U.S. computer networks totaling about $380 million in 2001 alone.

Science plays an important role in development tools for countering urban and computer terrorism and must provide well-founded methods for use by our states and the international community in this regard.

In our view, problems requiring scientific evaluation include the following:

• ensuring the security of the global information infrastructure and its national components
• ensuring control over the spread of technologies used in deriving or processing materials and compounds that could be used to inflict mass casualties
• developing a new approach to resolving problems of the spread of dual-use technologies and preventing them from falling into the hands of terrorists
• creating a system for detecting evidence of preparations for terrorist acts involving the use of high technologies

Of course, this list does not fully cover all the problems associated with the study of terrorism as a social phenomenon. It will probably be augmented significantly as a result of discussions on this topic at the seminars held at this workshop.

NOTE

1. Translator's note: The Collective Security Treaty countries are Armenia, Belarus, Kazakhstan, Kyrgyzstan, Russia, Tajikistan, Uzbekistan, and Ukraine.

Making the Nation Safer:
The Role of Science and Technology in Countering Terrorism—
A Report of the U.S. National Academies

Lewis M. Branscomb
Harvard University

This discussion is derived from the study by the National Academy of Sciences, National Academy of Engineering, and Institute of Medicine of how science and technology might assist in countering catastrophic terrorism.[1] This study was initiated by the presidents of the three branches of the Academy shortly after initial discussion with a large group of experts on September 25, 2001. The project was carried out by a committee of 24, with Lewis Branscomb and Richard Klausner as cochairs. The committee was supported by a set of more specialized expert working groups, numbering 119.[2] The work of the committee and its panels was then subjected to 46 independent expert reviewers. To avoid any delay in the project, the work was entirely financed out of the Academies' own funds. The resulting 400-page report was presented to the Congress, White House, and public on June 25, 2002. It was released in book form by the National Academies Press on August 2, 2002. The discussion below, now one and one-half years after the event that triggered the need for the study, includes a number of extensions of material and ideas in the original report. For these the author takes personal responsibility.

The study set out to answer three primary questions:

1. How can science and engineering contribute to making the nation safer against the threat of **catastrophic terrorism**?
2. What key **actions** can be undertaken **now**, based on knowledge and technologies in hand? What are the key opportunities for reducing current and future risks even further through longer-term research and development activities?

3. How can government and society **make good decisions** about science and technology homeland security programs and activities? How can the government manage the necessary science and technology programs?

To understand how science and technology might contribute to countering terrorism, we must evaluate the nature of the threat, the vulnerabilities of targets in civil society, and the availability of technical solutions to the vulnerabilities that are most likely to be exploited by terrorists.

TERRORISTS' ADVANTAGES

The terrorists possess some advantages, despite their small numbers (relative to the security forces of a modern industrial nation). First, their actions are unpredictable, since their objectives are, at least those of ideological terrorists such as al Qaeda and Aum Shinrikyo, largely idiosyncratic and obscure.[3] Second, we must assume that the terrorist group has some part of their number in covert residence within the society they plan to attack. There may also be domestic terrorists who are citizens of the target society. Third, terrorists may be very patient; they have the initiative in deciding when an attack may occur. As a result, those defending against terrorism must be alert at all times; the terrorists need be prepared only when they choose to strike.

Finally, terrorists may have international bases of operations, and quite possibly enjoy the sponsorship and assistance of a rogue state. This combination of stateless terrorists who infiltrate target societies, supported by the resources of an irresponsible government, is a particularly dangerous combination. The U.S. government was obviously concerned that the Baathist government of Iraq might represent such a state, although evidence indicating a link to the September 11, 2001, attack is substantively outweighed by data to the contrary.[4]

ADVANTAGES OF INDUSTRIAL SOCIETIES
THREATENED BY TERRORISTS

Modern industrial societies have some offsetting advantages to terrorism. Their global intelligence and military presence, especially when they cooperate with one another, may keep the terror networks off balance and may be able to damage some of them. Military action, or the threat of it, may discourage rogue states from supporting the terrorists.

Through the application of available or new technologies, states can make targets less vulnerable, thus less attractive. They can limit the damage that may result from an attack, increase the speed of recovery, and provide forensic tools to identify the perpetrators.

U.S. GOVERNMENT STRUCTURE AND HOMELAND SECURITY

The U.S. federal government is organized for cold war, not for dealing with a serious threat of catastrophic domestic terrorism. Issues are compartmented into separate departments for military concerns and for civil justice, for domestic or foreign affairs, and for public or private responsibilities. Although the new Department of Homeland Security (DHS) comprises most of the agencies concerned with protecting the nation's borders and its imports and is intended to provide support for the police, fire, and medical first responders, almost all the science and technology experience and capability in the federal government lie in departments and agencies outside the DHS and in the private sector. Managing the organizational challenges facing the U.S. government will be a formidable task.

THREE MAIN CATEGORIES OF PUBLIC POLICY APPROACHES TO COUNTERING TERRORISM

First, foreign policies may, over time and if designed for the purpose, reduce poverty, injustice, authoritarian rule, and religious zealotry. This is a very long-term task, and there is certainly no guarantee of success.

Second, there are the tools of domestic policing through which the government attempts to identify and root out hidden terrorists. Creation of a domestic intelligence service to further this aim has been discussed by politicians, but these approaches may threaten the very civil liberties and constitutional rights the government is sworn to protect.

The third type of policy engages technology and management to harden domestic targets, reduce the damage, and enhance recovery. This is the focus of the Academies report, which found that science and technology can contribute substantially to making the nation safer but cannot assure that catastrophic attacks will not succeed.

TARGETS OF AND WEAPONS FOR TERRORIST ATTACKS

In the Academies report the targets of terrorist attacks are organized into the following eight categories:

1. nuclear and radiological attacks
2. human health and food systems
3. toxic chemicals and flammable or explosive materials
4. communications and information services
5. energy systems (power plants and distribution)
6. transportation systems (air, sea, and land)
7. cities and fixed infrastructure (buildings, water supply, tunnels, and bridges)

8. people (including their confidence in public institutions)

The terrorists' weapons include

- fissile nuclear and radiological materials
- biological organisms used against human and agricultural health systems
- military-type chemical weapons
- inflammable, toxic, and explosive chemicals and materials
- cyber- and electromagnetic pulse (EMP) attacks on electronic targets, such as telecoms, data, or controls
  - transportation and industrial materials systems used as weapons
  - explosives derived from, for example, fuel oil and nitrogen fertilizer

It is important to appreciate that this list is much larger than what in U.S. law are called weapons of mass destruction (WMD). These are nuclear, biological, and chemical weapons designed initially for military use and restricted (but not eliminated) by a series of treaties. It is essential that those concerned with counterterrorism bear in mind that while weapons of mass destruction are perhaps the most lethal, they also tend to be the most inaccessible to a terror organization, at least if it is not assisted by a technically competent government. The terrorists who attacked the World Trade Center on September 11, 2001, certainly created mass destruction, but the weapon used (a fully fueled airliner used as a manned cruise missile) was technically not a WMD—that is, it did not arise from a military system designed for mass destruction.[5]

ECOLOGICAL ECONOMICS:
COMMERCIAL EFFICIENCY CREATES VULNERABILITIES

The vulnerabilities of modern industrial societies result not only from the possible escape from government control of military WMDs but also from the possible use of products of commercial and industrial operations that may be used as weapons by terrorists. In the latter category are the use of agricultural fertilizer and fuel oil to make explosives, the possible release of toxic chemicals from railroad tank cars during shipment, interference with or modification of electronic messages used to control critical processes, and so forth.

There is a larger source of vulnerability of civil society, however, arising from the very efficiency of its competitive economic system. The competitive drive for commercial efficiency creates linkages and vulnerabilities in what are called *critical infrastructure* industries—industries governing energy, transportation, communications, food production and distribution, public health, and financial transactions.

The mechanisms through which the quest for industrial efficiency may threaten the industry's resilience to catastrophic terrorism include

- single-point failures, where costs are high and risks from small perturbations are low, for example, ultra-high-voltage transformers in electric power distribution
- insufficient stockpiles of spare parts to permit rapid restoration of services, especially where component costs are high and replacement times are long.
- excessive concentration in the quest for scale economies, for example, the concentration of chicken meat processing and distribution in several large firms or the aggregation of fuel in passenger liners in the largest commercial air transports
- coupling to other critical infrastructure systems to leverage their scale economies, for example, the dependence of transportation safety on the availability of electric power and secure computer networks

Thus, a competitive economy creates new vulnerabilities, which only government policy and industrial cooperation can reduce. The President's Council of Advisers on Science and Technology estimates that 85 percent of U.S. infrastructure systems are owned and run by private firms, not the government. If industry is to bear the cost of these investments, it must make public good investments without any reliable means of evaluating risk, and thus the justification for spending the capital. So, who will pay to make infrastructure more secure? What incentives will the federal government offer to the private sector?

WHO WILL PAY TO HARDEN CRITICAL INFRASTRUCTURE?

There are a variety of possible policies to motivate private investments in the hardening of critical infrastructure. Some of them are

- compulsion through regulation (which may require congressional legislation)
- subsidies of research and development to design hardening strategies through public-private research and development partnerships (This still leaves industry with the capital expense for implementing the strategy.)
- voluntary commitments with antitrust exemption (The chemical industry in the United States has an excellent record of voluntary standards for plant safety that might become a model for protections from terrorism.)
- reinsurance as an inducement to set a sliding scale of rates for terrorism loss insurance, reflecting the extent to which client firms have adopted hardening measures

DUAL-USE STRATEGIES FOR HARDENING INDUSTRY

In a limited number of cases, firms may be able to devise hardening strategies that also reduce costs or improve product or service value so that the total costs are minimized or are even negative. The experience of the way many firms responded to the Y2K threat offers some encouragement for this notion. The dual-use strategy is needed for at least three reasons:

1. to increase the likelihood that industry will invest in hardening critical infrastructure
2. to create a more sustainable public commitment to the costs and inconveniences of national efforts against terrorist threats
3. to integrate homeland security research and development with the rest of the societal research and engineering base to ensure that a fully national effort of high quality results

Because the targets and many of the weapons are imbedded in the civil economy, security issues cannot be neatly separated from the daily life of the civil population. Thus, the strategy for gradually restructuring many of our physical facilities, production processes, means for providing food distribution, and the like will have to reflect a complex balance of public good investments for which government will have to take the initiative and commercial investments aimed at competitive success. The political economy of the United States is not designed to make this marriage of conflicting interests and responsibilities very easy; European nations are more accustomed to this balance in their economies.

EXAMPLES OF THE ACADEMIES' RECOMMENDATIONS FOR DEALING WITH A VARIETY OF THREATS

A few examples of specific threats and the science and technology recommendations (selected from the 134 recommendations in the report) are summarized here.

Nuclear and Radiological Threats

If terrorists, with a minimal level of scientific knowledge, can acquire enough highly enriched uranium (HEU), they may be able to assemble an inefficient but effective nuclear weapon in a major city. Thus, the United States and Russia are cooperating in safeguarding fissile material and blending down stocks of HEU. Even more dangerous is the possible availability of finished nuclear weapons provided by rogue states with nuclear weapons capability if global cooperation for nonproliferation fails.

The U.S. public must be educated on the nature of radiological threats, both from "dirty bombs" and from damaged nuclear electrical power plants. Public ignorance about radiation hazards may induce a level of panic much more destructive than the radiation from which people may be fleeing.

Biological Threats to People and Their Food Supply

Research on pathogenesis of infectious agents, and particularly on means for early detection of the presence of such pathogens before their symptomatic appearance, is important. Nations will stockpile vaccines against known diseases, but the threat of genetic modification—while perhaps beyond the capability of most terrorists (but not of rogue states)—requires a vigorous research effort to find solutions for detection, evaluation, and response.

Although in the United States the Centers for Disease Control provides a robust capability in epidemiology, there is no equivalent capability for possible biological attacks on agriculture and farm animals. Thus, measures to protect the food supply and provide decontamination after an attack must have high priority.

Toxic Chemicals, Explosives, and Flammable Materials

Some highly lethal chemicals, such as those made for military applications, are relatively easy to make. There is even greater risk from industrial chemicals, which are widely accessible as they move in commerce. Dangerous chemicals in transit should be tracked electronically. To ensure that only first responders, and not terrorists, know what the tank cars contain, the rail cars should be equipped with encrypted electronic identification.

Sensor networks are required to detect and characterize dangerous materials, particularly when they are airborne. Self-analyzing filter systems for modern office buildings whose windows cannot be opened must not only protect the inhabitants but also detect and report the first presence of those materials (such as aerosols) that may be trapped in improved filters.

An example of quite long-range basic research that could prove rewarding would be the discovery of olfactory biosensors than can reach levels of sensitivity dogs already possess.

Energy Systems

The hazards associated with fossil fuel storage, shipment, and use are well known. Perhaps less apparent are the vulnerabilities of a modern electric power grid. Many of these systems have vulnerable, unique, extra-high-voltage transformers that do not have spares and thus represent a single-point failure. A solution recommended in the Academies report is the production of a substantial number of mid-sized transformers specifically designed to be reconfigurable in combination to replace one of the failed high-voltage transformers.

Another example is the replacement of operating engineers in power distribution control rooms with computer systems running Supervisory Control and Data Acquisition (SCADA) systems. These computer-based software systems are generally produced abroad; it is difficult to guarantee their integrity. In addition, while some electric utilities use encrypted traffic on fiber optics to communicate among the SCADA computers, some use clear traffic on the Internet, vulnerable to a cyberattack.

From the perspective of a longer time frame, adaptive power grids should be developed to make them harder to attack and to make recovery after attack much easier and quicker.

Communications and Information Systems

In the United States the most urgent issue is to reconfigure first responder communications so that police, fire, and medical personnel can communicate with one another and with the emergency operations center (EOC). Inability to do so greatly aggravated loss of life, especially among firefighters, in the World Trade Center attack. The main worry about cyberattacks is that they may be used, perhaps with EMP as well, to amplify the destructive effect of a conventional physical or biological attack. The longer-term concerns about human resources for research in computer and network security were also discussed in Dr. Wm. A. Wulf's paper. The goal must be the invention of fully secure operating systems.

Transportation and Borders

Sensor networks for inspection of goods and passengers crossing the nation's borders will be a research priority. The primary technical challenge will not be the design of sensors themselves, although much progress is needed here, but in the systems engineering of the networks of sensors together with data fusion and decision support software. Biometrics for more secure identification of individuals shows promise, and systems superior to the driver's licenses used by most travelers are promising. The range of threats to the transportation networks of a modern state is very great, and careful systems analysis to identify the weak points and find the most effective and economical means for protecting them is essential.

Cities and Fixed Infrastructure

The emergency operations centers in many large U.S. cities are quite vulnerable, not only to a destructive physical attack but also to a more indirect attack on their ability to access data and to communicate through a cyber- or EMP attack. Remedying these vulnerabilities must have high urgency; in many cases, the centers will have to be relocated.[6]

Much research is already under way to analyze the structural characteristics of high-rise buildings that may make them much more vulnerable than necessary. Without waiting for this research to result in revised building codes, the expert panel recommends immediate adoption and extension where appropriate of European standards for fire and blast, which were much improved following World War II. As already noted, air intakes for large buildings need to be less accessible and equipped with better air filters, perhaps with chemical analysis sufficient to determine that a toxic material is present. Instrumentation to allow first responders to detect toxic and hazardous materials; special provisions for protecting harbors, bridges, dams, tunnels, and dikes; and protection against attacks on urban water supplies downstream from the treatment plant are all discussed in the Academies report.

Response of People to Terrorist Threats

The study concludes that public fear and confusion are more likely than terror in response to most attacks. The main dangers are panic and destructive behavior resulting from a lack of credible public information. Thus, a loss of public confidence in those responsible for protecting the public can also be an attack amplifier. The government faces a number of dilemmas, for example, in using a color-coded warning system to alert the public to the perceived likelihood of additional terrorist attacks. Some citizens feel that this system itself may needlessly amplify the threat, thus doing terrorists' psychological job for them.

An urgent matter is for the government to train and introduce to the public well in advance of any attack a number of trusted and knowledgeable people, prepared to provide accurate and trustworthy information quickly and authoritatively.

TECHNICAL STRATEGIES

Admittedly, technical strategies can only make the terrorist's task more difficult and less consequential. Only effective detection and disruption of terrorist capabilities through intelligence and police work in the short term, and reducing the supply and motivation of terrorists in the long term can truly reduce catastrophic terror attacks. But neither of these strategies is assured of success; it would be irresponsible of government not to adopt the most cost-effective strategies for reducing vulnerability to terrorism.

From the great variety of threats studied by the Academies' experts, a few commonsense conclusions about technical strategy can be extracted.

- Repair the weakest links (single-point failures) in vulnerable systems and infrastructures.
- Use defenses-in-depth (do not rely only on perimeter defenses or firewalls).
- Use "circuit breakers" to isolate and stabilize failing system elements.

- Build security and flexibility into basic system designs where possible.
- Design systems for use by typical first responders (which will require unusually careful attention to the needs and capabilities of the end users of new technologies, since those needs are so different from the military, which the technical community has supported for so long).
- Focus priority attention on the "system of systems" technical challenge.

The last point is particularly important. Attacks are likely to involve multiple complex systems. There are a number of dimensions to the systems engineering challenge of homeland security. The multiple critical industrial infrastructures are closely coupled. Almost all of the responses to terrorist threats require the concerned action of federal agencies, state and local authorities, private companies, and in some cases friendly nations. The technologies used in counterterrorism will themselves be coupled complex systems. An evident example is the notion of complex networks of sensors that are coupled to databases, within which the network output is fused with other information and from which sensible information must be provided so that local officials in EOCs can use it. Thus, priority setting requires modeling and simulating attack and response and red teaming to test the effectiveness of proposed solutions.

The Academies' report attached a high priority to the establishment, within the new Department of Homeland Security, of a Homeland Security Institute to provide the systems analysis and decision support services to the senior officials in the department. Provision for such an institute is in the law creating DHS, although it is given only a three-year life unless extended by the Congress.

SUMMARY: FIVE POINTS ABOUT COUNTERING TERRORISM

1. Only a farsighted foreign policy, addressing the roots of terrorism and denying terrorist ideologies a foothold in other societies, can make the United States and its allies safer.

2. Weapons of mass destruction are potentially devastating, but the most probable threats will depend on the characteristics of the economy itself, as was the case on September 11, 2001.

3. Reducing vulnerabilities in critical infrastructure is a highly complex **systems** problem; it requires a tested strategy.

4. Policies for understanding who will pay to harden the critical infrastructure industry, and how the federal government and industry cooperate to this end, are required.

5. A unique degree of cooperation between industry, cities, and government is required.

NOTES

1. Making the nation safer: The role of science and technology in countering terrorism. 2002. Washington, D.C.: The National Academies Press. Website: *www.nap.edu*. Also available online in PDF at: *http://books.nap.edu/html/stct/index.html*.

2. The quality and timeliness of the report were in large part due to the effort of the project's National Research Council staff, Dr. Ronald Taylor and Dr. Elizabeth Grossman.

3. Politically motivated terrorists, such as the Irish Red Army, may have a specific goal, which, if achieved, might end their attacks. One can imagine an attempt to negotiate an end to their terrorism. This is not so for the al Qaeda terrorists who carried out the September 11, 2001, attack on New York City and Washington, D.C.

4. Gerald Holton anticipates just such a combination of individual terrorists supported by a rogue government in a paper presented at a terrorism conference at the Hoover Institution in 1976 and published at that time in *Terrorism, an International Journal*. He called this threat Type III terrorism. See G. Holton, Reflections on modern terrorism. Edge, 2002. Available online at *http://www.edge.org/3rd_culture/holton/holton_index.html*.

5. The traditional definition (in many U.S. statutes) of WMD is those weapons developed for military use complete with delivery systems. Thus the search in Iraq for chemical weapons of mass destruction focused on chemical warheads and the stocks and production facilities for charging them. Ordinary chemicals in commerce, such as chlorine, phosgene, and other such materials, have not been considered WMD as defined in U.S. law.

6. The EOC in New York City was located in the World Trade Center, surely not a good choice.

International Aspects of Creating a State System for Countering the Illegal Circulation of Radioactive Materials in the Russian Federation

Vladimir M. Kutsenko*
Department for the Protection of Information and Nuclear Materials and
Facilities, Ministry for Atomic Energy

I have been assigned the task of making specific recommendations for a program of joint activities in counterterrorism. These recommendations are based on practical measures we are taking in the Russian Federation to combat the potential for nuclear and radiological terrorism. Coming from a federal executive agency, our recommendations are of a purely practical nature in accordance with the purview of the Russian Ministry for Atomic Energy (Minatom).

We hope that the following five proposals correspond to the fundamental goal of the conference organizers by focusing specifically on what we should do and how we should do it.

1. On the initiative of Minatom in cooperation with the Russian Ministry of Internal Affairs (MVD), Federal Security Service (FSB), and Ministry of Foreign Affairs (MID), and with the involvement of other interested ministries and agencies, we have developed a draft of a provisional statute on a state system for countering the illegal circulation of radioactive materials within the Russian Federation and across its borders. This draft is being circulated for revision and approval by all relevant entities.

2. The draft statute includes the fundamental conceptual elements necessary for organizing the struggle against the illegal circulation of radioactive materials and for creating a state system linking and organizing the activities of the basic law enforcement and customs agencies, ministries, and departments dealing with the nuclear sector, and other interested organizations. The draft also defines the basic responsibilities and functions of these ministries, departments, and organizations, which primarily lie in preventing the possible criminal use of nuclear materials and radioactive substances.

*Translated from the Russian by Kelly Robbins.

3. To facilitate further consideration of matters related to cooperation among the structural components of the system, plans for the first stage of the project call for creating a model district in the Moscow region as an element of the system for countering the illegal circulation of radioactive materials. A possible structure for such a model district is presented in Figure 1.

4. A fundamental component in the creation of a state system for countering the illegal circulation of radioactive materials is the development of devices for their detection, location, and identification and the provision of such instruments to the structural components of the system. Taking into account the special requirements inherent in the use of such devices, Minatom has created and tested models appropriate for stationary and mobile use. They may be categorized by intended use as follows: (a) handheld gamma and gamma-neutron monitors and similar devices for concealed installation for the detection and location of radioactive materials and (b) portable spectrometric devices for the identification of radioactive materials.

5. The draft statute pays special attention to the question of creating a well-developed information system on matters related to combating the illegal circulation of radioactive materials, including a number of central and agency-specific databases. In creating such systems, Russia also deems it expedient to propose that the international community examine the question of joining forces and coordinating the activities of all interested countries.

The main goal of creating a model district and subsequently implementing other elements of the draft plan is to facilitate the development of a federal system of preventive measures for combating nuclear and radiological terrorism. In this regard, Minatom proceeds from the belief that the problem cannot be resolved through a division of efforts by the various agencies but rather requires federal coordination.

International cooperation in countering nuclear and radiological terrorism is an objective necessity. In this area, there are problems demanding the unification of international efforts and the coordination of activities. In our opinion, these fundamental problems include

- addressing matters related to the detection of nuclear materials
- equipping law enforcement agencies with the necessary technical means and providing general and technical training for their personnel
- dealing with organizational, legal, and other aspects of incident response

In dealing with all these problems as well as other matters, we feel it is necessary to create a joint working group operating under conditions of confidentiality.

We note that any form of terrorism presents a special threat to cities, with even greater consequences in national capitals. In this regard, creating a model

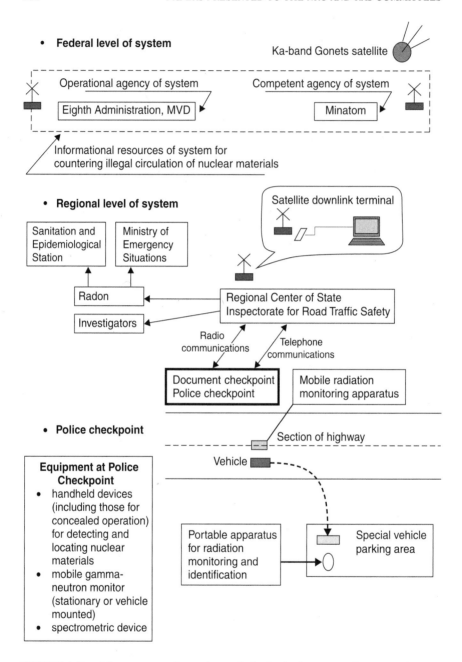

FIGURE 1 Possible structure of experimental district in the system for countering the illegal circulation of nuclear materials.

district in the Moscow region in 2003–2004 and obtaining practical results from its operation will make it possible to formulate a concept (system model) for protecting capital cities, especially those of United Nations Security Council member states, from the threat of nuclear and radiological terrorism.

At the same time, existing technical means for monitoring shipments of explosives, other hazardous cargo, weapons, and so forth, could be brought to bear in the creation of such a system. Work on addressing problematic questions in the model district could add substantial programmatic and practical impetus to efforts to deal with this urgent current problem.

Proposals to the International Atomic Energy Agency (IAEA) of an international program for countering and suppressing the illegal circulation of radioactive materials as a preventive measure in the struggle against nuclear and radiological terrorism could serve as a basis for cooperation. My preliminary estimate is that the establishment of monitoring devices in a model district will cost the equivalent of $250,000.

It should also be noted that all matters connected with the creation of this system are of a confidential nature and should not serve as instructions to terrorists in how to circumvent it.

Medical Aspects of Combating Acts of Bioterrorism

*Gennady G. Onishchenko**
Russian Ministry of Health

The national strategy for health protection against infectious diseases must also take into account the problem of combating bioterrorism, a problem that is the focus of increasing attention on the part of the government, the public, and specialists in many countries. Underestimating modern biological capabilities and the dangers they entail could have a disastrous impact on the national security of the state.

The imperfect nature of mechanisms for monitoring compliance with the chemical and biological weapons conventions, suspicions regarding the continuation of work on biological weapons programs, and a number of incidents involving attempts to intentionally use biological agents for terrorist purposes are evoking serious concerns that terrorists might actually use biological means as weapons.

One of the first and most illustrative examples of the use of bioterrorism was the intentional poisoning of residents of a small city in the state of Oregon (United States) in September 1984 by means of adding *Salmonella typhimurium* to the salad dressing at 10 of the city's most popular restaurants. The aim of this action was to cause a massive number of food poisoning cases and thus affect the outcome of local elections according to the interests of representatives of a cult sect. Two points are worthy of note. First, officials investigating the mass poisoning incident took a year to determine that the *Salmonella* had been introduced by terrorists. Second, the American authorities prohibited any information about this incident from being published for 12 years because of their concerns that it might serve as an example for other extremists throughout the country.

*Translated from the Russian by Kelly Robbins.

Other subsequent cases involving the attempted use of biological agents for terrorist purposes have triggered a flood of publications and numerous scientific conferences and have spurred many countries, especially the United States, to institute many legislative, legal, organizational, medical, and other measures aimed at countering bioterrorism. The United States has devoted substantial sums to the problem of fighting bioterrorism, including on matters of "internal preparedness," inasmuch as expert analyses, evaluations, and inspections have led to the conclusion that in most cases, public service agencies are not prepared to respond to terrorist attacks involving the use of biological weapons. Efforts are under way to implement a program to develop and create stockpiles of 18 new vaccines, including a new smallpox vaccine. In addition, funds have been allocated to create a stockpile of medicines and antibiotics, which are intended primarily for use by police, fire, and emergency medical personnel. Appropriate attention is being focused on the fight against terrorism in Russia as well. The Interagency Antiterrorism Commission was created in 1997, the State Duma passed the Law on Combating Terrorism in July 1998, and the Government of the Russian Federation issued a resolution establishing a federal targeted program in 1999.

Although many countries have well-prepared systems for combating ordinary terrorism and dealing with emergency situations (floods, earthquakes, accidents, and catastrophes), none has put in place a complete set of measures for meeting this new threat. This is because for many reasons it is extremely difficult to combat the use of biological agents for terrorist purposes (the large number of potential agents, the long incubation period, the lag time before symptoms of illness appear, the possibility of secondary infection and the further spread of the disease, and so forth).

Medical personnel must also play a special role when bioterrorist acts are carried out. They must understand the epidemiological situation and know the potential biological agents and the symptoms of the infectious diseases they cause, which as a rule would differ from those of naturally occurring illnesses. They must also be aware of treatment protocols and measures for preventing the spread of epidemics. However, the current state of affairs is such that most clinical microbiological laboratories have neither the capabilities nor the experience in real-life detection and identification of infectious agents from a list of those that might be used by bioterrorists, such as anthrax, brucellosis, botulism, cholera, plague, smallpox, hemorrhagic fever viruses, and others.

Biological agents of critical importance from the standpoint of civilian public service preparedness may be divided into the following three categories based on their characteristics:

1. **Category A**

- smallpox (*Variola major*)
- anthrax (*Bacillus anthracis*)

- plague (*Yersinia pestis*)
- botulism (*Clostridium botilinum*)
- tularemia (*Francisella tularensis*)
- hemorrhagic fevers (filoviruses, arenaviruses, and so forth)

2. **Category B**

- Q-fever (*Coxiella burnetii*)
- brucellosis (*Brucella spp.*)
- glanders (*Burkholderia mallei*)
- melioidosis (*Burkholderia pseudomallei*)
- viral encephalitis (Venezuelan equine encephalitis, Western equine encephalitis, Eastern equine encephalitis, and so forth)
- typhus (*Rickettsia prowazekii*)
- psittacosis (*Chlamydia psittaci*)
- foodborne agents (*Salmonella spp., Shingella dysenteriae, E. coli 0157:H7,* and so forth)
- waterborne agents (*Vibrio cholerae, Cryptosporidium parvum,* and so forth)

3. **Category C**

Newly emerging agents (antibiotic-resistant bacteria and tuberculosis, Nipah virus, AIDS, and so forth)

Without denying that health care institutions respond rather adequately to naturally occurring infectious disease outbreaks, it must be noted that a significant proportion of the methods currently used in Russia to identify pathogens do not meet the necessary standards for identifying biological agents that are used intentionally. These methods have become outdated and are unsatisfactory primarily from the standpoint of the time required to use them.

The system of scientific, organizational, and other measures aimed at improving the preparedness of the health care system for meeting the threat of bioterrorism must not undermine the measures already in place to combat infectious diseases. Instead, it should promote the constant improvement of the health care and biomedical research infrastructure and facilitate cooperation involving the capabilities of other agencies, such as the Ministry for Emergency Situations, regional units of the sanitary-epidemiological service, and relevant scientific research institutes. The most important measures to be taken in improving these efforts would include the following:

- The major regional centers, especially those with international airports, should have permanently operating infectious disease hospitals equipped to at least the P-3 biosafety level.
- These hospitals must be amenable to continuously improving their methods for treating infectious diseases, up to and including being willing to participate in clinical trials of new drugs and actually doing so.
- Regional clinical microbiological and immunological laboratories are also needed, and it is important that they be fully operational according to the highest modern standards. They should be associated with the infectious disease hospitals mentioned above and should be equipped to at least the P-3 biosafety level.
- These laboratories must be open to new technologies and methods of identifying, diagnosing, and deactivating infectious agents, and in this regard, they must support close linkages with the relevant scientific research institutes working in the given field.

The following actions should be taken as part of the Federal Scientific Research Program on Combating Bioterrorism:

- Develop new express immuno-enzyme and other test systems for detecting antigens and antibodies as markers for hemorrhagic fever viruses, smallpox, anthrax, tularemia, plague, legionellosis, malaria, and so forth.
- Develop various types of polymerase chain reaction (PCR) diagnostic tests, including those using biochip technology, for express diagnosis and detection of pathogens within a few hours or even minutes.
- Establish modern, well-equipped PCR laboratories in various regions of Russia.
- Conduct additional research on the pathogenic characteristics of especially dangerous infectious agents and search for new medications for treatment and emergency prophylaxis of individuals infected with these agents.
- Develop vaccines against infectious agents for which none yet exist or for which existing vaccines are inadequately effective or unsatisfactory for other reasons.
- Provide specialized training for medical personnel and laboratory workers in safe methods for handling, analyzing, and detecting such agents in research centers and clinics with real experience in this area.

Efforts in these areas will not only bring real results in the struggle against bioterrorism but will also improve the health care situation in general.

Roots of Terrorism

Robert McC. Adams
University of California at San Diego

In a meeting primarily devoted to enhancing the role of science and technology in reducing the threat of terrorism, this contribution takes a somewhat different perspective. The apparent suddenness of the emergence of that threat does not mean that its origins are irrelevant or impenetrable, but only that the formative and sustaining processes responsible for it deserve serious attention of a different kind. Clearly, there was a time not long ago when the international problem that now concerns us all was not yet regarded as particularly urgent anywhere, at least in the developed world. What changed, and what can we learn from those changes that may inform our efforts better to contain and eventually overcome it?

This problem primarily calls for social and behavioral science perspectives, not innovative advances in hardware or even software. Valery Tishkov and I are cochairs of an interacademy study[1] that began three years ago with a focus on ethnic violence, as terrorism had not yet drawn our attention. Having watched it rise sharply in visibility as our work continued after September 11, 2001, we have come to recognize a significant (if only partial) overlap between ethnic violence and terrorism that makes this a useful starting point.

Our committee's activities were first devoted to the North Caucasus, including a meeting with local and regional ethnic specialists and administrators. That led into a major Moscow symposium that considered not only Russian and former Soviet Union ethnic violence but also some comparative dimensions of the subject. Later, this was followed by candid and productive exchanges with senior officials in the governorate of Nizhny Novgorod, and with members of a conflict early warning network that had assembled and was functioning there. Next, there were meetings in Kazan to consider the radically different nature of pressure for change in the Tartar Republic. Most recently, in September 2002, meetings were held in Sochi concentrating on the reconstruction of the Chechen educational system as a strategic first step in reestablishing conditions for peace and reconstruction in that most difficult and tragic setting.

The challenge of diverse ethnic tensions within Russia itself has eased since the breakup of the Soviet Union, but there remains a heterogeneous group of largely Muslim, deeply entrenched ethnic and linguistic enclaves that are quasinational in outlook and character. In all, they amount to about 20 percent of the gross population of the Russian Federation. The restive members of this group, with behavior ranging from periodic threat and tension to fairly continuous, low-level hostilities, were the subject of an earlier interacademy collaboration (reported on in *Balancing and Sharing Political Power in Multiethnic Societies: Summary of a Workshop*, 1993). The ground was well prepared, in other words, to ask to what extent endemic ethnic violence was a related, possibly contributory, and sometimes perhaps even initiatory element in full-scale terrorism, as the latter became a central focus of our common concern and work.

Our existing project originated in 2000 with a Russian Academy of Sciences initiative, which the U.S. National Academies readily joined. The war in Chechnya had recently resumed in all its destructive intensity, with pitiless interpersonal violence on both sides but without the hallmarks of the al Qaeda variety of terrorism. What constructive involvement, as a convening authority if nothing more, could the two academies working jointly bring to the many ongoing and incipient problems of this kind in Russia and neighboring areas? In the days before September 11, 2001, our undertaking had from the outset a broader, more comparative, less crisis- and countermeasure-oriented agenda than would have been the case if we were beginning today.

As already noted at the outset, the new international wave of Islamist terrorism cannot be regarded as a direct derivative of, let alone a synonym for, ethnic violence. There are complex and important differences between the two. Ethnic violence is not only more diverse and geographically widespread but much more accessible to serious study than terrorism. Much but not all of it has religious overtones, with Muslims roughly as often the victims as the perpetrators.

A number of questions arise in an environment where ethnic violence is prevalent, and the phenomenon of ethnic violence and later its relationship to terrorism, whether religiously or politically motivated, can be approached from different angles. The entire committee finds itself devoting enhanced attention to the relationship of education to the control and reduction of violence and now the recruitment of terrorists. Of special concern is the problem of demobilized irregular militias who, having missed years of formal education, find themselves unemployed, unemployable, and without prospects. Among further questions the committee has been persistently concerned with are the following:

- May incidental violence spread through an internal dynamic of its own after an almost accidental origin, and then perpetuate itself and generate its own rationalizations?
- What is the role of essentially external factors, such as specific local inequities accompanying the ongoing globalization of the world's economy?
- What about center-periphery power imbalances within Russia and extending to successor states of the former Soviet Union?
- To what extent are "objective" conditions of the affected population—poverty, un- or underemployment, corruption, confiscatory tax codes or other governmental malfeasance, educational shortcomings—factors that, on the one hand, may precipitate or intensify violence but, on the other hand, may also be constructively addressed to keep it under control?
- What are the respective effects of a state's employment of military forces as opposed to civil authorities in negotiating with potentially violent groups?
- What steps are effective in building trust in order for peaceful negotiations to go forward?
- How can provisions for early warning be made more timely and useful?

These generic questions apply in the main to potentially violent ethnic tensions that are not substantially infused with religious differences. Where Islam becomes a medium of protest in its own right, many additional questions need to be addressed, for example,

- How fundamental are the differences between violent conflicts invoking national, secular, state, or ethnic group loyalties as opposed to those in which one party speaks in the name of a religion?
- What is the role of Koranic schools in this process, how are they established and staffed, how can their curricula be broadened to provide for something more than an extremely narrow, economically stultifying, religious education?
- To what extent is agitation for the replacement of civil with Sharia law, posed as a religious demand, perhaps primarily a reflection of the inadequacies of the prevailing, state-administered system of justice?

In short, we are trying to give more disciplined attention to the problem of religious versus ethnic identifications. But a widespread current heightening of the role of militant (versus moderate) Islamism in a number of regions of the Russian Federation is undeniable—even if it is often overstated in policy pronouncements and usually overestimated in public opinion at large.

A further and no less interesting and important set of questions is difficult to approach with relevant, reliable data. Those questions concern individuals who are recruited into violent movements.

- How coherent and sharply bounded are they as a generation? In what respects are their prior careers also distinctive?
- What are the feedback mechanisms that seem to reinforce their commitment?
- How do they find their places in a differentiated, inherently very centralized and hierarchical, protest structure? Do they experience regular episodes of alienation and detachment, and if so, under what conditions?
- Apart from the extreme stresses, such as military defeat in Afghanistan, how often, and how, is it possible for individuals to break away from the movement? What inducements can assist in this process?

Ideological terrorism does not arise in a vacuum from a few unstable individuals who go berserk. Highly relevant is a recent comprehensive review of terrorism in the Middle East by Scott Atran, "Genesis of Suicide Terrorism,"[2] which concludes that those involved exhibit "no appreciable psychopathology and are as educated and economically well-off as the surrounding communities." Rather, a group process generates true believers. "A first line of defense is to get the *communities* from which the suicide attackers stem to stop the attacks by learning how to minimize the receptivity of mostly ordinary people to recruiting organizations" [italics added]. The absolutist mentality often ascribed to terrorists has been observed upon inspection to be associated with pragmatic adaptive behavior closely attuned with reality.

It is also important to consider the environment in which ideological terrorism arises. Most non-Western societies, including Muslim societies, are disadvantaged in demographic and economic respects. High fertility places heavy demands on resources for growth and general well-being, with the high proportion of children and very young resulting in high dependency ratios, adverse pressure on educational systems, high unemployment, poor prospects for stable family formation, and regressive distribution of incomes—but at the same time, wide exposure to high expectations through media. Nondemocratic regimes are characteristic in many such societies, repressing even moderate forms of political opposition and thus opening doors to more radical, more effectively conspiratorial ones. In these circumstances, it is hardly surprising that social movements emerge with revivalist ideologies—perceiving threats to traditional values and institutions, and holding a vision of restoration of these societies to a state of traditional purity.

Islam lacks any central unifying doctrine or hierarchical structure. Given its vast heterogeneity and geographical diversity and its deep internal schisms and rivalries, the rapid spread of allegedly Islamic terrorism across many kinds of boundaries is a new and unprecedented facet. Helping to explain the spread of the new militancy, however, is that it surely feeds upon another development that is somewhat older but still new in its global dominance, that is, the bundle of trends commonly identified with globalization. We would like to think of economic integration and development as a positive force—and generally it has been in the industrialized world. However, this positive aspect is not truly global. The overwhelming bulk of North American trade takes place within the North American Free Trade Agreement (NAFTA) and of European trade within Europe. In the 1960s the richest fifth of the world's population had a total income 30 times greater than the poorest fifth. By 1998 the ratio had grown to 74 to 1. Making this trend even more dangerous is the imbalance between the location of the bulk of the world's scarce nonrenewable resources, such as petroleum, and the regions of consumption. The Middle East accounts for just 6 percent of oil consumption but has 65 percent of total known reserves, while the United States alone consumes 30 percent and has only 6 percent of reserves. How completely can we afford to ignore the impression that an irreplaceable resource is being wastefully consumed without regard to the wider, long-term interest of the global commons?

Market forces associated with globalization can increase inequalities within nation-states, not just across larger world regions. What assurance is there of justice and equity in the relations between centers and peripheries? May not the homogenization of commercial popular culture in the hands of media giants provoke a natural reaction of intensified ethnic identities? Moreover, the perception of injustice or the threat of cultural loss, and their frequently less than one-to-one correspondence with "objective reality," can have major community impacts that escape the notice of outside observers.

In contrast with what we are experiencing with modern terrorism, most ethnic conflicts fortunately do not normally involve implacable hostilities or merciless attacks upon the fabric of civil society. Therefore, it is often possible to find ways to reconcile them before some initial incident of violence degenerates into a spiral of retaliatory violence. Ethnic rivals are also less embedded in secretive planning than those who have crossed over the line into outright terrorism. Hence, we can learn about them and about the interplay of proximate and more remote forces contributing to their complex, multilevel manifestations directly from informants, and thus at least indirectly from participants. At least some of that understanding is transferable to the much more refractory subject of terrorist cells and planning.

More so than terrorist organizations like al Qaeda, potentially violent ethnic groups are rarely homogeneous. They frequently factionalize, break up, form new alliances, and are often not uniformly adversarial or supportive with regard to the states or other civil entities with which they deal. Issues and events that turn out to be polarizing and the immediate precipitators of violence are often symbolic rather than substantive and can be recognized only in retrospect. Careful study of particulars can be rewarding, since detailed knowledge on the part of negotiators conveys a useful sense of deep awareness and concern to be deployed during their meetings with representatives or spokespersons of ethnic communities. The abruptness of some threatening rate of change often turns out to be as important as the magnitude of change itself in precipitating violence. Real peacemaking and peacekeeping require transparency in the give-and-take of negotiation and readiness to work through all available third parties as partners. Purely military solutions are seldom if ever effective. Ultimatums, deadlines, and decisive positions not open to shadings and renegotiation tend to be major obstacles to peaceful solutions.

All of these tactics and attitudes are just as vital in dealing with terrorist groups even if there is absolutely no direct communication with them, for in that case we have to turn our attention to intermediaries and interlocutors wherever we can find them. We need to avoid at all costs seeing terrorists as discrete groups of fanatics to be met with narrowly specific countermeasures, instead seeing them as groups of extremists who depend on continuously interacting with and drawing recruits from an immense, largely passive population reservoir. The terrorists' tactic is to distort and magnify both their own exploits and the latent perceived senses of repression, exclusion, injustice, and impoverishment. This is what we must work tirelessly to correct.

The most immediately practical applications of this interacademy activity will largely be found in Russia, not in the United States. The U.S. members of our joint committee are acutely conscious of this fact, which dictates careful attention to maintaining a strictly consultative role. Our own contribution comes from engagement in dialogue, not from any misapprehension that such dialogue will be directly determinative of policy: Our presence supports efforts to maintain broader comparative perspectives, to explore the widest possible range of alternatives, and to maintain a concern for long-term outcomes as well as immediate ones and for human rights issues.

We believe additionally there is something highly constructive in the example of the effectiveness of the cooperation between U.S. and Russian groups of social scientists committed to a common problem such as the control and reduction of violence. The Russian members, with years of field experience, a well-developed, quantitative database, and many major analytical and descriptive publications to their credit, have an excellent command of the interplay of demographic and sociological factors, of formal employment and cost-of-living statistics, and of detailed event sequences. Their impressive early warning networks may be the best means available for forecasting and thus averting violence. Aspects of the informal economy and perceived outcomes of shifting patterns of land use and tenure are more difficult to monitor, as are sources of dangerous tensions. American investigators bring their particular strengths in the study of ethnic identity formation, concern for identifying symbolic sources of action, dissension, and boundaries, and perhaps in formulating alternative governance structures. The mix is proving to be a remarkably productive and harmonious one.

It may be helpful, as planning for further interacademy efforts gets under way in this field, to specify some operating parameters we have felt it important to follow consistently:

• Participants have been acutely conscious of the long and rewarding tradition of interacademy cooperation. In a sensitive, easily misunderstood area like this, it has been an essential principle to maintain candid, ongoing communication on the progress of our work with the leadership of both academies.

• Our objective is scientific inquiry, including the development of a more adequate theoretical base for the field as a whole. We take no part in intelligence gathering or planning for the active suppression of violence, while recognizing that these must go on in defense of civil society.

• While there are practical limits, inquiries of a scientific character require (fairly) open dialogue with informants, interlocutors, and sometimes even potential adversaries.

• Narrowly descriptive or event-oriented narratives are not always especially helpful, yet in actual ethnic confrontations, the factors at work are often highly complex and localized. Simplification comes at a cost, in other words. Moreover, ours is a field-oriented committee with an anthropological emphasis, accustomed to seeking out inputs from regional and local administrators and researchers rather than limiting itself to high-level meetings in national capitals. The balance we seek to strike accepts this orientation and yet seeks to abstract from it relatively generalized processes, factors, causes, and—very hesitantly and informally—recommendations.

In a setting devoted not so much to causes as to countermeasures, this account must aim at brevity. There are, however, a number of post-September 11, 2001, published studies and reports of the National Academies complex that cover some of the same ground more fully, albeit dealing with the issue in an almost exclusively U.S. domestic context. They include *Terrorism: Perspectives from the Behavioral and Social Sciences* (2002) and *Discouraging Terrorism: Some Implications of 9/11* (2002). In addition, behavioral and social science findings also figure in the comprehensive Academy report of the committee cochaired by Lewis Branscomb and Richard Klausner, *Making the Nation Safer: The Role of Science and Technology in Countering Terrorism* (2002).

To summarize, active defense of civil society against terrorist violence is, of course, necessary. Alongside it, however, there is a no less indispensable place for ongoing, multilevel, constructive dialogues with the central masses of ethnic populations. These dialogues not only vent grievances but also act upon every aspect of social rehabilitation, education, employment, health, and other needs, and to be effective they need to remain carefully independent of security personnel and most security considerations. Enhancement of the role of intermediaries; stress on long-term, mutual adjustments; a cultivation of trust; the maintenance of transparency in negotiations; and an avoidance of fixed, unyielding positions are all interlocking, key principles of behavior. But with every possible degree of care in consistently maintaining this stance, it remains clear that, in the near term, there are no swift and miraculous solutions that will lead to the eradication of the new and virulent wave of international terrorism.

NOTES

1. Project on Conflict and Reconstruction in Multiethnic Societies, Office for Central Europe and Eurasia, Policy and Global Affairs, the National Academies.

2. Atran, S. 2003. Genesis of suicide terrorism. Science 299:1534-39.

The Department of Homeland Security: Background and Challenges

*Raphael Perl**
Congressional Research Service

This presentation is divided into two parts. It begins with background on creation of the Department of Homeland Security (DHS) and addresses the issue of how and why this new department came to be. It then focuses on policy issues and challenges facing the new department.

WHY A DEPARTMENT OF HOMELAND SECURITY?

How did the idea of the establishment of a department of homeland security evolve into the biggest U.S. government reorganization in American history—and not only the biggest but also the most diverse merger of functions and responsibilities?

In the early 1990s, Americans increasingly became concerned about terrorism on our soil. This concern was fueled by the World Trade Center bombing in 1993, the Oklahoma City bombing, and the discovery of a bomb at the Atlanta Olympics in 1994. Moreover, it became increasingly evident to the American public that terrorism had a growing sophisticated and global reach, a perception fueled by overseas events such as the bombings in 1998 of the U.S. embassies in Kenya and Tanzania, and the subsequent bombing of the U.S.S. *Cole* in Yemen.

Hand in hand with this development came a recognition that the security environment after the cold war had shifted dramatically—that power was devolving from the nation-state to the individual and to transnational, or subnational, groups and organizations; that individuals and disaffected groups were seeking and might gain access to weapons of mass destruction; and that globalization,

---

*The views presented are those of the author and not necessarily those of the Congressional Research Service.

free trade, and the expansion of democratic regimes provided a relatively unregulated environment for terrorist and criminal groups worldwide.

The result was a series of U.S. commissions in the late 1990s that looked at differing aspects of U.S. national security, including the threat of weapons of mass destruction and terrorism—the Hart-Rudman Commission, the Gilmore Commission, and the National Commission on Terrorism. At the same time, individual members of Congress had expressed concern that the United States did not have a cohesive, threat-driven, counterterrorism strategy. Some in Congress also expressed concern over the difficulty of ascertaining how much money was allocated to combat terrorism and where it was going.

Many proposals for reform were announced, most recommending more centralized policy direction. Some favored keeping and strengthening existing institutions. Others proposed establishing a coordinating office within the office of the vice-president, and yet others sought to merge a few federal agencies into a larger one. Reform was debated, but before the attacks of September 11, 2001, counterterrorism was simply not the top priority of the U.S. law enforcement and intelligence communities.

After September 11, 2001, priorities changed rapidly and dramatically. There was strong pressure for Congress and the administration to act decisively, and there was strong pressure from the intelligence community to focus any dramatic organizational mergers and reassignment of responsibilities away from them. Shortly thereafter (October 2001), President Bush, arguably in an attempt to preempt action from Congress, created an Office of Homeland Security designed to coordinate domestic terrorism efforts. Some members of Congress and some experts in the field, however, recommended a new federal agency or full department to integrate and heighten antiterrorism efforts. In 2002 the Bush administration sponsored its own proposal along these lines, and on November 19, 2002, Congress passed the Homeland Security Act of 2002 (P.L. 107-296). The president named Tom Ridge, former director of the Office of Homeland Security, to be secretary of the new Department of Homeland Security created by the act. The Senate confirmed Ridge's nomination.

The creation of the new department constitutes the most substantial reorganization of the federal government agencies since the National Security Act of 1947, which placed the different military departments under a secretary of defense and created the National Security Council (NSC) and Central Intelligence Agency (CIA).

When we look at the emerging Department of Homeland Security, we see that it incorporates 22 government agencies and some 179,000 people into a single organization. We also see an organization with

- a proposed budget for FY 2004 of $36.2 billion—roughly one-tenth the size of the nation's military defense budget ($380 billion). Note that overall these amounts constitute roughly a 7 percent jump in domestic defense spending.

- customs and border protection responsibilities
- emergency preparedness and response functions
- an intelligence analysis and infrastructure protection mission
- a science and technology mission
- coordination functions involving the federal government, state and local governments, foreign governments, and the private sector
- narcotics control functions that at the same time house the Secret Service, Coast Guard, and Immigration and Naturalization Services (INS)

A DHS reorganization plan of November 25, 2002, sets out a blueprint for the new organization. Included are five directorates: (1) Border and Transportation Security, (2) Emergency Preparedness and Response, (3) Science and Technology, (4) Information Analysis and Infrastructure Protection, and (5) Management.

POLICY ISSUES AND CHALLENGES

What are some of the immediate and long-term policy issues and challenges facing the new department? At least seven are worthy of note:

1. building an effective organization, that is, start-up
2. assigning/dividing jurisdictional responsibilities
3. processing and sharing of intelligence
4. integrating science and technology
5. interacting with Congress
6. defining relationships with the military
7. adding value over preexisting structures and relationships

Woven throughout these challenges is an ongoing theme of increasing coordination from merging related organizations into a single focal point and by creating new and innovative interagency coordinating mechanisms.

Building an Effective Organization

The immediate challenge facing the new department is clearly start-up: How quickly can DHS be up and running? The department formally began operating on January 24, 2003, and by March 1 had absorbed representatives from most of its component parts. The formal process of transferring agencies is expected to be completed by September 30, 2003, but analysts suggest full integration of agencies will take at least several years.

Notwithstanding, as a practical matter, the new department today is preoccupied with day-to-day start-up issues: finding a physical location, improving communications capabilities, and personnel management tasks. Finding a location for the agency is key. DHS headquarters is currently at a temporary location with the majority of additional personnel scattered elsewhere. Practical staff questions about, for example, new office location and supervisor, remain for the most part unanswered.

Questions abound about how the new organizational components will communicate with each other. Linking phone systems and databases (most of the 22 agencies have their own internal computer systems and communications systems, as well as different e-mail systems) remains a pressing challenge of the first magnitude.

Human resources issues abound as well, for example, hiring, firing, retirement, processing of the payroll, and assignment to new tasks. Enormous pressure exists to fill positions. Yet, as of early March 2003, most of the senior and critical jobs in DHS were still unfilled. Only 3 of the department's top 23 managers had been confirmed by the Senate, and nominees for most of those jobs had not been decided.

What are some of the challenges and practical problems facing DHS as it seeks to integrate agencies such as the Coast Guard, the INS, and the Transportation Security Administration (TSA) into one organization, while at the same time not incorporating others, such as the FBI and CIA? Compounding this concern is the relative autonomy of some of the transferred federal agencies, such as the Coast Guard and Secret Service. What new controls and guidance will they face? In a broader context, the new department has been likened to an interior ministry but without a national police component.

A major challenge facing the department is how to effectively join border security functions and interior functions into an organization that has centralized leadership and decentralized operations. Moreover, DHS must coordinate a network of disaster response capabilities, while at the same time seeking to become a central focal point for analysis and dissemination of intelligence. At the same time, the organization is charged with joining research and development efforts to detect and counter potential terror attacks with the goal of shoring up vulnerabilities of the nation's critical infrastructures to include its ports, utilities, and food and water supply—no small task!

Assigning and Dividing Jurisdictional Responsibilities

A second issue relates to the functions that differing DHS components will perform. Clearly, in this new organizational arrangement, some agencies, such as the Coast Guard and Secret Service, will probably not change dramatically in the way they are managed and operate. However, the way that functions of other agencies will be orchestrated in this new setup is far from finalized. Yet to be seen are the additional functions or components that will emerge from the department. One new function is likely to be creation of a full-time, permanent red team that will simulate terrorist threats and test the security of installations, such as nuclear plants and government buildings. Another new function assigned to the department is oversight of visa processing. How will this be worked out with the State Department? Moreover, what, if any, will the operational role of DHS be in its many areas of responsibility?

Processing and Sharing of Intelligence

A third and crucial issue is how intelligence will be moved through the system and shared. It is not clear the degree to which the department will have its own intelligence analysis group. Absent a strong in-house intelligence analysis component, it may be that DHS will have to rely more heavily on predigested information from many other agencies. As it starts up, the new department's intelligence role will be limited, primarily linking analysis from a newly created interagency Terrorist Threat Integration Center (TTIC; see below) to efforts to strengthen the defenses of critical infrastructures.

On January 28, 2003, President Bush announced creation of the Terrorist Threat Integration Center. The new center will be responsible for fusing and analyzing domestic and foreign intelligence related to terrorist threats. It is chaired by the Director of Central Intelligence (DCI) and will be staffed by members of the intelligence community, the law enforcement community, and DHS. Reportedly, the center will have access to all intelligence information available to the U.S. government, both raw and processed.

Creation of the TTIC, however, is considered controversial by some in Congress who are concerned it undermines the language and intent of the Homeland Security Act, that is, that the TTIC's functions be performed within the Information Analysis and Infrastructure Directorate of DHS. Other analysts express concern that the TTIC structure will increasingly involve the DCI in domestic intelligence issues, a prickly arena potentially prone to collision with civil liberties safeguards.

One of the functions of the TTIC will reportedly be to maintain an up-to-date database of known and suspected terrorists that will be available to federal and nonfederal officials, as needed. This function is a terrorism counterpart to EPIC, the El Paso Intelligence Center. Currently, in the drug area, a policeman on the beat can, in real time, contact EPIC and get information on a suspect from a national drug trafficking database.

There are other complex issues as well. What role will DHS play in the flow of information from the national level to the first responder and vise versa? What role will the new department have in facilitating the flow of information to the public, to the private sector, to international organizations, and to foreign governments? Some argue that homeland security is in its essence global security. Thus, homeland security must be based on the underlying principle that security for one will never be achieved without security for all. Yet to be defined is how DHS will interact with the international community.

Integrating Science and Technology

An important issue is what role will DHS play in the area of promoting and integrating science and technology into the homeland security policy equation. The pragmatic answer here is "more," especially in the area of threat and vulnerability assessment. The National Academies' report _Making the Nation Safer: The Role of Science and Technology in Combating Terrorism_ has outlined a policy framework.

A current policy debate within DHS centers on whether the new information analysis directorate should focus on vulnerabilities or threats. Whatever the outcome, analysts predict that increasingly systems analysis and risk management will be brought to bear on this debate. The Office of Management and Budget (OMB), the General Accounting Office (GAO), and the NAE have emphasized the importance of the risk management sciences to the nation's homeland security effort. Moreover, the intelligence community is increasingly employing such methodologies. At some point, we are likely to see widespread use—and perhaps even daily use—of a broad range of terrorist threat-based risk assessment matrixes by government officials charged with homeland security decision making.

In September 2002 the President's Council of Advisors on Science and Technology issued a report on maximizing the contribution of science and technology to homeland security. Stressed was a need for flexibility for research and development programs in terms of organization, personnel, and budget. Moreover, the report proposed a DHS organizational structure for research and development to be headed by an undersecretary for science and technology, an idea subsequently adopted. The report also recommended the use of risk management, based on risk assessment, in the budgeting process and in research and development programs to determine infrastructure interaction models. The new DHS Science and Technology Directorate will coordinate research and development programs, including preparation for and responding to threats from weapons of mass destruction. A major responsibility of the new DHS Science and Technology Directorate is to join research and development efforts to detect and counter potential terrorist attacks. The DHS requests for funding for research and development totaled $761 million for fiscal year 2003 and $1 billion for fiscal year 2004.

Relationship with Congress

An important question is how will Congress relate to this new entity as the legislature performs its traditional functions of overseeing, legislating, and appropriating money. Much of this depends on how Congress chooses to organize, either with a new structure or by restructuring its committees. Both the new department and the threats it addresses defy traditional jurisdictional power structures. Today in Congress, 88 committees and subcommittees have oversight responsibilities for agencies that have been folded into DHS.

Because of this, both houses of Congress have recognized a need for integrating these jurisdictional complexities. In the House of Representatives, the leadership has created a new House Select Committee on Homeland Security. The committee is chaired by Representative Christopher Cox of California, who sees one of the major challenges of the committee as integrating the efforts of FBI, CIA, Pentagon, and intelligence communities into a homeland security framework.

The House committee has five subcommittees, which mirror the five directorates at DHS. The five subcommittees are

1. Infrastructure and Border Security
2. Rules
3. Emergency Preparedness and Response
4. Cybersecurity, Science, and Research and Development
5. Intelligence and Counterterrorism

In addition, new Subcommittees on Homeland Security under both House and Senate Appropriations Committees have been created.

When discussing government failures preceding September 11, 2001, the focus tends to be on failures of the executive branch, but questions have also been raised about the effectiveness of legislative activities. The Subcommittee on Rules is studying whether Congress should structure itself to more effectively perform its responsibilities in light of the new policy and organizational focus afforded the issue of homeland security.

Defining, or Redefining, Relationships with the Military

An issue of emerging importance is the role of the military in homeland security—of the Department of Defense (DOD), the National Guard, and in some instances the state militias.

On October 1, 2002, DOD activated a new regional combatant command, Northern Command (NORCOM), which plays the lead role in homeland defense for missile or air attack defense. Yet unclear is where DOD will fit into a support role for other homeland security missions, such as intelligence analysis; intelligence gathering and law enforcement; research and development, particularly in the chemical/biological area; and use of reserves and the National Guard in functions ranging from protecting airports and borders to assisting in the wake of national disasters.

We must be mindful that if we look at missions from the DOD perspective, much interest centers on keeping overseas military operations as the department's primary focus. Providing personnel and resources to the support of a homeland security mission, though important, is not DOD's top priority.

Value Added

Finally, we must ask ourselves what added value, if any, will DHS provide over preexisting structures and relationships. Arguably, it will better integrate state and local government activities with national antiterrorism and homeland defense efforts, and it will provide better coordination of law enforcement functions among component federal agencies and thereby enhance the efficiency of such operations.

There is an expectation that DHS will provide a more effective use of science and technology in combating terrorism and supporting homeland defense. Certainly, we can expect an enhanced role for science and technology because of DHS activity. To the degree that DHS lends support to science and technology projects on a large scale, a challenge will be not to overlook smaller, creative, and perhaps more independent projects that may look at things differently. In this regard, independent input from organizations such the National Academies may contribute much to preserving a spirit of open and promising scientific inquiry.

Last, it is hoped that DHS will provide a better model for government structures in an increasingly borderless, jurisdictionless, interconnected, interdisciplinary world. However, civil libertarians are quick to remind us that a potential downside of centralization of power in institutions is the possibility of a climate less conducive to open inquiry and dissent.

CONCLUSION

Who would have thought even 10 years ago that the United States would so dramatically reorganize the federal government? In one sense, what the DHS model attempts to do is deal a serious blow to the nineteenth century musket assembly-line model of government, where every agency had a separate piece of the action, and where at the end of the day, the pieces fitted together fairly well. Although in most instances such compartmentalized models served us relatively well for certain functions, they may be losing relevance in the world of today and the world of the future. If successful, DHS will enhance homeland security. Perhaps even more important, a smoothly functioning DHS could well provide the United States with a government that will function more efficiently and serve as a model for other organizational fusions in our nation and abroad.

It is possible to take a solid or sound path to the wrong destination. It is also possible to take a good path to the right destination at the wrong time. Clearly, there are downsides to massively reorganizing the federal government especially at a time when the nation perceives itself at war. There is strength in the argument that at such critical times, individual and organizational efforts should be focused on combating the threat of terrorism and not diverted by a need to find office space, define turf, or get working telephones.

On the other hand, if not now, when? Is it realistic to expect threats to the homeland of any nation to diminish in the immediate future? Without the events of September 11, 2001, it is unlikely that any reorganization of substance would have had the impetus to go further than the planning stage. A fully operational DHS is expected to have the resources readily available for controlling borders, fighting terrorism, and combating illegal activity generally and the power to prioritize such resources and use them more efficiently.

What will the impact of DHS actions be on earlier priorities and policies? Will anticounterfeiting efforts suffer because the Secret Service is no longer in the Treasury Department? Will marine safety activities of the Coast Guard lose their importance in a homeland security organization? Will antidrug efforts be helped, or harmed, by infusion of new resources along the U.S. border, resources directed by DHS, not by the Department of Justice?

The issue is part of a broader question: Is the nation overreacting by overprioritizing terrorism? We must ask ourselves, to what degree does America's expenditure of unending energy and countless billions of dollars constitute a follow-on victory for al Qaeda by weakening our economy and relatively open, unregulated lifestyle? As a society, are we diverting money and attention in an area, or in areas, that are not productive?

What can science, technology, and engineering offer here? How can the scientific and engineering community support government and industry decision making in a world of increasing terrorist risk? The National Academies and other scientific organizations continue to face these questions head on.

APPENDIXES

Appendix A

Agendas

U.S.-Russian Workshop on the Problems of Urban Terrorism

Presidium, Russian Academy of Sciences
Moscow
March 17, 2003

Opening of Workshop
    Nikolai A. Platé—Vice President, RAS
    Konstantin V. Frolov—Director, RAS Institute of Machine Science, Cochair
    George Bugliarello—President Emeritus and University Professor,
    Polytechnic University, Cochair

Analysis of the Threats and Consequences of Acts of Urban Terrorism
    Vladimir Z. Dvorkin, RAS Institute of World Economy and International
    Relations

Urban Security and September 11, 2001, in New York City
    George Bugliarello, Polytechnic University

Lessons Learned from the Terrorist Acts During the Performance of *Nord-Ost*
in Moscow from the Point of View of Enforcement Agencies
    Yevgeny A. Kolesnikov, FSB

Discussion

Complex and Dangerous Impacts of Terrorist Acts with Severe Consequences
    Igor A. Kirillov, GNT, Kurchatov Institute

Protection of Chemical Enterprises in Cities
    Pavel A. Storozhenko, Scientific Center, GNIIKhTEOS
Measures for Prevention of Catastrophic Results from Bioterrorism in Cities
    Vladimir G. Ivkov, RAS Pushchino Scientific Center

Toxic Chemicals and Explosive Materials: Terrorism-Related Issues for the
Research Community, Chemical Industry, and Government
    Alexander MacLachlan, Dupont (retired)

Discussion

Role of the Ministry of Internal Affairs in Ensuring the Security of Housing
and Commercial Buildings
    Sergey A. Starostin, All-Russian Scientific Research Institute, Ministry of
    Internal Affairs

The Three R's: Lessons Learned from September 11, 2001
    Robert Prieto, Parsons Brinckerhoff Inc.

Discussion

Bioterrorism
    Russ Zajtchuk, Chicago Hospitals International

Role of Ministry for Extreme Situations and Executive Agencies of the City of
Moscow in Extreme Situations Resulting from Acts of Terrorism
    Aleksandr M. Yeliseev, Moscow Main Administration for Civil Defense
    and Emergency Situations

Protection of the Transportation System from Acts of Terrorism
    Konstantin V. Frolov, RAS Institute of Machine Science

General Discussion

Summary of Results of the Workshop
    Konstantin V. Frolov—Director, RAS Institute of Machine Science, Cochair
    George Bugliarello—President Emeritus and University Professor,
    Polytechnic University, Cochair

U.S.-Russian Workshop on the Problems of Computer Terrorism

Presidium, Russian Academy of Sciences
Moscow
March 18, 2003

Opening of Workshop
Igor B. Fedorov—Rector, N. E. Bauman Moscow State Technical
University, Cochair
Anita K. Jones—University of Virginia, Cochair

A Perspective on Cybersecurity Research in the United States
Wm. A. Wulf, President, NAE

Analysis of the Threat of Cyber Attacks in Russia to Large-Scale Systems for
Control of Transportation
Mikhail B. Ignatyev, St. Petersburg State University of Aerospace
Instrumentation

Discussion

Cyberattacks as an Amplifier in Terrorist Strategy
Lewis M. Branscomb, Harvard University

Cybercrime and Cyberterrorism
Mikhail P. Sychev, N. E. Bauman Moscow State Technical University

Discussion

Comments on IT Safety
Anatoly Streltsov, National Security Council

Protecting Bank Networks from Acts of Computer Terrorism
Boris I. Skorodumov, Institute of Banking Affairs of the Association of
Russian Banks

Comprehensive Training of Specialists to Counter Information Security Threats
Nikolai V. Medvedev, N. E. Bauman Moscow State Technical University

Discussion

Computer Security Training for Professional Specialists and Personnel
Associated with the Necessity for Countermeasures to Computer Attacks
    Aleksey I. Tolstoy, Moscow Engineering Physics Institute

Information Assurance Education in the United States
    Anita K. Jones, University of Virginia

Discussion

Protection of Electronic Documents in Computer Systems
    Valery A. Konyavsky, Scientific Research Institute of Problems of
    Computer Technology and Information, Ministry of Communications and
    Information

Experience of International Cooperation in the Field of Scientific Support for
Antiterrorist Activity
    Anatoly P. Sudoplatov, Moscow State University

Certain Aspects of the Development of Conditions Favorable to Cyberterrorism
and the Main Areas of Cooperation in the Struggle Against It
    Igor A. Sokolov, RAS Institute for Informatics Problems

About the Activity of the Publicly Funded Center of Internet Security
    Aleksey A. Soldatov, GNT Kurchatov Institute

General Discussion
    Consideration of the Possibility of Joint Projects

Summary of Results of Workshop
    Igor B. Fedorov—Rector, N. E. Bauman Moscow State Technical
    University, Cochair
    Anita K. Jones—University of Virginia, Cochair

Program for the Meeting of the RAS and NRC Counterterrorism Committees for Development of a Program of Joint Activities

March 19–20, 2003

March 19, 2003

Opening

- Opening of the Meeting of Joint Committees, Cochairs Yevgeny P. Velikhov, Kurchatov State Research Center of Atomic Energy, and Siegfried S. Hecker, Los Alamos National Laboratory
- Welcoming Remarks, Yury S. Osipov, RAS President
- Welcoming Remarks, Wm. A. Wulf, NAE President
- Welcoming Remarks and Presentation, Valentin A. Sobolev, Secretary, Security Council of the Russian Federation

Session on Counterterrorism Activities in Russia and the United States and Selected Themes

- International Cooperation and Russian Activities in Counterterrorism, Anatoly Y. Safonov, Deputy Minister for Foreign Affairs
- National Academies Activities in Counterterrorism, Wm. A. Wulf, NAE
- Activities of Russia in the Struggle with Transnational Crime and Terrorism, Anatoly S. Kulikov, Duma
- RAS Activities in Counterterrorism, Nikolai P. Laverov and Nikolai A. Platé, RAS Vice Presidents
- Report of Committee of the National Academies, *Making the Nation Safer: The Role of Science and Technology in Countering Terrorism*, Lewis M. Branscomb, Harvard University
- Countering Illegal Circulation of Radioactive Materials, Vladimir M. Kutsenko, Minatom

Session of Joint Committee on Selected Themes

- Medical Aspects of Controlling Acts of Bioterrorism, Gennady G. Onishenko, First Deputy Minister of Health and Chief Public Health Doctor of Russia
- Ethnic Roots and Problems of Terrorism, Valery A. Tishkov, RAS Institute of Ethnology and Anthropology; Robert McC. Adams, University of California at San Diego

- Report of Cochairs of Two Workshops, George Bugliarello, Polytechnic University, and Konstantin V. Frolov, RAS Institute of Machine Science; Anita K. Jones, University of Virginia, and Igor B. Fedorov, N. E. Bauman Moscow State Technical University
- Views on Bioterrorism, Aleksandr S. Spirin RAS Protein Institute, Russ Zajtchuk, Chicago Hospitals International

Meeting of Joint Committee

- Consideration of the U.S.-Russian Joint Program (goals, approaches, anticipated results, priorities), Yevgeny P. Velikhov, Kurchatov State Research Center of Atomic Energy, and Siegfried S. Hecker, Los Alamos National Laboratory
- Membership and Interactions of Committee, Velikhov and Hecker

March 20, 2003

Session of Joint Committee on Selected Themes

- Electromagnetic Terrorism, Vladimir Ye. Fortov, RAS Moscow High Temperature Institute (Yury V. Parfyonov, Institute for High Energy Densities); Siegfried S. Hecker, Los Alamos National Laboratory
- Nuclear and Radiological Terrorism, Leonid Bolshov, RAS Nuclear Safety Institute
- Department of Homeland Security: Background and Challenges, Raphael F. Perl, Congressional Research Service

Meeting of Joint Committee

- Adoption of a Program of Joint Activity (goals, approaches, anticipated results)
- Consideration and Agreement of Priorities for Cooperation
- Plans for Committee Activities
- Near-Term Steps and the Next Meeting

Agenda for Visits to Ministries of the Russian Federation

NRC Committee on Counterterrorism Challenges for Russia and the United States

March 21, 2003

Ministry of Emergency Situations
Deputy Minister Mikhail I. Faleev
Gen./Prof. Vasily V. Baterev
Maj. Gen. Mikhail A. Shakhramanian
Vladimir Novikov, Head of the Department for Emergency Prevention and Response

Ministry of Internal Affairs
Gen. Sergey Ivanovich Girko, Head of Institute
Fedor Gregorovich Sery, Head of Scientific Laboratory Responsible for Combating Terrorism, Kidnapping, etc.
Sergey A. Nyrikov, Head of Scientific Laboratory Responsible for Research on Terrorism and Transportation
Yuri Maravovich Antonyan, Head Scientific Contributor to VNII MVD
Vitaly Y. Kvashis, Chief Research Fellow, Distinguished Scholar
Sergey A. Starostin, VNII MVD

Ministry of Foreign Affairs
Deputy Foreign Minister Anatoly. Y. Safonov

Ministry of Atomic Energy
Vladimir Petrovich Kuchinov, Head of International Relations Department

APPENDIX B

Annex 2

To the Agreement of Cooperation in Science, Engineering, and Medicine Between the Russian Academy of Sciences and the U.S. National Academies

Russian-American Cooperation in Counterterrorism

The U.S. National Academies and the Russian Academy of Sciences, recognizing the urgent need for collaborative science- and technology-based efforts across the broad spectrum of areas related to prevention, response, and mitigation of terrorism, will undertake a new joint program under the guidance of Russian and American standing committees. The committees will organize joint studies on how to cope effectively with emerging threats and challenges related to terrorism. The program will provide an independent avenue for scientists and specialists to perform studies and analyses; to exchange data and findings; to hold workshops, seminars, and conferences; to train specialists; to educate representatives of the media and other relevant organizations; and to recommend future cooperative programs and projects between appropriate organizations.

Areas of particular interest for this effort may include but are not necessarily limited to

- radiological terrorism, including protection of radioactive sources and wastes
- access by terrorists to nuclear materials and technologies and the security of nuclear materials and facilities
- bioterrorism against both humans and the food supply, including preventing access by terrorists to dangerous pathogens and application of new technologies for prevention and detection of terrorist incidents and for responses to them

- chemical terrorism, including prevention of access by terrorists to dangerous chemicals and application of new technologies for prevention and detection of terrorist incidents and for responses to them
- electromagnetic terrorism and the prevention of damage to electronic equipment sensitive to electromagnetic effects
- safety of vulnerable industrial and energy infrastructures and transportation facilities
- cyberterrorism, including education and training of specialists
- improvement and harmonization of the international and national legal basis for combating terrorism
- the social, economic, and ethnic roots of terrorism

In furtherance of the above-mentioned activities, the two committees will commission papers and analyses in specific areas of high priority involving American and Russian specialists with relevant expertise. Likely initial topics will be cyber-, radiological, and biological terrorism.

The committees will consist of up to 10 members each. The chairs and members of the committees will be approved by the U.S. National Academies and the Russian Academy of Sciences. Their activities will be appropriately coordinated with other interacademy activities and with intergovernmental programs.

APPENDIX C

Comprehensive Training of Specialists to Counter Information Security Threats

Nikolai V. Medvedev*
Information Security Department,
N. E. Bauman Moscow State Technical University

One of the most difficult problems encountered when connecting corporate or local networks and individual users to the Internet is that of ensuring the security of information resources. To resolve this problem, a number of technologies are used, each of them intended to counter particular classes of security threats. These include intrusion detection systems (IDS), public key infrastructure (PKI), virtual private networks (VPN), antivirus software, cryptographic systems, identification and authentication systems, security scanners, and so forth. Firewalls represent another significant type of such technologies, and their skillful application can substantially reduce the risks associated with unauthorized access to data. However, comprehensive efforts to prevent the realization of threats of unauthorized access will be successful only through the development of an optimal information security policy involving the integration of the theoretical foundations of information protection with the best possible selection of protection mechanisms to be put in place.

Only a major leading university with the appropriate methodological base is in a position to provide training for highly qualified specialists in this field. The main areas of training for specialists of this sort at N. E. Bauman Moscow State Technical University are as follows:

- theoretical foundations of engineering and technology for information protection
- methods and practices of engineering and technology for information protection

*Translated from the Russian by Kelly Robbins.

- devices and operating principles involved in automated systems
- methodology for the design, construction, and operation of secure automated systems
  - criteria and methods for assessing the security of automated systems
  - means and methods of unauthorized access to information in automated systems
  - architecture of secure computer networks
  - software, devices, and hardware for creating secure networks
  - principles of building and managing secure networks
  - rule for the organizational, technical, and legal protection of information
  - the use of software and device technologies for protecting information
  - building and operating secure databases
- systems approach to the problem of protecting information in database management systems
- mechanisms for protecting information in databases and database management systems and opportunities for circumventing them
- concepts of engineering- and technology-related means of information protection
- organizational foundations for the use of engineering- and technology-related means of information protection

After receiving training in this discipline, specialists must have an understanding of the following:

- promising areas for the development of computer security theory
- methods for information security threat analysis
- architecture of secure automated systems
- principles for the construction of secure systems
- typical attacks on secure systems
- promising areas for the development of network security technologies
- current problems of information security science and the role and place of network information security in overall efforts to ensure comprehensive information security

Specialists must know the following:

- methodological and technological foundations for comprehensive automated systems security
- threats and methods of violating systems security
- formal models providing a foundation for security systems
- standards for assessing systems security and their theoretical foundations
- methods and means of building secure systems
- methods and means of verifying and analyzing the reliability of secure systems

- methodological and technological foundations of ensuring the information security of networked automated systems
- threats and methods of violating the information security of networked automated systems
- physical processes related to technical means and systems facilitating the leakage of secure information
- typical models of attacks aimed at overcoming the security of networked automated systems, conditions under which such attacks could occur, potential consequences, and means of preventing them
- the role of the human factor in ensuring network security
- opportunities, means, and rules for applying basic software- and device-based means of protecting information in networks
- principles of the operation of basic secure network protocols
- fundamentals of using firewalls for network security
- rules for setting network security policy
- standards for evaluating secure network systems and their theoretical foundations
- methods and means of designing, building, and evaluating secure network systems
- concepts of engineering- and technology-related means of information security
- fundamental principles and methods of information security
- fundamental regulatory and reference documents regarding engineering- and technology-related means of information security
- procedures for the organization of engineering- and technology-related means of information security

They must be able to

- analyze automated systems from the standpoint of ensuring computer security
- develop security models and policies using known approaches, methods, means, and the corresponding theoretical foundations
- apply standards to evaluate the security of automated systems while analyzing and designing information security systems for them
- put in place information security systems in accordance with security assessment standards
- analyze networked automated systems from the standpoint of ensuring information security
- develop network security models and policies using known approaches, methods, means, and theoretical foundations

• apply standards to evaluate secure networked systems while analyzing and designing information security systems for automated systems

• put in place secure protocols and firewalls necessary for constructing information security systems in networks

• implement measures to counter detected threats to network security using various software- and device-based means of ensuring security in accordance with the rules for their use

• put in place information security systems in automated systems in accordance with standards for the evaluation of secure systems security

• detect threats and technical channels for data leakage

• describe (model) security targets and information security threats

• apply the most effective engineering- and technology-related methods and means of information security

• monitor the effectiveness of security measures

They must have skills in the following areas:

• working with automated systems for distributed computation and data processing

• working with automated systems documentation

• using criteria for the evaluation of automated systems security

• constructing formal models of information security systems for automated systems

• constructing and operating computer networks

• designing secure networks

• providing comprehensive analyses and evaluations of network security

• working with means for interface support with various categories of users of database management systems

• working with database management systems in various platforms

• working with means of ensuring the integrity of database management systems

• working with means of ensuring database confidentiality

• serving as a database security administrator

• conducting device-based evaluation of the energy parameters of side radiation emitted by hardware and systems

• conducting an engineering assessment of the parameters of the security zone

The special disciplines involved in helping students meet these training objectives are listed in Sections 1 through 7. Theoretical aspects of computer security are included in Sections 1 and 2.

SECTION 1: STRUCTURE OF COMPUTER SECURITY THEORY

1.1 Analysis of information security threats. Threats to confidentiality, integrity, and accessibility of information; discovery of information system parameters

1.2 Structure of computer security theory. Basic levels of information security, protection of machine data carriers, means of interaction with such carriers, and data representation and content

1.3 Basic types of attacks on automated systems. Classification of basic attacks on automated systems as well as malicious software programs

1.4 Network architecture. Distributed data processing, classification of networks by data distribution methods, comparative characteristics of various types of networks

1.5 Network organization and operation. Network standards and protocols; network operating systems; means of coordinating processing in networks; client-server systems; local, corporate, and global networks; unique computer networks; fundamentals for classifying network threats and attacks; examples of types of attacks and recommendations for building security systems; impact of the human factor on network security

SECTION 2: METHODOLOGY FOR CONSTRUCTING SECURE AUTOMATED SYSTEMS

2.1 Security models. Description of security systems using access matrixes, Harrison-Ruzzo-Ullman model, solvability of security problems, Take-Grant model for access rights distribution, expanded Take-Grant model, analysis of information channels, description of the Bell-LaPadula model, foundations for the security theorem of the Bell-LaPadula model, equivalent approaches to defining the Bell-LaPadula security model

2.2 Building systems to protect against threats of data confidentiality violations. Organizational security regimes, protection against unauthorized access, construction of password systems, cryptographic protection methods, protection against threats of confidentiality violations at the information content level

2.3 Protection of network topology. Routers, firewalls, basic outlines for using firewalls, subscription coding, virtual private networks

2.4 Means of improving the reliability of network operations. Protecting against power outages, device-based and software-based means, monitoring and distributing network loads

2.5 Basic criteria for evaluating automated systems security. Criteria and classes of protection of computer hardware and automated systems, standards for evaluating automated systems security, the Trusted Computer Systems Evaluation Criteria (TCSEC or "Orange Book") standard for evaluating computer systems security, fundamental requirements for systems security under TC-SEC, TCSEC security classifications

2.6 Concept for protecting automated systems and computer hardware according to reference documents from the State Technology Commission of the Russian Federation. Classification of computer hardware and automated systems according to documents from the State Technology Commission, requirements for security classifications

2.7 The Common Criteria for information technology security. Fundamental provisions of the Common Criteria, security requirements, protection profiles

2.8 Regulatory documents in the area of computer network security. Security standards for networks and their components, legal bases for network data security

Aspects of ensuring network security are covered in Sections 3 and 4.

SECTION 3: CONSTRUCTING SECURE NETWORKS ON THE BASIS OF NETWORK OPERATING SYSTEMS

3.1 NetWare, Windows, and UNIX network operating systems. Basic protocols; services; operations; security features; management and control features; application generation and development; compilation of application-related manuals and reference materials

3.2 Security policy. Concept of security policy, typical elements of security policy, recommendations on creating security policy, basic steps to implement security policy, maintaining and modifying security policy

3.3 Criteria for evaluating the security of network operating systems. Fundamental criteria for analyzing network security, general analytical procedures, methods for preparing expert recommendations

SECTION 4: COMPUTER NETWORK SECURITY

4.1 Internet standards and protocols. Internet standardization process, basic transmission control protocol/Internet protocol (TCP/IP), network management protocols, applied protocols and services, electronic document exchange

4.2 Operation, development, and creation of reference documents for Internet applications. Special features of creating and linking applications in various platforms, programming for the World Wide Web (WWW), Internet access to databases

4.3 Development trends. Limitations on the current architecture of the Internet, new standards and protocols, language-related tools for presenting information on the Internet, intranet networks, basic principles for ensuring security and managing distributed resources, ensuring the reliability of the Internet infrastructure

4.4 Protecting Internet communications channels. Types of communications channels used over the Internet, special characteristics involved in their protection, use of firewalls, virtual private networks

4.5 Vulnerabilities and protection of basic protocols and services. Routing protocols, TCP/IP family, search services, WWW and e-mail security, Java security

4.6 Protection of electronic document exchange. Standards and protocols for secure electronic document exchange

4.7 Protection of the Internet user's workstation. Protecting workstation software, protecting personal data, preventing viruses

4.8 Comprehensive security for Internet connections. Security of various types of Internet connections, integrating local networks into regional and global networks, controlling and analyzing the security of Internet connections

Aspects involved in ensuring the security of databases and database management systems are listed in Sections 5 and 6.

SECTION 5: CONCEPT OF DATABASE SECURITY

5.1 Understanding database security. General and specific threats to database security, requirements for database security, protecting against unauthorized access, protecting against deletions, database integrity, auditing, responsibilities and methods of database security administrators

5.2 Multilevel security. Types of security control—flow control, deletion control, access control

SECTION 6: THEORETICAL FOUNDATIONS OF SECURITY IN DATABASE MANAGEMENT SYSTEMS

6.1 Criteria for database protection. Criteria for evaluating the reliability of computer systems, the concept of security policy, joint application of various security policies as part of a single model, interpretation of TCSEC for reliable database management systems (TDI), the concept of the State Technology Commission

6.2 Security models for database management systems. Classification of models, aspects of studying security models, special points involved in applying security models to database management systems, discretionary (selective) and mandatory (authorization) security models, databases with multilevel secrecy (MLS), polyinstantiation in databases

6.3 Threats to the integrity of database management systems. Basic types of and reasons for threats to integrity, means of countering them

6.4 Metadata and data dictionaries. Creating a data dictionary, access to the data dictionary, contents and presentation of the dictionary

6.5 The transaction concept. Defining a transaction, forward and back functions, control point, rejection, the transaction as a means of isolating users

6.6 Blocking. Blocking regimes, rules for the coordination of blocking, two-phase protocol for synchronization of blocking, recognizing and eliminating dead-end situations

6.7 Reference integrity. Declarative and procedural reference integrity, external keys, means of supporting reference integrity

6.8 Rules (triggers). Goals of using rules, means of issuing commands, implementation points

6.9 Events. Defining a mechanism for events, event signals, types of event notifications, components of event mechanisms

6.10 Classification of threats to the confidentiality of database management systems. Causes, types, and basic methods of confidentiality violation, types of leaks of confidential information from database management systems, partial revelation of information, relation between data security and data access, use of logical conclusions to obtain unauthorized access to confidential information, methods of prevention, special aspects involved in using cryptographic methods

6.11 Means of identification and authentication. General information, organization of linkages between database management systems and base operating systems

6.12 Means of access management. Fundamental concepts: subjects and objects, user groups, privileges, roles, and representations; language-based means of limiting access; types of privileges: security and access privileges; conception and implementation of role mechanisms; relation between access rights under operating systems and those under database management systems; security targets; use of representations to ensure the confidentiality of information in database management systems

6.13 Auditing and subordination. Subordination of user actions, auditing of event security, journaling, registration of user actions, management of events registered, analysis of registration information

6.14 Means for maintaining heightened readiness. Device- and software-based support, cluster-based organization of database servers, parameters for building database management systems, means of creating backup copies and restoring databases

6.15 Operations administration. Administrative tasks, means, and regimes; monitoring of database management system servers

6.16 Functional saturation of database management systems. Forms of redundancy, device redundancy, data redundancy, construction of software mirrors, data printing

6.17 High-readiness systems. Description, purpose, examples

6.18 Distributed computing environments. Distributed information processing in a client-server environment, the concept of the distributed computing environment (DCE), distributed databases in computer networks, technology for remote access to database systems

6.19 Threats to the security of distributed database management systems. Threats to the accessibility, integrity, and confidentiality of data; prevention mechanisms; security for the Informix-DCE/Net system

6.20 Distributed data processing. The concept of the distributed transaction, model for transaction processing, transaction processing monitors, corporate transaction processing environment

6.21 Fixation protocols. Fixation protocols, protected fixation protocols such as Advanced Secure Early Prepare (ASEP) and others, processing of distributed transactions in databases with multilevel secrecy

6.22 Data printing. Review of data printing methods, effecting printing algorithms, comparison of approaches to database printing (Sybase and Informix)

6.23 Integrating databases and the Internet. Current trends, review of existing technologies (WebDBC and others), security issues: threats and prevention methods, development prospects

Aspects related to the physical foundations of information security are covered in Section 7.

SECTION 7: PHYSICAL FOUNDATIONS OF INFORMATION SECURITY

7.1 Physical foundations of electromagnetic emissions and stray current. Acoustoelectric transformations, focusing and distribution of source of side emissions, the nature of electromagnetic radiation in near and far zones, parasitic generation in radioelectronic equipment, types of parasitic linkages and stray current, Picard's chain, physical phenomena causing data leakages on electric current chains, grounding and power-supply devices in buildings

7.2 Signal distribution in technical channels of information leakage. Distribution of acoustic signals in the atmosphere, water, and solid environments; special characteristics of the distribution of acoustic signals in buildings; distribution of optical signals in the atmosphere and in optical fibers; distribution of radio signals in various frequencies in space and over communications lines; fundamental indicators of the signal distribution environment that affect the distance of technical channels of leakage and the quality of information received in this manner

7.3 Physical processes for suppressing harmful interference. Suppression of harmful interference from acoustoelectrical transformers; screening of electrical, magnetic, and electromagnetic fields; requirements of firewalls; field compensation; suppression of harmful interference in power supply and grounding lines; use of barriers to suppress harmful interference

7.4 Engineering-based means of security and technical protection. Fundamental engineering devices used to prevent access to information sources by unauthorized outsiders; means of managing access; classification and characterization of intrusion, fire/intrusion, and fire alarm systems; video-monitoring and video-alarm systems; means of threat neutralization; means of notification management and transmission; automated integrated security systems

7.5 Means of preventing data leakage through technical channels. Means of masking and disinformation in the optical and radio frequency ranges; means of sound isolation and absorption; means of detecting, localizing, and suppressing signals of auxiliary devices; means of suppressing signals from acoustoelectrical transformers and power supply and grounding lines; linear and spatial noise generators

The special disciplines presented above include lectures, practical training and laboratory-based exercises, and internships working with real information security equipment and software. In receiving this training, the specialist acquires practical skills in countering cyberterrorism and is capable of independently developing an enterprise-wide information security policy involving the application of a range of integrated features.

APPENDIX D

Excerpts from "Bioterrorism: A National and Global Threat"

*Gennady G. Onishchenko**
Ministry of Health of the Russian Federation

According to a study conducted by U.S. researchers in 1994, there have been more than 244 incidents involving the use of biological and chemical weapons since the end of World War I.[1] A total of 110 additional suspicious episodes were later identified in which terrorists or members of criminal groups used, acquired, threatened, or displayed interest in biological weapons.[2] There are only scattered cases of the use of biological agents for terrorist purposes from the standpoint of the current definition of terrorism. Until recently, the only proven case was the 1984 contamination of salad bars in a U.S. city through the addition of *Salmonella typhimurium* to the salad dressings.[3]

Experts had been predicting the growing threat of bioterrorism long before the events of September 11, 2001. Russian foreign intelligence services noted in 1993 that "the evident trend toward the broad proliferation of biotechnologies (which as a rule are dual use in nature) and the difficulties in controlling the production and use of biological agents and toxins increase the likelihood that 'third-world' countries will use biological weapons in local military conflicts as well as for sabotage and terrorist purposes."[4] The report also emphasized the advantage of biological weapons over nuclear and chemical weapons in that they make it possible to inflict serious economic damages on the enemy by the initial-

---

*Gennady G. Onishchenko, First Deputy Minister of Health and Chief Public Health Physician of the Russian Federation; Lev S. Sandakhchiev, General Director of the Vector State Science Center for Virology and Biotechnology; Sergei V. Netesov, Director of the Scientific Research Institute for Molecular Biology, Vector; Raisa A. Martynyuk, Deputy General Director for the Coordination of Scientific Research, Testing, and Design, Vector. Translated from the Russian by Kelly Robbins. Full article originally published in *Vestnik Akademii Nauk* [Herald of the Russian Academy of Sciences] 73(3):195-204, March 2003; reprinted with permission.

ly covert use of biological weapons against crops or livestock. Such actions could also be carried out for the purpose of "economic warfare."

Whereas potential chemical weapons agents are well studied, and methods to counter most of them have been created, the situation is fundamentally different for biological agents. It is important to recall that biological agents do not act immediately but have an incubation period during which the carrier of an illness could end up in completely different geographical conditions from the location where the biological agents were released. Such cases are very difficult to detect and differentiate from natural outbreaks; therefore, comprehensive and potentially time-consuming epidemiological analysis is required to prove that an outbreak is of a bioterrorist nature. In the case of the contamination of the salad bars with salmonella, it was only after a year that it was proven a terrorist act, and the U.S. public learned of the incident only many years later.[5]

Neither should we forget that the natural environment that surrounds us is an inexhaustible source of microorganisms—viruses, bacteria, and fungi—that cause diseases in humans, plants, and animals. The World Health Organization (WHO) deems infectious diseases to be the world's second leading cause of death and the leading cause of premature death. According to WHO estimates, 2 billion people annually suffer from infectious diseases, of whom 17 million die. Some 50,000 deaths per day result from infectious diseases, and half of the world's population is threatened by epidemic diseases.[6]

There are also other reasons for which biological agents could be a preferred tool for terrorists, primarily including their accessibility; their ease of preparation, storage, and shipment; and their capacity for covert use. The threat of bioterrorism requires the health care sector to maintain an exceedingly high level of readiness to detect the most dangerous agents and eliminate the consequences of their intentional use.

•   •   •

Russia began taking measures to counter bioterrorism in 1997. The Interagency Antiterrorism Commission of the Russian Federation was created to handle operational matters, and it includes a section on bioterrorism, the members of which are specialists from a number of ministries and agencies. In 1999, on the initiative of the Russian Ministry of Health, the commission was presented with a concept describing how state agencies are to act in the event of emergencies due to terrorism involving the use of biological or chemical weapons. The same year saw the approval of the Federal Targeted Program on the Creation of Methods and Means of Protecting the Population and the Urban Environment from Dangerous and Especially Dangerous Pathogens in Emergency Situations of Natural and Industrial Origin during 1999–2005 (hereafter referred to as the Pathogens Defense Program). This program sets forth the following priorities: basic research on pathogens; forecasting of infectious disease outbreaks; and specific methods for detecting, diagnosing, preventing, treating, and protecting against pathogens (means and methods of infection). The Center for Special Laboratory Diagnostics and Treatment of Dangerous and Exotic Infections was created, and the Federal Interagency Center for the Training of Specialists and the Testing of Means and Methods of Detecting Especially Dangerous Pathogens was organized.[7]

After the events of the fall of 2001, amendments to the Law on Combating Terrorism were drafted in our country, and a number of ministries are working on the Concept for the Biological Security of Russia.[7] The Russian Academy of Medical Sciences and the Russian Ministry of Health are developing a program featuring a plan of actions for rendering medical and psychological assistance to the population during potential bioterrorism threats. The plan includes special training for medical personnel as well as guidance for the population on how to protect themselves against the threat of bioterrorism.[9]

Created in 2000, the national Program of Basic and Applied Research on the Smallpox Virus is becoming increasingly significant. The current generation of doctors has no experience diagnosing or treating this infection. Modern diagnostic methods and treatment medications are lacking, and the vaccine supply is limited.[10] The Russian Ministry of Health has prepared a Concept for Reviving the Smallpox Vaccination Program and submitted it for government review in 2002.

A substantial share of Russian scientific and organizational measures to counter bioterrorism are being carried out in conjunction with the existing system for combating infectious diseases. The main objectives in this system are

- increasing the effectiveness of epidemiological monitoring of infectious diseases on the basis of comprehensive use of computerized information and analytical systems, environmental monitoring, and collective immunity of the population
- developing regulations and methodologies for infectious disease prophylaxis
- implementing federal and regional programs to promote the sanitary-epidemiological welfare of the population
- improving the infectious disease vaccination system
- expanding the public information system for persuading the population to take personal and societal measures for infectious disease prophylaxis
- strengthening the material and technical infrastructure of laboratories in the treatment and prophylaxis institutions and centers of the State Sanitary-Epidemiological Observation Service, providing them with the necessary equipment, and introducing modern methods for detecting infectious disease pathogens (PCR and others)
- increasing scientific research in diagnostics, epidemiology, treatment, and prophylaxis of infectious diseases[11]

Readiness for possible acts of bioterrorism will be enhanced by having infectious disease hospitals equipped at the necessary biosafety level (at least P-3) and operating on a 24-hour basis in major regional centers, especially those with international airports. Regional clinical microbiological and immunological laboratories that must cooperate with infectious disease hospitals and relevant scientific research institutes should also be equipped at the same biosafety level.

Complementing the existing system for combating infectious diseases, this set of measures for countering the threat of bioterrorism is intended to improve the health care infrastructure, enhance the quality of biomedical research, and promote better cooperation among the various ministries and agencies, institutions of the Sanitary-Epidemiological Service, and relevant scientific research institutes.

•   •   •

In the wake of the events of the fall of 2001, it became even more obvious that more international cooperation is needed in the fight against the threat of bioterrorism. Work is under way at various levels to consolidate the efforts of states in this struggle.

The presidents of Russia and the United States issued a joint declaration in November 2001 stating that the two countries will work together to counter the threat of bioterrorism. The two sides declared their adherence to the 1972 convention banning the development, production, and stockpiling of bacteriological, biological, and toxin weapons and calling for their destruction.[12]

Also in November 2001, the United States and six other countries joined the Ottawa Plan, which calls for increased international cooperation in preventing acts of biological terrorism. The countries agreed to establish joint cooperation in supplying vaccines and antibiotics, to participate in a constructive dialogue on harmonizing laws and regulations on the creation of vaccines, particularly the smallpox vaccine, and to provide further support for the existing World Health Organization disease monitoring network and for WHO efforts to develop a coordinated strategy for curbing disease outbreaks. The plan also calls for exchanging plans for preparing for and recovering from emergency situations, reviewing opportunities for joint personnel training, and organizing exchanges of observational data from national medical laboratories, information on actual or threatened incidents of food contamination, and strategies for food supply security.[13]

The theme of joining forces to fight terrorism was discussed by officials from the U.S. and Russian ministries of foreign affairs, defense, health, and science at a working conference held in Moscow in May 2002.[14] The question of actions to be taken by the public health care sector in response to the intentional use of biological, chemical, or radiological weapons was considered at the Fifty-fifth World Health Assembly in May 2002. The assembly secretariat noted the importance of fighting epidemics arising under natural conditions, for example, Ebola. Special attention was devoted to measures for protecting water and food products from contamination with chemical and biological agents.[15]

The world possesses resources to fight infectious diseases, and these resources can be used to counter bioterrorism. In 1997 an international network for data collection and monitoring of outbreaks of the most dangerous diseases was created based on national centers and laboratories collaborating with the WHO. There are hundreds of WHO centers specializing in specific infections, as well as a network of laboratories of the Pan-American Health Organization, the International Clinical Epidemiology Network, the network of Pasteur institutes, and the network of research centers under the U.S. National Institutes of Health, which also includes universities.[16]

Much attention is currently being devoted to creating an automated system for epidemiological detection and response. The United States has already implemented several systems for improved monitoring both of infectious diseases and of cases of bioterrorism in major cities. The so-called Lightweight Epidemiology Advanced Detection and Emergency Response System (LEADERS) is operational at 79 U.S. military hospitals.[17] An automated system has been developed to process information from patient visits and telephone calls to doctors' offices and clinics.[18]

Modern geographic information systems, or GIS technology, could provide substantial help in analyzing various epidemic situations. The first epidemiological research conducted in Russia with the help of GIS technology showed that they facilitated the study of infectious disease distribution patterns, the prediction of the future course of outbreaks, and the analysis of potential consequences of acts of bioterrorism.[19]

Special teams (epidemiological brigades) created under WHO auspices have traditionally been used to deal with disease outbreaks. They quashed epidemic outbreaks of Marburg hemorrhagic fever in the Congo in 1999, encephalitis caused by the Nipah virus in Malaysia in 1999, Rift Valley fever in Saudi Arabia in 2000, and yellow fever in Liberia in 2001.[20]

To enhance the effectiveness of the struggle against infectious diseases, Donald A. Henderson, chief scientific adviser to the U.S. secretary for health and human services, proposes the organization of a network of 15 regional centers. These centers should have infectious disease clinics, diagnostic research laboratories, and epidemiological brigades operating as an epidemiological intelligence service and monitoring a region with 2–5 million residents, and educational and training facilities for domestic and international personnel. This network should cooperate with organizations such as the U.S. Centers for Disease Control and Prevention (CDC), the U.S. National Institute of Allergy and Infectious Diseases, and other centers. To ensure their legitimacy and operational stability, the regional centers must be closely linked to the WHO and to governmental departments and agencies in the countries where they are located.[21]

Efforts are currently under way to organize a single European Center for Infectious Diseases, which will begin operating in 2005. Similar to the U.S.

CDC, the European center will coordinate scientific research work, monitor infectious diseases, and conduct professional training. It is expected that the new center will help to optimize the activities of existing national structures in Europe such as the Pasteur Institute (France), the Karolinska Institute (Sweden), and the Robert Koch Institute (Germany), and enhance Europe's readiness to counter the threat of bioterrorism.[22]

A unique system designed for combating and monitoring infectious diseases is already functioning in Russia, and it is unlike any other in the world. The State Sanitary-Epidemiological Service has 89 regional and 1,700 district centers. An antiplague system, including 5 scientific research institutes, 11 stations, and 14 brigades, operates in areas where plague is endemic.[23]

Considering foreign experience, the idea of creating regional infectious disease centers in Russia based on relevant existing scientific research centers and institutes is of interest. Under the leadership of the Russian Ministry of Health, these regional centers could carry out programs aimed at detecting and eliminating natural or terrorist-caused outbreaks of infectious disease in their territories. The geographical zones such centers would serve should be determined based on the economic and geopolitical significance of the various regions to Russia's national security. Later, these Russian regional centers could become part of the international biological security network.[24]

Success in countering biological and chemical terrorism is impossible without coordinating the efforts of the various departments and agencies involved, for example, the Russian Ministries of Defense and Health, the Russian Academy of Medical Sciences, the Russian Academy of Sciences, and the Russian Academy of Agricultural Sciences. The experience accumulated by these institutions can serve as a foundation for creating a national system for countering terrorist acts. Attention should also be focused on the system developed by the Russian Ministry of Agriculture for monitoring especially dangerous and little-studied exotic diseases, including zooanthroponotic infectious diseases of animals.[25]

An obvious condition for ensuring Russia's biological security is sufficient and stable state funding for basic and applied biomedical research aimed at developing a new generation of diagnostic tools and medications for treatment and prevention.[26] At the Eighth Congress of Epidemiologists, Microbiologists, and Parasitologists, which was held in Moscow in March 2002, participants emphasized the need for fundamental expansion of scientific research, design, and testing efforts in the following areas:

- new rapid pathogen detection methods and tools based on cutting-edge research in the fields of biotechnology and nanotechnology
- new-generation vaccines and live recombinant vaccines based on viral vectors developed through genetic engineering methods, live polyvalent antiviral vaccines, and DNA vaccines
- new chemical substances and formulations of new disinfectant agents[27]

Efforts should also be continued to search for, test, and organize production of more effective preparations for treating infectious diseases. Further study of the molecular diversity and molecular variability of infectious agents will facilitate not only the rapid identification of a variety of infectious agents causing outbreaks but also the forecasting of the appearance of new pathogens based on their natural evolution or as a result of the covert actions of bioterrorists aimed at artificially changing their properties.

In conclusion, we believe it is necessary to reemphasize that the state's capacity to counter the threat of bioterrorism—one risk factor for the appearance and spread of infectious diseases—is determined by the condition of the health care system and its readiness to detect, localize, and eliminate infectious outbreaks regardless of the origins of the pathogens causing them. Another key factor in state preparedness is the quality of basic and applied research conducted both to study pathogens at the molecular and epidemiological levels and to create the diagnostic, prophylactic, and therapeutic tools necessary for preventing or eliminating disease outbreaks. Undoubtedly, Russia's entry into the international biological security system that is currently being formed will promote a successful outcome in the struggle against bioterrorism.

NOTES

1. McGeorge, H. J. 1994. Chemical and biological terrorism: Analyzing the problem. Applied Science and Analysis Newsletter 42 (June 16).

2. Carus, S. J. 1998. Bioterrorism and biocrime: The illicit use of biological agents in the twentieth century. Washington: Center for Counterproliferation Research, National Defense University.

3. Chemical and biological terrorism: Research and development to improve civilian medical response. 1999. Washington: National Academies Press. *http://www.nap.edu.*

4. The new post-cold war challenge: The proliferation of weapons of mass destruction. 1993. Open report of the Russian Foreign Intelligence Service (SVR). *http://svr.gov.ru/material/2-1.html.*

5. Martynyuk, R., S. Netesov, and L. Sandakhchiev. 2002. International centers as a foundation for combating infectious diseases and countering bioterrorism. Nuclear Control 2.

6. Ban, J. 2001. Health, security, and U.S. global leadership. Special Report 2. *http://www.cbaci.org.*

7. Onishchenko, G. G., L. S. Sandakhchiev, S. V. Netesov, and S. V. Shchelkunov. 2000. Bioterrorism as a national and global threat. Journal of Microbiology, Epidemiology, and Immunobiology 6.

The epidemiological situation in the Russian Federation and basic areas of activity aimed at stabilizing it. Materials for the report of G. G. Onishchenko, chief state public health physician of the Russian Federation, at the VIII All-Russian Congress of Epidemiologists, Microbiologists, and Parasitologists, Moscow, March 26–28, 2002. Moscow: Ministry of Health of the Russian Federation.

8. Scientists' response. 2001. Meditsinsky Vestnik [The Medical Herald] 31. *http://www.medvestnik.ru/Gazeta/2001/031/p02-03.html.*

9. Russia developing national action program for possible bioterrorism threats. 2001. *http://www.strana.ru/stories/01/10/16/1776/86465.html.*

10. The specter of smallpox: Efforts to implement national program for creating defenses against fatal infection. 2002. Izvestia, *http://www.izvestia.ru/science/article17850.*

11. The epidemiological situation in the Russian Federation and basic areas of activity aimed at stabilizing it. Materials for the report of G. G. Onishchenko, chief state public health physician of the Russian Federation, at the VIII All-Russian Congress of Epidemiologists, Microbiologists, and Parasitologists, Moscow, March 26–28, 2002. Moscow: Ministry of Health of the Russian Federation.

12. Fact sheet: U.S.-Russian cooperation against bioterrorism. 2001. Website of the U.S. Department of State, *http://usinfo.state.gov/topical/pol/terror/01111314.htm.*

13. U.S. joins Ottawa Plan to fight bioterrorism. 2001. Website of the U.S. Department of State, *http://usinfo.state.gov/russki/topics/terror/1113t-bio.htm* [in Russian] or *http://usinfo.state.gov/topical/pol/terror/01110807.htm* [in English].

14. Reducing the threats from weapons of mass destruction. Building a global coalition against catastrophic terrorism. Working for a safe world. Moscow, May 27, 2002.

15. Deliberate use of biological and chemical agents to cause harm. 2002. WHO 55th World Health Assembly. A55/20.

16. Martynyuk, R., S. Netesov, and L. Sandakhchiev, op. cit.

17. Zaitsev, K. Medical news: a hospital leader. *http://www.medlinks.ru/article.php?sid=1470&mode=thread&order=0&thold=0* [undated].

18. Lazarus, R., K. Kleinman, I. Dashevsky, et al. 2002. Use of automated ambulatory-case encounter records for detection of acute illness clusters, including potential bioterrorism events. Emerging Infectious Diseases 8(8).

19. Boyev, B. V., V. M. Bondarenko, A. A. Vorobyov, and V. V. Makarov. 2002. Problems of protecting against acts of bioterrorism under current conditions. Agrarnaya Rossiya [Agrarian Russia] 2.

20. WHO report on global surveillance of epidemic-prone infectious diseases. 2002. *http://www.who.int/emc/surveill/index.html.*

21. Martynyuk, R., S. Netesov, and L. Sandakhchiev, op. cit.

22. Tibayrenc, M. 2001. A European center to respond to threats of bioterrorism and major epidemics. Bulletin of the World Health Organization 79(12).

23. Website of the Russian Ministry of Health, *http://www.minzdrav-rf.ru.*

24. Martynyuk, R., S. Netesov, and L. Sandakhchiev, op. cit.

25. A system for epizootiological monitoring of especially dangerous, exotic, and little-studied diseases including zooanthroponotic diseases of animals. 2001. Moscow: All-Russian Research Institute of Veterinary Virology and Microbiology.

26. Paltsev, M. A. 2002. Biological weapons: A problem for Russia's national security. Natsionalnaya Bezopasnost [National Security] 5.

27. The epidemiological situation in the Russian Federation and basic areas of activity aimed at stabilizing it. Materials for the report of G. G. Onishchenko, chief state public health physician of the Russian Federation, at the VIII All-Russian Congress of Epidemiologists, Microbiologists, and Parasitologists, Moscow, March 26–28, 2002. Moscow: Ministry of Health of the Russian Federation.

Appendix E

Biological Terrorism

Russ Zajtchuk and David Franz[1]

The thought of an outbreak of disease caused by the intentional release of a pathogen or toxin in an American city was alien just 10 years ago. Many people believed that biological warfare was only in the military's imagination, perhaps to be faced by soldiers on a faraway battlefield, if at all. The "anthrax letters" and the resulting deaths from inhalation anthrax have changed that perception. The national, state, and local governments in the United States are preparing for what is now called "not if, but when and how extensive" biological terrorism.

In contrast to the acute onset and first responder focus with a chemical attack, in a bioterrorist attack, the physician and the hospital will be at the center of the fray. Whether the attack is a hoax, a small foodborne outbreak, a lethal aerosol cloud moving silently through a city at night, or the introduction of contagious disease, the physician who understands threat agent characteristics and diagnostic and treatment options and who thinks like an epidemiologist will have the greatest success in limiting the impact of the attack. As individual health care providers, we must add the exotic agents to our diagnostic differentials. Hospital administrators must consider augmenting diagnostic capabilities and surveillance programs and even making infrastructure modifications in preparation for the treatment of victims of bioterrorism. Above all, we must all educate ourselves. If done correctly, preparation for a biological attack will be as "dual use" as the facility that produced the weapon. A sound public health infrastructure, which includes all of us and our resources, will serve this nation well for the control of the disease, no matter what the cause of the disease.

INTRODUCTION

Before 1990, little thought was given to the possibility of biological warfare or a biological terrorist attack on U.S. cities. Even as recently as 1997, the U.S. Department of Defense spent approximately $137 million on biodefense to protect the deployed force, while academia, industry, local governments, and the rest of the federal government were oblivious to—and in some cases, doubtful about—the threat of biological warfare.[2] In fiscal year 2000, the United States committed more than $1.5 billion to military biodefense and another $1 billion to domestic preparedness for biological attack. The responsibility for research, development, policy, and planning is now spread among the Departments of Justice, Health and Human Services, Defense, and Energy, with the Department of Justice responsible for crisis management (intelligence, law enforcement, and education of first responders) and the Department of Health and Human Services responsible for consequence management (surveillance, epidemiology, reference laboratory and field diagnostics, triage, and postexposure prophylaxis and therapy). Anthrax letters have resulted in American deaths from inhalation anthrax, the first since 1978. Although the loss of life has been minimal—we lose 20,000 to 80,000 Americans to influenza each year—the psychological and economic effects have been significant. Before September 2001, our emergency responders were dealing with about 200 biological hoaxes each year, up from approximately 20 to 30 in 1997. In just weeks since the anthrax letters, we have seen many thousands of biological hoaxes and copycat letter attacks.

THE DUAL-USE NATURE OF BIOLOGICAL WARFARE PROGRAMS

The process of research, development, and production of biological weapons is an extremely difficult intelligence target because legitimate vaccine and agricultural production facilities can be used to make illegal biological weapon agents. Basic research can be done in academic, industrial, or government public health laboratories. The scale-up of agent lots can be done in pharmaceutical or agricultural facilities. Weaponization and field testing may be more difficult to disguise, but the previous Iraqi regime successfully tested aerosol dissemination equipment on aircraft by flying modified crop-dusting equipment out of a crop-dusting airfield. Although the previous Iraqi regime had successfully developed and field-tested biological agents (*Bacillus anthracis,* botulinum toxin serotype A, and aflatoxin) in bombs, rockets, and agricultural sprayers on conventional aircraft, our best information suggests that they were nothing more than high-level bioterrorists.[3]

TODAY'S AND TOMORROW'S THREATS TO OUR CITIES

Classic Cold War Agents

During the cold war, which reached its peak in the 1980s, the Soviet Union and the United States and its allies, Great Britain and Canada, developed biological weapons. These nations' programs were developed independently as highly classified endeavors. Yet, of the thousands of bacteria, viruses, and biological toxins available in nature, the proliferators typically selected fewer than 20 agents for weaponization—and their lists were strikingly similar. (There is evidence that the Iraqi program agent list was influenced by the previous work of others.) The agents of anthrax, plague, and tularemia were commonly selected bacterial agents throughout the past 60 years. The easily grown and highly infectious encephalitic alphaviruses (for example, Venezuelan equine encephalitis, or VEE) were favorites, and the botulinum toxins were always tried, at least in the beginning of developing programs.

The proliferators of the past selected their agents for pathogenicity or toxicity, ease of production into weapons, and stability during production, processing, storage, and dissemination. It is no wonder that anthrax came to the top of everyone's list. The would-be terrorist is constrained by most of the physical and biological rules that plagued the biological warfare proliferators of the past. To lethally infect 100,000 people in a city, the terrorist must lay down a cloud in a respirable particle size that will allow pulmonary or airway retention of the agent. The cloud must hug the ground and not be dispersed and diluted in the atmosphere as on a warm, sunny day. Although some experts disagree, we believe that to accomplish such a deed efficiently, the terrorist would be dependent on state sponsorship—by a state at least as accomplished as Iraq was in 1999— and would have to use one of the "dirty dozen" agents selected by yesterday's bioweaponeers. To infect 500 to 1,000 people through the air-handling system of a large office building, the meteorological constraints would be eliminated, but many of the others would remain.

Highly Contagious Agents

In one type of attack a direct relation between effort by the terrorist and result on the target may not apply. We have said that intent, access to agents, research and development, scale-up, weaponization, testing, and favorable meteorological conditions are necessary for the successful execution of an attack with a respirable biological agent. The highly contagious agents such as variola (smallpox) or an influenza strain similar to that which killed approximately 20 million people in the early 1900s may allow terrorists to accomplish a truly horrific attack with intent and access to the agent only.

Biological Toxins

Of the hundreds of biological toxins in nature, only a very small number are potent enough to be used. Because they must be delivered as respirable aerosols, a toxin's utility as a battlefield—or urban—weapon is limited by its potency and ease of production. It is apparent that, ignoring other characteristics, if a toxin is not adequately potent, sufficient quantities cannot be produced to make even one weapon. Because of low potency, hundreds of toxins can be eliminated as ineffective for use as mass casualty weapons in our cities. Certain plant toxins with marginal potency, such as ricin, could be produced in large (ton) quantities. These toxins could possibly be weaponized by a competent organization. At the other extreme, several bacterial toxins are so lethal that mass casualty quantities are measured not in tons but in kilograms, quantities much more easily produced. Such toxins are potential threats to our cities. The botulinum toxins are so potent that lethal aerosol mass casualty weapons could be produced with quantities that are attainable relatively easily with current technology. Botulinum toxin, serotype A, is 10,000 to 100,000 times more potent than most of the well-known chemical warfare agents.

THE EPIDEMIOLOGY OF BIOTERRORISM

The Attack

Assume that an individual or group can obtain a high-quality, talcum powder-like dry agent with adequate viability and release it in one of our cities under the right meteorological conditions and at the right time of day without notice. The result would be a footprint of potential exposure, with high and low concentration eddies caused by buildings and city effect. The extent of exposure would be greatly dependent on time of day, season, weather, and chance. Dose received by those exposed would follow a broad distribution, and for many agents, onset of clinical disease would vary directly with dose and possibly with age and physical condition. Many of the diseases associated with the agents we have discussed present as a flu-like illness. In our society, many individuals would attempt self-medication, and some few who visited their physicians early would be sent home with analgesics, forced fluids, and bed rest.

It may not be immediately obvious that there has been a biological attack. We may have to differentiate such an attack from a spontaneous outbreak in an endemic area or a spontaneous epidemic of an emerging or unknown disease. With a spontaneous outbreak, there may be seasonal clues and a gradual increase in incidence and traditional cycles of transmission. With a biological attack, whether aerosol or foodborne, there may be a compressed epidemic curve, even when considering varying exposure doses and differing states of health of the exposed population.

Identification of the agent may be difficult and is of critical importance. Without identifying the agent, rational postexposure prophylaxis will be impossible. If a weapon or container is found, samples may be taken directly and delivered to a reference laboratory for analysis. Formulation of a case definition is important for several reasons. During epidemiological investigation, the case definition allows investigators widely separated geographically to use the same criteria in evaluating the extent of the outbreak and the attack rate. It allows the outbreak to be described, and the clinically based definition supports diagnostic and triage efforts even if definitive diagnostic tools are not widely available. The case definition is even more important for investigating a potential biological attack because of the increased likelihood of hysteria and confusion caused by rumor, misinformation, and fear of the unknown. The city that collects good, seasonally adjusted background rates for influenza, gastrointestinal disease, and other common public health threats will be better prepared to identify and describe the unusual outbreak.

Description of the Outbreak

The outbreak must be described to assist in identifying and caring for victims and for forensic purposes. Circumscribing the footprint of an aerosol attack will be necessary to assist in notifying, testing, and treating the potentially exposed. The aerosol attack differs from traditional insect-borne or patient contact exposure and disease spread. Onset data would be compressed and exposure data, especially for a noncontiguous aerosol, would reflect a snapshot-in-time location map of the victims. Therefore, knowing whether the release occurred during rush hour or at 2:00 a.m. would greatly change the exposure footprint if not the actual cloud footprint. An attack on a city would be complicated by complex wind patterns that prevail among multistory buildings and by the microenvironment produced by unique temperature gradients. Obtaining meteorological information from local airports or weather stations can be helpful. Several government agencies now have computer plume-prediction models, which can also be helpful, if some sense of source and routine meteorological data are available. The investigation of the Sverdlovsk accident, even 20 years after it occurred, benefited from historic meteorological data, and airport weather station data proved useful in confirming that the spores had been windborne.[4] Historically, in a disaster, a relatively large percentage of any population leaves their homes and flees. Flight after a biological aerosol attack is, of course, the wrong thing to do. Movement from the area not only complicates the investigation but also takes patients away from help and with contagious agents may facilitate spread of the outbreak. Knowledgeable, respected medical leadership in the city will be needed to appeal to the population for their trust and cooperation with the response personnel.

Identification of Exposed Individuals

Human beings who have been exposed, even to replicating agents, will not have measurable amounts of the agent in their blood or serum for several days at the earliest, nor will they have a measurable immune response. However, after inhalation exposure of replicating agents or toxins, nasal mucosal swab samples may contain sufficient agent to allow identification by PCR (polymerase chain reaction) or ELISA (enzyme-linked immunosorbent assay). Nasal swab analysis may be useful for anthrax, for example, but not for the alphaviruses or some of the viral hemorrhagic fevers with extremely low infective doses.

Treatment and Patient Management

Once the agent has been identified, decisions can be made regarding triage and postexposure prophylaxis. Is specific therapy available? How much time do we have to treat primary exposures? Is there a chance of secondary spread? If the causative agent of inhalation anthrax, pneumonic plague, or possibly tularemia, with its 35 percent case-fatality rate, is identified from field or nasal swab samples, a rapid response becomes the first priority. With these agents, postexposure prophylaxis within the first 24 to 48 hours can mean the difference between life and death. If the agent were VEE, much less could be done for individual victims, but mosquito control and equine immunization might be critical. The appropriate response may range from door-to-door treatment teams to simply providing the public good information through the media. If the decision is made to treat the population within the cloud footprint, it may be done door-to-door, at central collection points—schools, churches, or civic centers—or using both approaches.

In the aftermath of a terrorist attack, many victims may self-admit to hospitals. City hospitals may have overwhelming admissions and emergency room visits the day of the attack. If the agent used was not life threatening, crowd control procedures may suffice in dealing with large numbers of hospital visits. If the agent causes severe illness or death, hospitals must be prepared to increase capacities by adding beds and reducing routine patient load.

Preparation for Biological Attack: What Can a Medical Center Do?

It is the physician and the medical facility, not necessarily the paramedics, police, and fire service, that will take the brunt of a biological terrorist attack. The prepared physician, hospital, and medical center have the potential of making an enormous difference in outcome after an attack. Therefore, preparation at this level is critical. Fortunately, much of what should be done in anticipation of a biological terrorist attack is also applicable to any public health disaster or infectious disease outbreak. Sound preparation, like production of biological weapons, is truly dual use.

Education and Training

At the top of the list of priorities are education and training. Much of what is needed in a hospital or medical center that faces a spike in the patient load after an attack is simple application of the standard principles of medicine with which the professional and support staffs are already intimately familiar. However, if the disease faced is not in the doctor's differential or the doctor is unaccustomed to thinking about "herd health," the way ahead may seem fraught with danger. Education and training must include the general characteristics of biological agents versus chemical agents; clinical presentation, diagnosis, prophylaxis, and therapy of the most important diseases; and sample handling, decontamination, and barrier patient care. Training, planning, and drills must prepare the physicians and staff for mass casualty patient treatment, respiratory support for unusual numbers of patients, and distribution of medications or support of the local government in vaccination programs. The engineering staff must be taught to establish improvised containment in patient rooms or suites. To apply the knowledge we already have or to use the facilities already in place in a mass casualty resulting from a biological terrorist attack is the least difficult, least expensive, and probably the most important thing we can do to prepare.

Routine Surveillance

Although most surveillance programs may be initiated at the national or state level, hospitals and medical centers should consider establishing their own. This is more easily done today than in the past because of automation. For example, large numbers of flu-like illnesses seen at emergency rooms, severe gastrointestinal syndromes, or evidence of an increased caseload of communicable disease or simply nontrauma admissions or even deaths should be cause for taking a second look from an epidemiological view. The pharmacy service might consider monitoring selected antibiotics or antidiarrheal medications and flagging dispensing levels greater than the norm. For a covert attack, surveillance may provide the first indication of an attack. For either a covert or overt attack, a sound surveillance system may help circumscribe the geographic extent of the attack and provide essential information regarding where postexposure prophylaxis and therapy should be initiated.

Infrastructure Modifications

For biological attack, two categories of modification to the hospital building may be required. The first, related to decontamination and segregation of patients, is probably less important for biological attack than for chemical attack. As described above, patients exposed to a true respirable aerosol may have little or no contamination externally. For most agents that are not highly infectious, simple surface decontamination of the face and nares may be sufficient. The second modification that should be considered is some sort of preparation for dealing with highly contagious or dangerous infectious patients. Fortunately, this might not be necessary for many of the agents that might be selected by the bioterrorist.

NOTES

1. Reprinted from Disease-a-Month, 48, Franz, D.R.; Zajtchuk, R.; Biological Terrorism: Understanding the Threat, Preparation, and Medical Response, 489–568, Copyright (2002) with permission from Elsevier.

2. U.S. Department of State. 1998. Report of the United States of America to the United Nations Department of Disarmament Affairs. Washington, D.C.: Department of State.

3. Trevan, T. 1999. Saddam's secrets: The hunt for Iraq's hidden weapons. London: Harper Collins.

4. Meselson, M., J. Guillemin, M. Hugh-Jones, et al. 1994. The Sverdlovsk anthrax outbreak of 1979. Science 266:1202–1208.

APPENDIX F

Top-Priority Problems for Scientific Research on the Information Security of the Russian Federation

This list of priority problems was developed and approved by the Information Security Section of the Science Council of the Security Council of the Russian Federation (Protocol 1 of March 28, 2001).*

Humanitarian Problems of Ensuring the Information Security of the Russian Federation

1. Study of the place and role of information security problems in the transition to a modern information society.

2. Study of the problems of ensuring a balance of the interests of the individual, society, and the state in the information sphere.

3. Study of the role and place of information security in ensuring military, economic, environmental, and other types of national security.

4. Development of a unified conceptual framework (terms and definitions) in the information security sphere.

5. Provision of a scientific foundation for the basic activities of state governmental structures in ensuring the information security of the Russian Federation.

6. The national interests of Russia and cyberconflict in the modern world.

7. The ethical orientation of the individual, the information-related foundations of this orientation, and information security.

8. Information security and political ethics.

*Appendix 4 from Streltsov, A. A. 2002. Ensuring Russia's Information Security. Moscow: Moscow Center of Continuing Mathematical Education. Translated from the Russian by Kelly Robbins.

9. The information space and the problem of the integrality of the Russian state.

10. Study and forecasting of the sociopsychological consequences of the introduction and broad dissemination of modern information technologies.

11. Study of the historical aspects, current status, and prospects for development of the information-related activities of foreign states involving the use of Russian information systems for promoting their own interests.

12. Development of and provision of a scientific foundation for a system for monitoring the status of the information security of the Russian Federation.

13. Development of an information-dynamic model of the balance between the demand for free exchange of information and allowable limits on its distribution.

14. Development of legal mechanisms for ensuring the constitutional rights and freedoms of citizens in the information sphere.

15. Problems of providing legal protection and assigning property and profit rights with regard to the results of scientific-technical activities and compensating authors and persons facilitating the use of intellectual property.

16. Study of the place and role of the mass media in addressing issues related to the information technology-related aspects of the state policy of the Russian Federation.

17. Development of regulations aimed at preserving and legally protecting Russian intellectual property in the information sphere.

18. Improving the legal base regulating the creation and use of databases and other information resources of federal significance.

19. Study of problems of legal regulation in the area of technological independence.

20. Development of a mechanism for legal regulation of the protection and use of dual-use technologies.

21. Development of models and mechanisms for providing insurance coverage for information-related risks.

22. Development of legal mechanisms for cooperation among members of the Commonwealth of Independent States in ensuring collective information security.

23. Study of problems of legal regulation on issues of investment policy in the area of information technologies.

24. Development of legal mechanisms for regulating the creation and utilization of cryptographic products.

25. Development of legal mechanisms regulating the circulation of electronic documents.

26. Problems of providing a legal foundation for the creation and operation of a system for monitoring the threat of information attacks on critically important segments of the information infrastructure of the Russian Federation.

27. Improvement of the legal and regulatory base for conducting expert reviews and monitoring of the quality of protection afforded to information and information resources.

28. Development of mechanisms in international law to restrict cyberconflicts.

29. Harmonization of domestic and foreign standards in the information technology sphere.

30. Problems of the formation of the international system for information security.

31. Development of models and legal mechanisms for facilitating cooperation on information security matters between the federal government and the various entities making up the Russian Federation.

32. Development of models and legal mechanisms for facilitating cooperation on information security matters between oblast, republic, and territory governments and the various local governments.

33. Development of and provision of a scientific foundation for means of ensuring the information-psychological security of the individual and society.

Scientific-Technical Problems of Ensuring the Information Security of the Russian Federation (Physical-Mathematical, Technical)

34. Development of an integrated conceptual framework of the information space and the content of information resources.

35. Problems of creating and developing the information component of a special-purpose information-telecommunications system in the interests of government departments and agencies.

36. Study of the problems of ensuring information security of national payment systems based on Russian intellectual resources.

37. Study of the problems of creating and developing a national system for managing digital certificates.

38. Search for ways of resolving the problem of creating a unified system of technical standards for information exchange (protocols, data formats, interface specifications) taking into account existing international standards and prospects for their future development.

39. Study of approaches to the creation of a Russian system of industrial standards for the design and development of information and telecommunications systems taking into account existing international standards and prospects for their development.

40. Studies aimed at the creation of a range of Russian technical means for designing information systems.

41. Problems of improving Russian software.

42. Development of and provision of scientific foundations for systems for certifying hardware or software containing foreign-produced components.

43. Analysis of the potential for using technological production features of the latest foreign and domestic microelectronics to perform destructive IT-related functions.

44. Study of the problems of creating and operating a national standard database of software found to be reliable.

45. Study of the problems of creating and developing protected information-telecommunications systems, including developing methods for selecting the architecture and calculating the parameters for such systems, mathematical models and control technologies, systems software and applications with integration protection functions, networking devices and software, and devices for the transfer and distribution of information.

46. Development of models of system security threats and means of carrying them out, determination of methods and means of monitoring to detect unauthorized operations, development of methodologies and a conceptual framework for assessing damages from the impacts of information security threats.

47. Development of methods and means for conducting expert analyses and quality control regarding the protection of information and information resources, including matters related to assessing fundamental systems software in accordance with information security demands.

48. Development of methods and means of ensuring the information security of information and telecommunications systems, including automated safety control systems, methods and means of key distribution and protection of information and information resources from unauthorized access and destructive actions, antivirus technologies, methods and means of monitoring the protection of modern and cutting-edge equipment and communications channels against unauthorized access, resolution of the problem of guaranteed deletion of data on magnetic media, study and development of methods for constructing protected systems that include elements that are unreliable (from an information security standpoint), including the problem of testing such systems.

49. Study of problems of the security of the Russian information infrastructure as a whole as it is being integrated into the global infrastructure.

50. Study of problems of ensuring the information security of special-purpose information-telecommunications systems, including the development of regulatory and technical security documentation, automated security control systems, and a unified range of means for cryptographic protection taking into account the information processing technologies used in such special-purpose systems.

51. Study of problems of the information security of corporate networks, including the science and education networks (as part of the comprehensive program of the Russian Ministry of Science and Industry entitled "Scientific, Methodological, Material-Technical, and Information Support for the Education System").

52. Problems of licensing activities in the area of information-telecommunications systems.

53. Analysis of trends in the development of the global information network and the status of Russian participation in it.

54. Study of fundamental problems of theoretical cryptography and fields of mathematics.

55. Study of cryptographic problems of creating cutting-edge Russian encryption systems (particularly high-speed systems).

56. Development and provision of scientific foundations for new methods for the cryptographic analysis of modern encryption systems.

57. Development of cutting-edge cryptographic protocols facilitating collaboration among users of complex hierarchical global networks and distributed information-analytical systems.

58. Study of existing open-key systems and development of new ones, along with related authentication and electronic signature protocols.

59. Improvement of the regulatory and methodological base regarding questions of information protection using cryptographic means.

60. Analysis of basic areas and development trends with regard to domestic and foreign means for the cryptographic protection of information.

61. Analysis of opportunities for using advances in physics and engineering to access information processed on modern hardware, including a study of physical bases for information leakage through side channels and of problems related to the analytical processing of side signals.

62. Study of the algorithmic and technological characteristics of the latest foreign and domestic technical means for information processing.

63. Study of the problems and methods of accessing information in communications channels.

64. Development of protection assessment methodology, creation of comprehensive methods and means of protecting information processing hardware from physical-technical methods of unauthorized access, and improvement of the relevant regulatory base.

65. Study of the problem of creating information processing hardware that is protected against physical-technical methods of information access.

66. Comparative analysis of development trends with regard to physical-technical problems of information protection in Russia and abroad.

67. Study of the architectural options for constructing high-output computer systems and algorithms and software taking into account current cryptographic demands.

68. Study of problems of constructing automated systems for the processing of cryptographic information in a heterogeneous computing environment.

69. Study of problems of the management of distributed computing processes.

70. Study of and provision of scientific foundations for threat models and strategies for protection against technical intelligence gathering.

71. Development of methods and means for countering technical intelligence gathering with an eye to the efficiency of their operation.

72. Development of methods and means for monitoring the status and sufficiency of measures taken to counter technical intelligence gathering at protected targets.

73. Development of modern methodology to ensure that technical intelligence gathering is countered at protected targets.

74. Development and theoretical and experimental study of modern methods of steganography and other means of hiding messages, as well as for protection against forgery and counterfeiting.

75. Study and development of Russian protection screens taking into account models of threats to existing and cutting-edge digital automated telecommunications systems.

Problems of Ensuring the Availability of Personnel to Deal with the
Information Security of the Russian Federation

76. Creation of a well-founded vision, structure, and operational plan for a unified system of personnel training in the area of modern information technologies and information security.

77. Definition of the structure and functions of the Training and Methodological System for the Training, Retraining, and Continuing Education of Personnel in the Information Security Sphere.

78. Development of state educational standards for new specialists graduating from institutions of higher professional education.

79. Creation of laws and regulations for a special licensing system with regard to information security-related educational activities.

80. Problems related to laws and regulations on the training of specialists in information security and related areas.

81. Development of a regulatory base aimed at preserving the intellectual potential of the state higher educational institutions of the Russian Federation that train specialists in modern information technologies and information security.

82. Development of methods and specialized educational literature pertaining to specialties in the information security sector, including development of training aids for use in the preparation of specialists in cryptography.

83. Development of methods and specialized educational literature pertaining to the study of general questions of information security for use by students being trained in other areas besides information security.

84. Development of a set of fundamental multimedia educational resources for use in training specialists in information security and related countermeasures.

85. Development of methods and specialized educational literature for use in retraining and continuing education courses on information security.

86. Software and hardware necessary for the integration of modern information technologies into the educational process.

87. The problem of including in the educational process various types of educational and research-oriented games related to information security.

APPENDIX G

Proposal for a Chem-Bio Attack Response Center (CBARC) for Chicago, Illinois, U.S., 2003

Russ Zajtchuk, M.D.
Chicago Hospitals International

Joe Petrovic
InteleDatics, Inc.

BACKGROUND

Civilian and military trauma care systems in the United States need a support framework for managing chemical and biological (chem-bio) emergencies. The continuing proliferation of chemical and biological weapons throughout the world poses an increasing threat, as demonstrated by the 1995 sarin attacks in the Tokyo subway, which injured more than 5,000 people. To prepare for and defend against such threats, sophisticated sensor and emergency telemedicine networks must be extended in capability to support identification, containment, and emergency medical care if a chem-bio emergency occurs.

This paper proposes a plan for the creation of a center in Chicago, Illinois, to develop response techniques and technologies for advanced trauma care of victims from chem-bio attacks that will support government and private medical groups and first responders. Tasks conducted under this center will involve collaboration between technical research and development companies and schools, and tertiary health care providers and their affiliated hospitals, clinics, and medical schools.

OBJECTIVE

The objective of this program is to establish a center for the development of advanced emergency medicine for application in response to a chem-bio attack. The center is configured as a virtual institute, including several organizations involved in the technical and clinical aspects of advanced emergency medicine and chem-bio environments. Functions performed by the center include information and research services and an advanced emergency medicine test bed to

229

gauge the technical effectiveness and clinical efficacy of advanced procedures and technologies. Near-term achievements involve a review and assessment of current telecommunication, medical informatics, and medical procedures as applied to chem-bio emergency medicine. Long-term goals include the development, testing, and deployment of advanced telecommunications, for example, high-bandwidth wireless system, sensors for identification of agents, medical informatics as applied to chem-bio emergencies and advanced trauma care, and chem-bio protection and isolation equipment.

PARTICIPANTS

The proposed approach for a nationwide (and global) program for improving emergency medical service for chem-bio incidents is to establish a Chem-Bio Attack Response Center (CBARC). This would be a virtual institute involving organizations specializing in advanced medicine, telecommunication technology, sensor technology, medical informatics, and chem-bio response procedures and equipment. To be compliant and integrate with the general area of advanced medicine, the CBARC must be embedded into a complete telemedicine architecture where all components of telecommunications and medical informatics are involved. The specific types of organizations to be included are

- tertiary health care providers
- affiliated urban hospitals and clinics, including primary care providers
- primary care emergency rooms
- medical schools and universities
- technical research and development companies
- local fire departments
- national guard units
- federal government (Department of Defense [DOD], National Institutes of Health [NIH], and so forth)

FUNCTIONS

CBARC will provide advanced emergency medical expertise, software development and engineering services, and equipment in the following categories:

- **Information Services**—These services are focused on the collection, analysis, processing, and dissemination of telecommunication and clinical data relevant to emergency telemedicine and medical informatics in a chem-bio environment. Information will include results of efficacy studies, telemedicine hardware configurations, chem-bio protection and isolation equipment, cost-benefit analysis, and other data compiled in databases that are available for access and search via the Internet.

- **Research Services**—These services are focused on unbiased, highly technical research and engineering in applying existing technologies, emerging technologies, and basic research in the areas of chem-bio sensors and sensor networks, medical informatics, clinical techniques, clinical efficacy studies, chem-bio protection and isolation equipment, data formatting and compression, and telecommunications as applied to chem-bio emergency telemedicine.
- **Chem-Bio Attack Response Test Bed**—This function includes establishing a Chicago-area test bed for testing emergency medicine concepts using the large trauma center at Cook County Hospital to gather data, Rush-Presbyterian-St. Luke's Medical Center to conduct efficacy studies, and InteleDatics, Inc., to provide technological solutions to emergency telemedicine problems.

IMPLEMENTATION

The specific organizations proposed for CBARC are all located close together in Chicago, Illinois, and include

- Rush-Presbyterian-St. Luke's Medical Center (RUSH)
- Cook County Hospital Emergency Services (CCH)
- InteleDatics, Inc. (IDI)
- Chicago Fire Department (CFD)
- University of Illinois at Chicago (UIC)

These organizations provide the expertise to develop and operate CBARC and have already established working relationships through present and past programs and contracts with industry and government.

Rush-Presbyterian-St. Luke's Medical Center is a tertiary care provider. It is the central component of the Rush System for Health, a comprehensive, cooperative health delivery system designed to serve 1.5 million people in northern Illinois and Indiana through its own resources and in affiliation with seven other Illinois hospitals. The Rush System for Health is vertically integrated, with an academic health center (Rush-Presbyterian-St. Luke's Medical Center, Johnston R. Bowman Health Center for the Elderly, and Rush University), a teaching hospital, community hospitals, and managed care offices that serve Chicago-area communities of diverse socioeconomic and cultural backgrounds. A major component of RUSH comprises a system of 49 advanced life support ambulances covering 240 sq mi. These ambulances relate to five level-1 trauma units.

Cook County Hospital, which has an academic affiliation with RUSH, is centrally located within the city and is close to Rush Medical Center. It is a world-renowned academic medical center that has one of the world's largest and busiest emergency departments. More than 120,000 adults, 45,000 children, and 4,500 major trauma patients are treated per year. CCH would be the primary trauma center for victims of a terrorist attack in the Chicago area, and its emergency physicians are acquainted with treatment procedures for people exposed to chemical and biological agents.

InteleDatics, Inc., is a small business providing high-technology consulting that helps hospitals and physicians project their expertise to distant locations and creates innovative devices and software applications that extend the forefront of medical specialties. The current staff of IDI has many years of experience from previous employment at research institutes, technical schools, and medical-related companies. This staff brings cutting-edge technology in the areas of telecommunication systems, integrated wireless sensor networks, and medical informatics.

The Chicago Fire Department will be one of the first units to respond (first responder) to a chem-bio attack. It is the largest fire department in the Midwest, serving a population of 3 million, with response procedures for hazardous materials and emergency medical services, including those for a chem-bio attack. The CFD would notify the Illinois National Guard of a possible emergency and would be the primary city service directly in contact with the victims.

The primary support to the local first responder will be the Illinois National Guard RAID (Rapid Assessment and Initial Detection) element. The RAID element will have the principal role in assisting the incident commander, for example, the fire chief, in providing early assessment, initial detection, and technical advice in response to a weapons of mass destruction (WMD) incident. Local response to an emergency may not be enough, and the incident commander may request state or regional assets through the State Office of Emergency Services. The RAID element is the military first responder with the goal of a four-hour response time. The RAID element will also have the necessary equipment for a large WMD incident with the capability to conduct reconnaissance; provide medical advice and assistance; perform detection, assessment, and hazard prediction; and provide technical advice concerning WMD incidents and agents.

The University of Illinois at Chicago is the largest institution of higher education in the Chicago area, is one of the top 100 research universities in the United States, and is dedicated to the land-grant university tradition of research, teaching, and public service. It has 13 academic colleges and professional schools and offers 92 undergraduate, 85 master's, and 55 doctoral programs in architecture, art, associated health professions, business administration, dentistry, education, engineering, humanities, kinesiology, mathematics, medicine, nursing, performing arts, pharmacy, public administration, public health, sciences, social sciences, social work, and urban planning. UIC has an enrollment of 25,000 students, including more than 8,000 graduate and professional students. It has an excellent engineering school and a state-of-the-art Microfabrication Applications Laboratory for support of CBARC science, technology, and engineering tasks.

The proposed program plan is based on the use of a networked health care test bed involving representative components of the entire telemedicine and chem-bio environment. This test bed allows for testing of maturing telemedicine systems, techniques, and procedures in a civilian application. The chem-bio Attack Response Test Bed (CBART) includes a network of community hospitals affiliated with a tertiary care institution and a mobile paramedic system and first responder unit linked to a level-1 trauma unit. In this environment, physicians caring for victims of a chem-bio attack can transmit information and communicate with physicians in a tertiary care hospital without being exposed to chemical or biological agents. The test bed provides a stable and controlled link between all components. The network of hospitals is widely dispersed throughout the urban and rural areas and can be linked through either wired or wireless communication networks.

Following is a typical configuration for a chem-bio environment. A terrorist attack occurs in the subway system and the first responders (local fire department and National Guard RAID teams) start to evacuate the victims. The victims are provided with special equipment that will isolate them and contain the chem-bio agents as they are taken to a nearby transfer zone. In the transfer zone the isolation gear is decontaminated, which allows for the contaminated victims to be placed in clean vehicles (ambulances and helicopters) for transfer to local hospital emergency rooms or a designated, contained treatment facility. The Chicago CBARC will allow for the development of equipment and procedures involved in all elements of the chem-bio scenario. In an actual attack, several such sectors will exist for rescuing victims and safely transferring them to medical emergency rooms without exposing the clinical staff to the chem-bio agents. Using the CBARC sector as a test bed (CBART) will allow for the development of advanced chem-bio response techniques and technologies that can be transferred and applied to other locations throughout the world in addition to the system assembled for use in Chicago—one of the top three target areas identified in the United States.

TECHNICAL APPROACH

Technical Areas Information Center

There is a need to establish a Chem-Bio Attack Response Information Center (CBARIC) for the purpose of collecting, analyzing, synthesizing, and disseminating worldwide scientific and technical information on emergency telemedicine, medical informatics, and medical response procedures for chem-bio attacks. The CBARIC would be a mechanism to prevent duplication in studies, enhance the effectiveness of current studies, and centralize information for use in studies and for distribution. Also, such a center would work to promote and oversee standardization of equipment and techniques.

IDI's extensive experience with DOD Information Analysis Centers (IACs) will be applied directly, which will eliminate start-up labor costs. The CBARIC will leverage off IAC information technology developments, provide a repository for data, and develop standards for chem-bio telemedicine for the community. The latest information retrieval techniques will be used to allow users to search massive text databases and retrieve relevant information.

Wireless Sensor Networks

The use of sensors in an emergency telemedicine environment and their interface to telecommunication systems are a required element of advanced trauma care. Sensors may be used for monitoring critical patients and for monitoring casualties in the field at all times. Networks of sensors will need to be deployed soon for chem-bio defense and will need to be assembled in civilian and military areas where there is a potential threat, such as subway stations, airports, office buildings, and convention centers. These sensor networks will transmit alarms following the detection of a chem-bio agent and will need to be networked into an emergency telemedicine infrastructure in order to disseminate this information to appropriate emergency response authorities and trauma centers. The design of a telecommunication infrastructure will need to consider the integration of sensor networks into that infrastructure in order to enhance the current emergency telemedicine environment with new technologies and capabilities.

Telecommunications

A telecommunications infrastructure must be established for use in emergency telemedicine. Rural, disaster, and terrorist-invoked emergency telemedicine will require systems that use mobile satellite and cellular telecommunications for video, voice, and telemetry data transmission from an emergency site or vehicle to a trauma center. Telemetry systems need to be designed for various emergency instrumentation that does analog-to-digital (A/D) conversion and uses telecommunications to transfer vital signs data from a forward emergency area and during transit. Also, video, voice, and data need to be transferred from emergency room personnel to a forward-area vehicle or site. The forward-area vehicle would provide the long-range telecommunications link to a trauma center. Chem-bio emergencies will require satellite, cellular, and other wireless technologies to provide links to an emergency area and to communicate with sensor networks that monitor an area for agents.

A primary source of telecommunications technology that will be used in this subtask is the Fly-Away Package (FAP). Various sections of the FAP relate directly to the communications need for mobile emergency telemedicine communications. The overall objective in conducting the FAP task is to experimentally verify the ability to assemble a full-service communications system that can support requirements in remote as well as developed areas. This support includes the proper transfer of data for successful operation from the point of view of total situation awareness and information dominance. Achievement of these objectives calls for a communications system having multiple voice channels, video conferencing, and high data rate transfers. Seamless connections to private telephone networks, mail systems, commercial telephone systems, various dial-up services, and the Internet are the required service goals in the design of the system.

To increase the amount of information transmitted over telecommunications channels, data must be formatted and compressed. In a military environment, the communication bandwidth (*bandwidth* here denotes transmission capacity rather than the width of a frequency band) necessary for the timely, secure, and reliable transport of information is scarce. In a civilian environment, high communication bandwidth for mobile wireless communication is relatively expensive in equipment cost and service rates. Thus, to bring tangible improvements in battlefield and civilian medical care, telemedicine information services must be carefully designed and deployed. It is important to prioritize these services and to design them to operate flexibly and degrade gracefully so that telemedicine operations can adapt to constraints imposed by the dynamic environments.

Since telemedicine services are based on the processing, transmission, storage, and retrieval of information (signals, digital data), it is essential to represent and organize the information efficiently and flexibly. To enable the delivery of the best grade of telemedicine services, the information must be represented (coded) to furnish various properties such as compactness, error tolerance, non-decipherability, scalability, modularity, extensibility, and openness. Many of these properties are essential to any open-architecture system. A compact representation conserves transmission bandwidth and can be achieved via compression or source coding. An error-tolerant representation can be achieved by means of channel coding; privacy of data, using public key encryption; integrity of data, using message digest calculation; and authentication, via digital signatures.

Current clinical information systems are mostly text based, with image and other signal data relegated to separate archives, for example, Medical Diagnostic Image Support System, or MDIS. The plethora of proprietary clinical information systems presents a major obstacle to inter-networking. To aid the trend of harmonizing diverse systems through the implementation of common interchange formats, for example, Digital Imaging and Communication in Medicine (DICOM), and protocols, focus will be placed on developing and applying coding algorithms that are based on standards that are or are likely to be widely accepted. Most coding standards do not specify exactly how to encode a given type of source signal. These standards can be regarded as "toolboxes" or as precisely defined languages that can be used to tackle a range of applications. For a specific application, there is usually substantial latitude allowed for designing and optimizing a coder algorithm conforming to the standard. Thus, considerable effort must be devoted to designing, applying, assessing, optimizing, and extending or enhancing standard-based coding algorithms, for example, JPEG, H.261, H.263, MPEG, and JBIG, to compress radiological images and image sequences.

Medical Informatics

To enhance the quality and timeliness of emergency care via telemedicine, information required for emergency care will need to be provided to the caregiver from historical records and from real-time data about the trauma victim. Data sent over telecommunications channels may be (1) near-real-time data gathered in the field that must be received by the trauma center and stored in the appropriate databases associated with the patient, (2) patient history data sent from the trauma center to the field, and (3) voice and video feeds between the remote site and trauma center. These data modalities will require software interfaces between existing databases and the telemedicine system, data transmitted to be secure, and new databases to be built for telemedicine session information.

The current state of storing patient information falls short of a single unified patient record. A number of systems are working toward unifying information that is scattered across many databases. The Defense Advanced Research Projects Agency (DARPA) has funded programs to address unifying a patient record. These systems had to devise their own formats for specific systems, such as the Trauma Care Information Management System (TCIMS). Those working on other government thrust areas, such as the Expert Tertiary Care Host, are attempting to deploy systems to project medical expertise forward to the battlefield.

To enhance emergency medicine, a Computerized Patient Medical Record System (CPR) must be used. The system should be able to work over a hospital intranet and possibly the Internet and preferably have a browser-based user interface. The emergency telemedicine user interface must be able to handle multimedia formats for video, voice, and data. It must interface with the patient medical record, various disparate hospital databases, and the live link to the field and bring all these sources of information together in a clear priority-oriented format that is easily interpreted by the emergency room physician and other personnel. Also, the paramedics in the field will need a user interface that will provide multimedia capability to display information sent from the hospital to the field. This may include patient record information, images, and video of the emergency room physician. If a communication or hardware problem occurs, these user interfaces must be easy to use, control, and start. The patient record will also be stored on a Personal Information Carrier (PIC) that will be on the patient at all times. This device will hold the patient medical record, including images, lab tests, and audio up to 80 MB on a dog tag-like device that can be worn on a chain around the neck or on the wrist or carried with the patient on a key chain. The device, called a Medi-Tag, will interface with the CPR system, and patient record data will be able to be downloaded onto the storage device or uploaded into the CPR. The Medi-Tag is a rugged, durable, and hermetically sealed device that can withstand shocks, tolerate extreme temperatures, and be sealed against water, fuels, and other harmful fluids. It is also resistant to wind-driven dust and sand and is not affected by saltwater, rain, or ice, making it an ideal device for use in a emergency situation anywhere in the world.

For disaster-related emergencies, including a chem-bio attack, an information infrastructure must be in place to disseminate and update information about the emergency. Emergency information must flow from a disaster site via a telemedicine network for treatment purposes and to disseminate alerts and emergency information via a networked infrastructure.

Network Surveillance for Chem-Bio Attack

The first priority in defense against weapons of mass destruction is the early detection of mass exposure. Whether the agents used are chemical or biological, there is currently no reliable method for early detection of victims with unsuspected agent exposure. One of the most fearsome events is occult attack, where victims who become contaminated at a scene do not exhibit symptoms until much later. They may be widely dispersed geographically by the time they feel sick. This is usually from exposure to a biological agent. The protection of the populace will require more than sensor use. This is especially true for a silent, unsuspected biological agent exposure. Because most biological agents have initially mild or subclinical symptoms accompanied by their communicability, the threat is devastating. The subsequent crippling of urban infrastructures, for example, hospitals, in this type of event is easily possible, resulting in marked limitations in the ability to provide health care to the populace.

In addition to detection by environmental sensors, another key protective mechanism that should be in place is the detection of exposure victims as they present to local area emergency departments. Unfortunately, current surveillance systems of population diseases have not kept pace with present-day information technology. Monitoring of these occurrences is done in a retrospective fashion. Even infectious disease surveillance of reportable conditions is limited to phone, fax, or mail communication from treating physicians to local public health departments. It is also dependent on recognition of the disease by the treating physician, which may be limited when considering rare, unfamiliar diseases such as anthrax or botulism. Processing and review of health surveillance information in this fashion offer no potential for rapid early detection and intervention if there is mass exposure to a biological or chemical agent with delayed symptoms.

A surveillance network capable of real-time detection of disease patterns suggesting unrecognized exposure to chemical or biological agents would address all these threats. The victims of exposure to biological agents with delayed effects frequently suffer symptoms that are first mistaken for unusual variants of such common diseases as influenza. Even when there are many patients in a geographic area, each health care worker in area emergency departments may see only one or two. Current detection of a mass exposure depends on an alert health care worker noticing an unusual but small increase in suspicious cases. Nobody will suspect a common exposure until a cluster of similar cases is noticed. To avoid losing valuable time, a real-time Internet-based surveillance system is proposed. This system will create a single database linking the clinical details of patients from the many hospital emergency departments of a geographic region. By combining the simultaneous experience of many health care providers, this system will be capable of rapidly detecting significant but small increases in patients treated for medical problems consistent with biological or chemical weapons exposure in a defined geographic area.

ATLS-Compatible Chem-Bio Protection and Isolation Equipment

Equipment must be designed and created that can be used for evacuation of chemically and biologically contaminated victims and provide isolation of victims and allow for trauma care to be administered. Some of the equipment must be able to provide for full ATLS (Advanced Trauma and Life Support) intervention while maintaining isolation of the victim. Equipment must be designed for mass casualties that can be used under severe environmental conditions of extreme hot, cold, dry, humid, and rainy conditions.

Internet-Based Training Course

One of the cornerstones of domestic preparedness against an attack by weapons of mass destruction will be coordinated, well-trained emergency response teams and hospital personnel. Although the U.S. Domestic Preparedness Program provides for low-cost training packages via CD-ROM and other inexpensive media, there exists no comprehensive, customized web-based program for use by first responders and medical staff. The current instructional process is accomplished using traditional teaching models such as lectures, slides, and video. This type of training has several limitations. First, there is rapid decay in knowledge on subjects rarely encountered, such as a nuclear, chemical, and biological weapon attack. Second, the multitude of possible agents and the enormous volume of information mean that most students will not absorb all the material on the first exposure. Third, there is an inherent difficulty in standardizing this type of presentation, since there are multiple trainers, each with a different background, experience, and style. There is also the difficulty and expense in meeting the need for mass training and periodic retraining. Last, updating traditional materials based on new knowledge or a detected weakness is expensive.

The design of a web-based, comprehensive interactive training program in nuclear, chemical, and biological weapons will address the problems given above. The features of this training program are as follows:

- The web-based format will allow students to retake part or all of the course at will without increasing costs.
- The multimedia interactive environment will engage student interest and increase active participation, leading to better learning.
- The variability in course presentation because of multiple instructors is reduced to nil.
- Anyone can take the course at any time. This relieves pressure on rescue and hospital departments who must release personnel simultaneously for traditional course presentation. This ensures that all target trainees can receive instruction without disrupting important department functions.
- Computer-based teaching materials are more easily and cheaply updated.
- In the traditional model, testing follows instruction. This mutes the learning advantage that can be received when immediate feedback is given for wrong answers. The student is no longer vested in the topic by the time a failing grade is returned. A second chance to reassess and correct deficiencies may be long delayed until the next course is offered in the geographic area. The proposed course will immediately recycle students through topics where they are weak to ensure the best trained personnel possible.